高等职业教育专业英语系列教材

汽车专业英语图解教程

主　编　高　扬　秦晓燕　雷长友
参　编　李晓蕾　袁立嘉　关皓天

机械工业出版社

本书以汽车构造英语为基础，增加了汽车生产和新能源汽车英语内容。全书主要包括汽车概述、汽车生产，发动机两大机构五大系统、排放控制系统、涡轮增压器，底盘部分汽车传动系统、行驶系统、转向系统、制动系统，汽车电气电子系统，以及纯电动汽车、混合动力汽车、插电式混合动力汽车、燃料电池汽车、自动驾驶汽车等专业英语内容。

本书充分考虑汽车专业英语的特点，以结构图或原理图的"图解"形式，将枯燥的专业英语和形象的汽车结构图结合起来，易学易用。全书共5章，每章主要包括课文、关键词中文翻译、句子翻译示例、思考与练习、实车案例、汽车专业英语词汇特点和翻译。附录提供了每章课文的翻译，供读者学习参考。本书力求体现学以致用的理念，取材精炼，优化组合，理论内容以实用为主，够用为度，以达到理论与实践更好的结合。

本书可供高职高专院校、技师学院、中职技校的汽车类各专业使用，也可供成人高校、函授大学、电视大学相关专业及相关工程技术人员、企业管理人员参考使用。

本书配有电子课件和视频，凡使用本书作为教材的教师均可登录机械工业出版社教育服务网 www.cpmedu.com 下载。咨询电话：010 - 88379375。

图书在版编目（CIP）数据

汽车专业英语图解教程/ 高扬，秦晓燕，雷长友主编. —北京：机械工业出版社，2018.7（2024.7重印）
高等职业教育专业英语系列教材
ISBN 978 - 7 - 111 - 60071 - 8

Ⅰ.①汽… Ⅱ.①高… ②秦… ③雷… Ⅲ.①汽车工程-英语-高等职业教育-教材 Ⅳ.①U46

中国版本图书馆CIP数据核字（2018）第124179号

机械工业出版社（北京市百万庄大街22号　邮政编码100037）
策划编辑：杨晓昱　　　　责任编辑：杨晓昱　徐梦然
责任校对：张文贵　　　　责任印制：常天培
固安县铭成印刷有限公司印刷
2024年7月第1版·第6次印刷
184mm×260mm·15印张·367千字
标准书号：ISBN 978 - 7 - 111 - 60071 - 8
定价：49.00元

电话服务　　　　　　　　网络服务
客服电话：010 - 88361066　机　工　官　网：www.cmpbook.com
　　　　　010 - 88379833　机　工　官　博：weibo.com/cmp1952
　　　　　010 - 68326294　金　书　网：www.golden-book.com
封底无防伪标均为盗版　　　机工教育服务网：www.cmpedu.com

前　言

为了适应汽车新技术快速发展，高职院校汽车专业学生不仅要掌握专业知识和技能，更需要掌握汽车专业英语。汽车专业英语已经成为专业技术人员学习和研究国外新技术的必备工具。

高职院校汽车专业英语的教学，主要是培养学生阅读和翻译汽车英文资料的能力。本书根据企业现代化改造、生产一线对应用型高等技术人才在汽车制造与维修技术方面的技能要求，结合汽车新技术的发展趋势，将传统教材内容加以取舍、整合，以汽车构造为主线，将发动机、底盘、电气电子系统与新能源汽车，以及现代汽车制造技术的发展趋势等相关内容有机结合在一起，编成一种全新形式的教材。

本书充分考虑汽车专业英语的特点，以结构图或原理图的"图解"形式，将枯燥的专业英语和形象的汽车结构图结合起来，易学易用。全书共5章，每章主要包括课文、关键词中文翻译、句子翻译示例、思考与练习、实车案例、汽车专业英语词汇特点和翻译。书后提供了每章课文的参考译文，供读者学习参考。全书尽量避免理论过深、专业太强及与实际应用关系不大的内容，符合汽车类相关专业高等职业教育人才培养目标的要求和高等职业教育的特点。本书各章节相对独立，不同专业可根据具体的教学需要进行调整和取舍。

本书由高扬、秦晓燕、雷长友担任主编，李晓蕾、袁立嘉、关皓天参加编写。其中高扬编写第1章、第2章、第5章和附录，雷长友编写第3章，秦晓燕编写第4章，李晓蕾、袁立嘉、关皓天参与了资料的收集整理工作。全书由高扬统稿。在编写过程中曾参考国内外出版的图书资料和权威汽车知识网站，谨向各位编者表示衷心的感谢。感谢在编写过程中提供技术支持的华晨宝马汽车有限公司杜鹏工程师、崔健工程师，上海通用北盛汽车有限公司杨雷工程师。感谢机械工业出版社杨晓昱老师和各位编辑同志的辛勤工作。由于编者水平有限，书中难免存在不妥之处，敬请广大读者批评指正，以便改进和提高。

编　者

目 录
Contents

Preface 前言

Chapter 1　Automobile Overview 汽车概述 …………………………………… 1
  1.1　Structure of an Automobile 汽车构造 ………………………………… 1
  1.2　Car Production 汽车生产 ……………………………………………… 3
  Case Study 实车案例 ……………………………………………………… 8
  Production Process of BMW i8 宝马 i8 的生产流程
  汽车专业英语词汇特点和翻译 …………………………………………… 9

Chapter 2　Engines 发动机 …………………………………………………… 10
  2.1　Car Engines Introduction 汽车发动机概述 ………………………… 10
    2.1.1　Classification of Engines 发动机的分类 ……………………… 11
    2.1.2　The Four-Stroke Cycle 四冲程循环 …………………………… 12
  2.2　The Engine Block 发动机缸体 ……………………………………… 15
  2.3　Two Mechanisms 两大机构 ………………………………………… 17
    2.3.1　The Crank Mechanism 曲柄连杆机构 ………………………… 17
    2.3.2　The Valve Mechanism 配气机构 ……………………………… 21
  2.4　Five Systems 五大系统 ……………………………………………… 23
    2.4.1　The Fuel Supply System 燃料供给系统 ……………………… 23
    2.4.2　The Lubrication System 润滑系统 …………………………… 27
    2.4.3　The Cooling System 冷却系统 ………………………………… 31
    2.4.4　The Ignition System 点火系统 ………………………………… 35
    2.4.5　The Starting System 起动系统 ………………………………… 38
  2.5　Emission Control Systems 排放控制系统 …………………………… 42
  2.6　Turbochargers 涡轮增压器 …………………………………………… 47
  Case Study 实车案例 ……………………………………………………… 50
  BMW's New V12 Engine 宝马新 V12 发动机
  汽车专业英语词汇特点和翻译 …………………………………………… 52

Chapter 3　Chassis 底盘 ……… 54

3.1　The Transmission System 传动系统 ……… 54
- 3.1.1　Clutches 离合器 ……… 54
- 3.1.2　The Manual Transmission 手动变速器 ……… 61
- 3.1.3　The Automatic Transmission 自动变速器 ……… 64
- 3.1.4　The Continuously Variable Transmission 无级变速器 ……… 67
- 3.1.5　Propeller Shafts & Universal Joints 万向传动装置 ……… 69
- 3.1.6　The Driving Axle Assembly 驱动桥 ……… 72

3.2　The Running System 行驶系统 ……… 75
- 3.2.1　Frames 车架 ……… 75
- 3.2.2　Suspensions 悬架 ……… 78
- 3.2.3　Wheels and Tires 车轮和轮胎 ……… 88

3.3　The Steering System 转向系统 ……… 94
- 3.3.1　Manual Steering Systems 机械转向系统 ……… 95
- 3.3.2　Power Steering Systems 动力转向系统 ……… 97

3.4　The Braking System 制动系统 ……… 102
- 3.4.1　The Hydraulic Braking System 液压制动系统 ……… 103
- 3.4.2　The Parking Brake & Anti-Lock Brake System 驻车制动器和防抱死制动系统 ……… 111

Case Study 实车案例 ……… 114
Pillars of the 2016 Prius 2016年普锐斯的支柱
汽车专业英语句法特点和翻译 ……… 116

Chapter 4　Electrical & Electronic Systems 电气电子系统 ……… 118

4.1　Power Supply Systems 电源系统 ……… 118
- 4.1.1　Lead-Acid Batteries 铅酸蓄电池 ……… 118
- 4.1.2　Charging Systems 充电系统 ……… 121

4.2　Lighting, Signal and Dashboard Instruments 照明、信号和仪表装置 ……… 125
- 4.2.1　Lighting Systems 照明系统 ……… 125
- 4.2.2　Signal Systems 信号系统 ……… 129
- 4.2.3　Dashboard Instruments 仪表装置 ……… 131

4.3　Accessories for Comfort and Safety 安全舒适附件 ……… 134

v

    4.3.1 Electrical Accessories 电气附件 …………………………………… 134
    4.3.2 Heating and Air Conditioning Systems 暖风和空调系统 … 137
    4.3.3 Automotive Electronics 汽车电子器件 ……………………………… 141
  4.4 Test Equipment 检测设备 ……………………………………………………… 145
    4.4.1 Common Test Equipment 常用检测设备 ………………………… 145
    4.4.2 On-Board Diagnosis 车载诊断系统 ……………………………… 147
  Case Study 实车案例 ……………………………………………………………… 150
  Waymo's Autonomous Cars　Waymo 自动驾驶汽车
  汽车专业英语句法特点和翻译 ……………………………………………………… 153

Chapter 5 Electric Vehicles 电动汽车 ……………………………………… 154

  5.1 Introduction 概述 ……………………………………………………………… 154
    5.1.1 Differences between Electric and Traditional Vehicles
      电动汽车和传统汽车的区别 ……………………………………… 154
    5.1.2 Types of Electric Vehicles 电动汽车的类型 …………………… 155
  5.2 All-Electric Vehicles 纯电动汽车 ……………………………………………… 158
    5.2.1 Drive Systems 驱动系统 …………………………………………… 159
    5.2.2 Batteries 电源系统 ………………………………………………… 161
    5.2.3 Additional Systems 辅助系统 …………………………………… 162
  5.3 Hybrid Electric Vehicles 混合动力汽车 ……………………………………… 164
    5.3.1 Structure 构造 ……………………………………………………… 164
    5.3.2 Two Basic Configurations 两种基本结构 ……………………… 165
    5.3.3 Three Advanced Technologies 三项先进技术 ………………… 166
  5.4 Plug-In Hybrid Electric Vehicles 插电式混合动力汽车 ………………… 168
  5.5 Fuel Cell Electric Vehicles 燃料电池电动汽车 …………………………… 171
  5.6 Autonomous Vehicles 自动驾驶汽车 ………………………………………… 174
  Case Study 实车案例 ……………………………………………………………… 179
  Toyota Prius Hybrid Electric Vehicle 丰田普锐斯混合动力汽车
  汽车专业英语句法特点和翻译 ……………………………………………………… 180

Translation for Reference 参考译文 ……………………………………………… 181
References 参考文献 ……………………………………………………………… 233

Chapter 1
Automobile Overview

━━━━ ▪ 基本要求 ▪ ━━━━

1. 掌握汽车的基本组成的英文表达。
2. 掌握汽车生产的四大工艺的英文表达。

━━━━ ▪ 重点和难点 ▪ ━━━━

1. 翻译汽车发动机、底盘、车身和电气系统的简要英文描述。
2. 翻译汽车生产的冲压、焊接、涂装和总装四大工艺的英文描述。

━━━━ ▪ 导入新课 ▪ ━━━━

Few inventions in modern times have had as much impact on human life and on the global environment as the automobile. Automobiles and trucks have had a strong influence on the history, economy, and social life of much of the world. How much do you know about automobiles?

1.1 Structure of an Automobile

Automobile, byname auto, also called motorcar or car, a usually four-wheeled vehicle designed primarily for passenger transportation and commonly propelled by an internal-combustion engine using a volatile fuel. The modern automobile is a complex technical system employing subsystems with specific design functions. The major structure of an automobile (Figure 1-1) are the engine, chassis, body and the electrical system. This will be found in every form of motor vehicle.

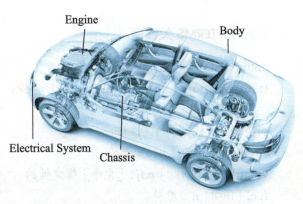

Figure 1-1 Major Structure of an Automobile

1

Engines

The engine—the "heart" of the automobile—operates on internal combustion, meaning the fuel used for its power is burned inside of the engine. The four-stroke engine is the most common type of automobile engine. The engine is comprised of pistons, cylinders, tubes to deliver fuel to the cylinders, and other components. Each system is necessary for making the automobile run and reducing noise and pollution.

Chassis

The chassis is the framework to which the various parts of the automobile are mounted. The chassis must be strong enough to bear the weight of the car, yet somewhat flexible in order to sustain the shocks and tension caused by turning and road conditions. The chassis is divided into four systems: the transmission system, the running system, the steering system and the braking system.

Body

The body of a car is usually composed of steel or aluminum, although fiberglass and plastic are also used. While the body forms the passenger compartment, offers storage space, and houses the automobile's systems, it has other important functions as well. In most instances, its solid structure protects passengers from the force of an accident. Other parts of the car, such as the front and hood, are designed to crumple easily, thereby absorbing much of the impact of a crash.

Electrical Systems

Electricity is used for many parts of the car, from the headlights to the radio, but its chief function is to provide the electrical spark needed to ignite the fuel in the cylinders. The electrical system is comprised of a battery, starter, alternator, distributor, ignition coil, and ignition switch.

▶ KEY TERMS 关键词

automobile [ˈɔːtəməbiːl] *n*. 汽车
transportation [ˌtrænspɔːˈteɪʃn] *n*. 运输；交通
propel [prəˈpel] *vt*. 推动
engine [ˈendʒɪn] *n*. 发动机
volatile [ˈvɒlətaɪl] *adj*. [化学] 挥发性的
fuel [fjʊəl] *n*. 燃料
subsystem [ˈsʌbˌsɪstəm] *n*. 子系统
chassis [ˈʃæsi] *n*. (*pl*. chassis) 底盘

body [ˈbɒdi] *n*. 车身
electrical [ɪˈlektrɪkl] *adj*. 有关电的，电气科学的
vehicle [ˈviːkl] *n*. 车辆；交通工具
piston [ˈpɪstən] *n*. 活塞
cylinder [ˈsɪlɪndə(r)] *n*. 气缸
component [kəmˈpəʊnənt] *n*. (机器、系统等的) 零件
framework [ˈfreɪmwɜːk] *n*. 框架，结构

mount [maʊnt] v. 安装
flexible [ˈfleksəbl] adj. 灵活的；柔韧的
wheel [wiːl] n. 车轮
steering [ˈstɪərɪŋ] n. 操纵，转向
brake [breɪk] n. 制动器 vi. 刹车
suspension [səˈspenʃn] n. 悬架
aluminum [əljuːmɪnəm] n. 铝
fiberglass [ˈfaɪbəɡlɑːs] n. 玻璃纤维；玻璃丝
compartment [kəmˈpɑːtmənt] n. 车厢
crumple [ˈkrʌmpl] vi. 皱缩；被扭弯

crash [kræʃ] n. 撞碎
headlight [ˈhedlaɪt] n. 车头灯；前大灯
spark [spɑːk] n. 火花
battery [ˈbætəri] n. [电] 电池，蓄电池
alternator [ˈɔːltəneɪtə(r)] n.（尤指汽车上的）交流发电机
distributor [dɪˈstrɪbjətə(r)]（发动机的）分电器
coil [kɔɪl] n. 线圈
switch [swɪtʃ] n. 开关

SENTENCES 翻译示例

❶ The major systems of an automobile are the engine, chassis, body and the electrical system.
汽车的主要结构是发动机、底盘、车身和电气系统。

❷ The engine is comprised of pistons, cylinders, tubes to deliver fuel to the cylinders, and other components.
发动机由活塞、气缸、输送燃料至气缸的管道和其他部件组成。

❸ The chassis must be strong enough to bear the weight of the car, yet somewhat flexible in order to sustain the shocks and tension caused by turning and road conditions.
底盘必须足够坚固，以承受汽车的重量，但为了承受转弯和路况所带来的冲击和张力，也得有一定的灵活性。

❹ In most instances, its solid structure protects passengers from the force of an accident.
在大多数情况下，它的坚固结构可以保护乘客免受事故的伤害。

❺ Electricity is used for many parts of the car, from the headlights to the radio, but its chief function is to provide the electrical spark needed to ignite the fuel in the cylinders.
电力用于汽车的许多地方，从车灯到收音机都用电，但其主要功能是提供点燃气缸内燃料所需的电火花。

ASIGNMENTS 思考与练习

1. List the major structure of an automobile.
2. What's the function of the chassis?
3. What is the chief function of the electrical system?

1.2 Car Production

Car production is a complex process consisting of step-by-step creation of a new car.

Before leaving the assembly line, a car will pass through five main processes as follows.

The Press Shop (Figure 1-2)

It's here that steel is shaped and moulded to form the panels that will become a bare bodyshell.

Figure 1-2　The Press Shop

The first step in the production process is to prepare the raw steel that will be used to make our vehicles. Sheet steel arrives in rolls before it is chopped and formed to make the individual components that will be welded together to make each car.

Before the steel is shaped, it has to be prepared. Each steel roll is delivered to a machine that unrolls the coil and smoothes the metal so it is perfectly flat. The metal is then cut into sheets and stamped into the individual panels that make up the car's basic structure. The finished panels are gathered into racks, where they are passed in sequence to the welding shop.

The Welding Shop (Figure 1-3)

In the welding shop, pressed panels are welded together to create a bodyshell. Each bodyshell is given an identity tag that will remain with it right the way through the production process. Created by the production system, this tag determines the car's colour, engine specification, trim, etc.

In its simplest form, the welding shop can be divided into two — the welding stations staffed by skilled people, and those powered by machines. Both stations bring together thousands of individual steel components to create a new bodyshell.

Components are built up into sub-assemblies, which are brought together to create a car. At the end of the bodyshell line the bonnet and boot are attached to the car by hand. The team here also

Figure 1-3　The Welding Shop

makes a final visual inspection, ensuring that the bodywork is perfectly joined and that the panels are smooth without dents, abrasives or other deformations that could create a finishing problem when undergoing the painting process. From here they are lifted onto a conveyor that takes it into the paint shop.

The Paint Shop (Figure 1-4)

When it comes to cleanliness, the paint shop leaves nothing to chance. Maintaining a spotlessly clean, dust-free environment is critical to the quality and consistency of each car's paint job. Now, in order to make the quality standard for line-off, there are four layers in painting including: ED, Sealer & PVC, Primer and Topcoat (gloss and color).

Surface pretreatment: After leaving the welding shop, the surface of the body will be cleaned to increase the anti-rust property and adhesion of the ED step.

Figure 1-4 The Paint Shop

ED: After the surface pretreatment step, the body will be embedded in the ED paint tank (Electrophoretic Painting Process — E coat). This process is also known as electrodeposition to make a better painting on the surface. After being taken out of the ED paint tank, the body would be dried in an oven to a high temperature for drying the paint and created the hardness of the coating.

Sealer & PVC: This step helps seal the edges of steel, against the external impacts during driving (waterproof and antinoise).

Primer: It increases the adhesion of the topcoat as well as the gloss and color. After the primer layer, the body will be in the drying process with high temperature.

Topcoat: It is the painting layer that creates the beauty for vehicles and shows a true color of the vehicle. Therefore, its requirements are included in three words "gloss, durability and reality." The color will be sprayed onto the primer layer by electrostatic painting process. After that, body will be dried in an oven to a high temperature for drying the surface.

Upon completion, the full body will be checked with a fine finish before moving to the assembly shop.

The Assembly Shop (Figure 1-5)

As soon as the bodyshell arrives in the assembly shop, the doors are removed and sent to another line to have their trim, glass, speakers and mirrors installed. The body, meanwhile, has covers laid in strategic locations to protect the paintwork and components from potential damage.

Because assembly is so complex, the whole task is divided into several parts: the trim line, the power train line and the final line.

Inspection (Figure 1-6)

It was the final step in the production process before delivery to dealers. In order to ensure the highest quality products, all vehicles must go through the final check where its engine is audited, its lights and horn checked, its tires balanced, and its charging system examined. Any defects discovered at this stage require that the car be taken to a central repair area, usually located near the end of the line. When the vehicle passes final audit, it is given a certificate and driven to a staging lot where it will await shipment to its destination.

Figure 1-5　The Assembly Shop　　　　Figure 1-6　Inspection

In a few hours, it has been transformed from a sheet of bare metal to a high-quality car.

KEY TERMS 关键词

steel [stiːl] n. 钢铁

mould [məʊld] vt. 浇铸

panel ['pænl] n. 板；平板

bodyshell ['bɒdɪʃel] n. 车架；车身外壳

stamp [stæmp] vt. (用机器或工具)冲压制成

rack [ræk] n. 架子

identity tag 识别标志；身份标签

trim [trɪm] n. 装饰；内饰

bonnet ['bɒnɪt] n. 发动机罩；发动机盖

boot [buːt] n. (汽车后部的) 行李箱

dent [dent] n. 压痕，凹陷

abrasive [ə'breɪsɪv] n. 研磨料

deformation [ˌdiːfɔːˈmeɪʃn] n. 变形
conveyor [kənˈveɪə] n. 传送机；传送带
anti-rust adj. 防锈的
adhesion [ədˈhiːʒn] n. 附着力
electrophoretic [ɪˌlektrəfəˈretɪk] adj. 电泳的
electrodeposition [ɪˌlektrəʊˌdepəˈzɪʃn] n.
　　［化学］电沉积；电镀
oven [ˈʌvn] 烘箱，烤箱
gloss [ɡlɒs] n. 光泽度；光泽
primer [ˈpraɪmə(r)] n. 底漆

durability [ˌdjʊərəˈbɪləti] n. 耐用度；持久性
horn [hɔːn] n. 喇叭
tire [taɪə(r)] n. 轮胎
defect [ˈdiːfekt] n. 缺点，缺陷
a staging lot 临时位置
press shop 冲压车间
welding shop 焊接车间
paint shop 涂装车间
assembly shop 装配车间；总装车间

▶ SENTENCES 翻译示例

❶ Car production is a complex process consisting of step-by-step creation of a new car. Before leaving the assembly line, a car will pass through five main processes as follows.
汽车生产是逐步地创造一辆新车的复杂过程。在离开装配线之前，一辆汽车将通过以下五个主要工序。

❷ It's here that steel is shaped and moulded to form the panels that will become a bare bodyshell.
在这里，钢被塑造成型，形成即将成为车身外壳的面板。

❸ In the welding shop, pressed panels are welded together to create a bodyshell.
在焊接车间，冲压后的钢板被焊接在一起，形成一个车身外壳。

❹ Surface pretreatment: After leaving the welding shop, the surface of the body will be cleaned to increase the anti-rust and adhesion of the ED step.
表面预处理：离开焊接车间后，将清洗车身表面，以增加电泳涂装步骤的防锈和附着力。

❺ As soon as the bodyshell arrives in the assembly shop, the doors are removed and sent to another line to have their trim, glass, speakers and mirrors installed.
当车身外壳到达装配车间后，车门就会被拆卸，并被送到另一条线上，以便安装其饰板、玻璃、扬声器和车镜。

▶ ASIGNMENTS 思考与练习

1. What are the four processes of automobile manufacturing?
2. How many layers in painting? What are they?
3. Name out the three parts of the assembly task.

Case Study 实车案例

Production Process of BMW i8 宝马 i8 的生产流程

Innovative manufacturing technologies and the application of new materials characterize the production process for BMW i cars. Their production stands at the beginning of a value chain that is completely aligned with sustainability criteria. From the raw materials production to the energy-efficient vehicle operations and the recycling as the last step, the chosen approach makes a considerable contribution to the favorable overall life cycle assessment of the plug-in hybrid sports car BMW i8. In both the development and the production of the BMW i8, the outstanding technological expertise of the BMW Group comes to the fore.

The BMW Group's global lead in automotive engineering is demonstrated, among other things, in the industrial production of components made of carbon fiber reinforced plastics (CFRP). The development and production of both the combustion engine and the electric motor of the hybrid sports car are also carried out completely by the BMW Group.

The innovative vehicle architecture of the BMW i8 comprises two elements: the Life module, the passenger cell made of carbon fiber reinforced plastic (CFRP), and the aluminum Drive module, which incorporates the entire drivetrain and chassis technology. The Life Drive concept and use of CFRP allows production times to be cut by half compared to those required for

an equivalent car built along conventional lines. The process is less investment intensive as the high costs required for a conventional press shop and paint shop are no longer an issue and the Life and Drive modules can be manufactured alongside one another.

The BMW i production network comprises a plant in Moses Lake, Washington State, for the carbon fiber production and a plant in Wackersdorf for the processing into carbon fiber laminates. Both these facilities are operated by SGL Automotive Carbon Fibers (ACF), a joint venture set up by the BMW Group and the SGL Group. They are joined by the BMW Group's own plants in Dingolfing, Landshut and Leipzig.

汽车专业英语词汇特点和翻译

汽车专业英语中涉及大量的汽车专业词汇和术语，具有汽车专业领域里特定的含义，有的词汇甚至仅在汽车领域里使用。另外，有大量非专业词汇，它们虽然不具有专业性，但是在翻译中也呈现出不同的特点。

1. 纯专业词汇

在汽车专业英语词汇中，有的是纯专业词汇，属于机械领域所特有。如：engine（发动机），chassis（底盘），crankshaft（曲轴），generator（发电机），clutch（离合器），suspension（悬架）等，它们的特点是含义精确明晰，概念单一狭窄，在中英文中都有确定的名称。

2. 通用型词汇

有的专业词汇属于通用型词汇，广泛应用于不同专业，而且在不同专业中往往意义不同。如，power 一词，作为一般词汇是指"力量""权力""势力"等等，但是在数学中，它是指"幂"，在物理学中，它具有"电""电源""功率"等多种含义。这一类词汇的特点是一词多义，用法灵活，应用领域广泛，必须慎重翻译。又如 spring 一词，一般指"春季""泉源"，机械英语里指"弹簧""发条"。

Chapter 2
Engines

———— 基本要求 ————

1. 掌握汽车发动机基本构造的英文表达。
2. 翻译汽车发动机的工作过程的英文表达。

———— 重点和难点 ————

1. 翻译汽车曲柄连杆机构和配气机构的英文描述。
2. 翻译汽车燃油供给系统的英文描述。
3. 翻译汽车润滑系统的英文描述。
4. 翻译汽车冷却系统的英文描述。
5. 翻译汽车点火系统的英文描述。
6. 翻译汽车起动系统的英文描述。
7. 翻译汽车排放控制系统的英文描述。
8. 翻译汽车涡轮增压器的英文描述。

———— 导入新课 ————

Have you ever opened the hood of your car and wondered what was going on in there? A car engine can look like a big confusing jumble of metal, tubes and wires to the uninitiated. You might want to know what's going on simply out of curiosity. Or perhaps you are buying a new car, and you hear things like "3.0 liter V-6" and "dual overhead cams" and "tuned port fuel injection". What does all of that mean?

2.1 Car Engines Introduction

The purpose of a gasoline car engine is to convert gasoline into motion so that your car can move. Currently the easiest way to create motion from gasoline is to burn the gasoline inside an engine. Therefore, a car engine (Figure 2-1) is an internal combustion engine—combustion takes place internally.

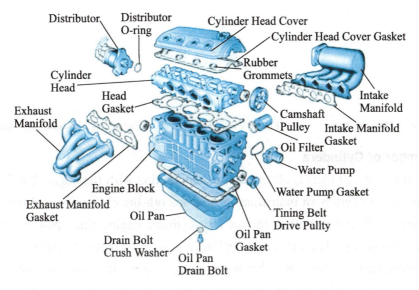

Figure 2-1 Engines (Exploded View)

2.1.1 Classification of Engines

Car engines vary in design, but certain elements are common to all engines and are used for engine classification. The following are the ways engines are classified.

1. Fuel Burned

Fuel burned provides a broad engine classification. Two types of fuel are in general use: gasoline and diesel oil. Gasoline car engines use spark ignition whereas diesel engines use compression ignition (no spark). Alternate fuels such as liquefied petroleum gas (LP-gas), gasohol (90% gasoline, 10% alcohol), and pure alcohol are used in very limited situations.

2. Block Geometry

There are actually three different engine configurations commonly used in automobiles:

In-line type (Figure 2-2)—the cylinders are arranged in a line in a single bank.

V-type (Figure 2-3)—the cylinders are arranged in two banks set at an angle to one another.

Horizontally opposed type (Figure 2-4)—the cylinders are arranged in two banks on opposite sides of the engine.

Figure 2-2　In-Line Type　　　Figure 2-3　V-type　　　Figure 2-4　Horizontally Opposed Type

3. Number of Cylinders

The number of cylinders is often used in combination with the engine block geometry. The number of cylinders is an indication of how smooth the car engine will run. An eight-cylinder engine will run smoother than a four-cylinder engine since power strokes occur with greater frequency. The number of cylinders also contributes to power output; more cylinders, more power. However, this is not always a good indicator of power output. A turbocharged, four-cylinder engine can produce more power than a naturally aspirated six-cylinder engine.

4. Ignition Types

Two methods for igniting fuel are used, spark ignition and compression ignition. Gasoline car engines use spark ignition whereas diesel engines use compression ignition. This method compresses the air to the point where the resulting rise in temperature causes ignition to occur when diesel fuel is added.

2.1.2　The Four-Stroke Cycle

Almost all cars currently use what is called a four-stroke cycle to convert gasoline into motion. The four-stroke cycle is also known as the Otto cycle, in honor of Nikolaus Otto, who invented it in 1867. The four strokes (Figure 2-5) are: intake stroke, compression stroke, power stroke, and exhaust stroke.

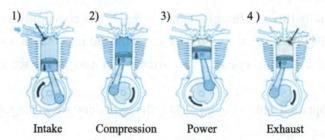

Intake　　Compression　　Power　　Exhaust

Figure 2-5　Four Strokes

Here's what happens as the engine goes through its cycle:

1. The piston starts from the top dead center, the intake valve opens, and the piston moves down to let the engine take in a cylinder full of air and gasoline. This is the intake stroke. Only the tiniest drop of gasoline needs to be mixed into the air for this to work.

2. Then the piston moves back up to compress this fuel/air mixture. Compression makes the explosion more powerful.

3. When the piston reaches the top dead center of its stroke, the spark plug emits a spark to ignite the gasoline. The gasoline charge in the cylinder explodes, driving the piston down.

4. Once the piston hits the bottom dead center of its stroke, the exhaust valve opens and the exhaust leaves the cylinder to go out the tailpipe.

Now the engine is ready for the next cycle, so it intakes another charge of air and gas.

In an engine, the reciprocating motion of the pistons is converted into rotary motion (Figure 2-6) by the crankshaft. The rotational motion is nice because we plan to turn (rotate) the car's wheels with it anyway.

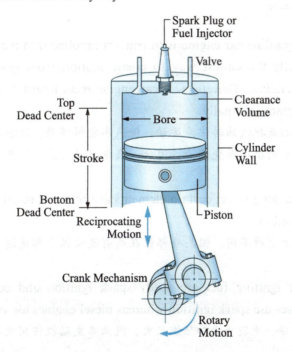

Figure 2-6 Reciprocating Motion is Converted into Rotary Motion

▶ KEY TERMS 关键词

gasoline [ˈɡæsəliːn] *n*. 汽油
internal combustion engine 内燃机
element [ˈelɪmənt] *n*. 元件
classification [ˌklæsɪfɪˈkeɪʃn] *n*. 分类
diesel [ˈdiːzl] *n*. 柴油
spark [spɑːk] *n*. 火花

ignition [ɪɡˈnɪʃn] n. 点火
compression [kəmˈpreʃn] n. 压缩
liquefied [ˈlɪkwɪfaɪd] adj. 液化的
petroleum [pəˈtrəʊliəm] n. 石油
gasohol [ˈɡæsəhɒl] n. （等于 gasoline and alcohol）乙醇汽油
configuration [kənˌfɪɡəˈreɪʃn] n. 配置；结构；外形
horizontally [ˌhɒrɪˈzɒntəli] adv. 水平地
turbocharged [ˈtɜːbəʊtʃɑːdʒd] adj. 涡轮增压的
aspirated [ˈæspəreɪtɪd] adj. 吸气的
emit [ɪˈmɪt] vt. 发出；放射

cylinder [ˈsɪlɪndə] n. 气缸
tailpipe [ˈteɪlpaɪp] n. 排气管
crankshaft [ˈkræŋkʃɑːft] n. 曲轴
intake manifold [动力] 进气歧管
oil filter [机] [车辆] 机油滤清器
oil pan 油底壳
exhaust manifold 排气歧管
top dead center [机] 上止点
bottom dead center [机] 下止点
spark plug [电] [机] 火花塞
fuel injector [动力] 喷油器
clearance volume 燃烧室容积
crank mechanism 曲柄连杆结构

SENTENCES 翻译示例

1 The purpose of a gasoline car engine is to convert gasoline into motion so that your car can move. Currently the easiest way to create motion from gasoline is to burn the gasoline inside an engine. Therefore, a car engine is an internal combustion engine — combustion takes place internally.

汽油车发动机的目的是把汽油转化为运动，使汽车能够移动。目前，把汽油转化为运动的最简单方法是在发动机内燃烧汽油。因此，汽车发动机是一种燃烧发生在内部的内燃机。

2 Car engines vary in design, but certain elements are common to all engines and are used for engine classification.

汽车发动机在设计上有所不同，但某些部件在所有发动机中都是通用的，并被用于发动机分类。

3 Two methods for igniting fuel are used, spark ignition and compression ignition. Gasoline car engines use spark ignition whereas diesel engines use compression ignition.

点燃燃料有两种方法：火花点火和压燃点火。汽油车发动机使用火花点火，而柴油发动机使用压燃点火。

4 Almost all cars currently use what is called a four-stroke cycle to convert gasoline into motion. The four-stroke cycle is also known as the Otto cycle, in honor of Nikolaus Otto, who invented it in 1867.

目前，几乎所有的汽车都使用四冲程循环，将汽油转化为运动。四冲程循环也被称为奥托循环，以纪念尼古拉斯·奥托，他在1867年发明了四冲程发动机。

5 In an engine, the reciprocating motion of the pistons is converted into rotary motion by the crankshaft. The rotational motion is nice because we plan to turn (rotate) the car's wheels with it anyway.

在发动机中，活塞的往复运动被曲轴转化为旋转运动。旋转运动很好，因为我们计划转动（旋转）汽车的车轮。

ASIGNMENTS 思考与练习

1. What is the difference between a gasoline engine and a diesel engine?
2. What is the difference between a two-stroke and a four-stroke engine?
3. Are there any other cycles besides the Otto cycle used in car engines?

2.2 The Engine Block

Today most engines for cars, trucks, buses, tractors, and so on are built with fairly highly integrated design. Thus "engine block", "cylinder block", or simply "block" are the terms likely to be heard in the garage or on the street.

The engine block (Figure 2-7) is the linchpin of vehicles that run on internal combustion, providing the powerhouse for the vehicle. It is called a "block" because it is usually a solid cast car part, housing the cylinders and their components inside a cooled and lubricated crankcase. This part is designed to be extremely strong and sturdy.

Engine blocks are normally cast from either a suitable grade of iron or an aluminium alloy. The aluminium block is much lighter in weight, and has better heat transfer to the coolant, but iron blocks retain some advantages and continue to be used by some manufacturers. Because of the use of cylinder liners and bearing shells, the relative softness of aluminium is of no consequence.

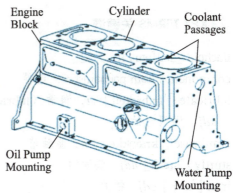

Figure 2-7 The Four-Cylinder Engine Block

A number of channels and passages inside comprise the cooling jacket and are designed to deliver water from the radiator to all the hot sections of the engine, preventing overheating. After the water is circulated in the engine, it returns to the radiator to be cooled by the fan and sent back through the engine.

The core of the engine block is the cylinders, capped by the cylinder head. The cylinder head (Figure 2-8) fastens to the top of the block, just as a roof fits over a house. The underside forms the combustion chamber with the top of the piston. The number of cylinders determines the size and placement of the block, with most cars having between four and eight cylinders. These cylinders house pistons, which provide motive energy for the vehicle through a series of controlled explosions inside the cylinders which push the pistons out, moving the crankshaft of the vehicle.

Attached to the bottom is the oil pan, which seals in the lubricating oil for the engine. The oil pan is usually formed of pressed steel. The oil pan and the lower part of the cylinder block together are called the crankcase (Figure 2-9).

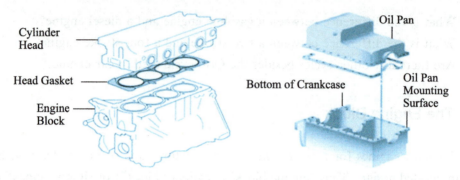

Figure 2-8　The Cylinder Head　　　　　Figure 2-9　The Crankcase

▶ KEY TERMS 关键词

linchpin [ˈlɪntʃpɪn] n. 关键
component [kəmˈpəʊnənt] n. 组件
lubricate [ˈluːbrɪkeɪt] vi. 润滑（lubricated adj. 润滑过的）
crankcase [ˈkræŋkkeɪs] n. 曲轴箱
sturdy [ˈstɜːdi] adj. 坚固的
iron [ˈaɪən] adj. 铁的
aluminum [ˌæljʊˈmɪniəm] n. 铝
alloy [ˈælɔɪ] n. 合金
bearing [ˈbeərɪŋ] n. [机] 轴承
shell [ʃel] n. 壳体
radiator [ˈreɪdieɪtə(r)] n. 散热器

circulate [ˈsɜːkjəleɪt] vi. 循环
piston [ˈpɪstən] n. 活塞
oil pan 油底壳
lubricating oil 润滑油
seal [siːl] vt. 密封
engine block 发动机机体
coolant passages 冷却剂通道
water pump mounting 水泵安装处
oil pump mounting 机油泵安装处
cylinder head [机] 气缸盖
head gasket 气缸垫；气缸盖密封垫片
oil pan mounting surface 油底壳安装面

▶ SENTENCES 翻译示例

❶ The engine block is the linchpin of vehicles that run on internal combustion, providing the powerhouse for the vehicle. It is called a "block" because it is usually a solid cast car part, housing the cylinders and their components inside a cooled and lubricated crankcase.

发动机缸体是内燃机车辆的关键部件，为车辆提供动力室。它被称为"缸体"，因为它通常是一个坚固的铸造汽车部件，在冷却和润滑的曲轴箱内安置气缸及相关的部件。

❷ Engine blocks are normally cast from either a suitable grade of iron or an aluminium alloy. The aluminium block is much lighter in weight, and has better heat transfer to the coolant, but iron blocks retain some advantages and continue to be used by some manufacturers.
发动机缸体通常由适当等级的铁或铝合金铸造而成。铝制缸体的重量轻得多，并能将热量更好地转移给冷却液，但铁制缸体保留了一些优势，并继续被一些制造商使用。

❸ A number of channels and passages inside comprise the cooling jacket and are designed to deliver water from the radiator to all the hot sections of the engine, preventing overheating.
缸体里面有许多通道，包括冷却水套，这样的设计是用来将水从散热器输送到发动机的所有热区，防止过热。

❹ The core of the engine block is the cylinders, capped by the cylinder head.
发动机缸体的核心是气缸，气缸顶部是气缸盖。

❺ The oil pan and the lower part of the cylinder block together are called the crankcase.
油底壳和气缸体的下部一起被称为曲轴箱。

⊙ ASIGNMENTS 思考与练习

1. Why is it called block?
2. What is the core of the engine block?
3. What is the function of the oil pan?

2.3　Two Mechanisms

2.3.1　The Crank Mechanism

　　The **crank mechanism** (Figure 2-10) is at the heart of the **reciprocating** piston engine, and its purpose is to translate the linear motion of the pistons into **rotary** motion for the purpose of extracting useful work. The crank mechanism is typically composed of pistons, connecting rods, the crankshaft, and a **flywheel** or power takeoff device.

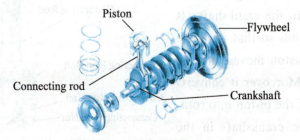

Figure 2-10　The Crank Mechanism

Pistons

A piston (Figure 2-11) is a cylindrical piece of metal that moves up and down inside the cylinder. The force exerted due to the combustion pushes the piston along the cylinder wall. This sliding movement along the cylinder transmits the exerted force to the connecting rod.

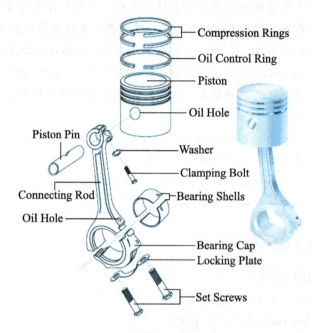

Figure 2-11 Pistons

In order to transmit the force efficiently, the inertia of piston is kept minimal by using aluminium pistons in combination with hollow structure. Two sets of piston rings are fitted on the piston to fill up the gap between the piston and cylinder. The upper set of rings is to provide air tight seal to prevent leakage of the burnt gases into the lower portion. The lower rings provide effective seal to prevent leakage of oil in the engine cylinder.

Connecting Rods

The connecting rod (Figure 2-12) connects the piston to the crankshaft. It can rotate at both ends so that its angle can change as the piston moves and the crankshaft rotates. Moreover it converts the sliding motion of the piston into rotational motion of the crankshaft in the working stroke. The Connecting rod

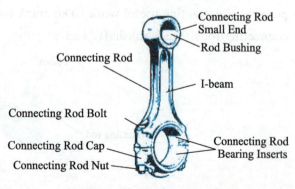

Figure 2-12 Connecting Rods

small end is connected to the piston through piston pin whereas the connecting rod big end is connected to the crankshaft through crank pin. Special steel alloys or aluminium alloys are used for the manufacture of the rods. A special care has to be taken while designing and manufacturing the connecting rod, as it is subjected to alternate tensile and compressive stresses along with bending stresses.

Crankshafts

The crankshaft (Figure 2-13) turns the pistons up and down motion into circular bigger part of motion. The shaft contains number of eccentric portions called "crank". The connecting rod big end is connected to the crank by the means of crank pin. Crank pins are the most crucial part in the crankshaft as the force transmitted through the piston is directly applied onto it.

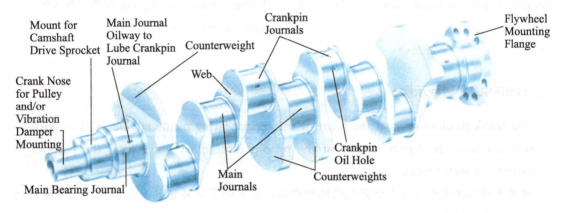

Figure 2-13   Crankshafts

Flywheels

The flywheel (Figure 2-14) is a large, heavy metal disk that mounts on the rear of an engine's crankshaft. Its purpose is to smooth out the shock caused by firing cylinders. The flywheel also provides a surface on which the clutch disc can engage and has a ring gear around the circumference to mate with the starter.

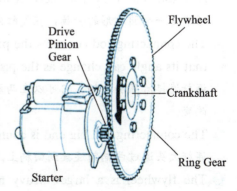

Figure 2-14   Flywheels

KEY TERMS 关键词

reciprocate [rɪˈsɪprəkeɪt] vi. 往复运动
rotary [ˈrəʊtəri] adj. 旋转的

flywheel [ˈflaɪwiːl] n. 飞轮
cylindrical [səˈlɪndrɪkl] adj. 圆柱形的

combustion [kəmˈbʌstʃən] n. 燃烧
inertia [ɪˈnɜːʃə] n. [力] 惯性
hollow [ˈhɒləʊ] adj. 空的；中空的
gap [gæp] n. 间隙
leakage [ˈliːkɪdʒ] n. 泄漏
tensile [ˈtensaɪl] adj. [力] 可伸长的；可拉长的
circular [ˈsɜːkjələ(r)] adj. 圆周的
eccentric [ɪkˈsentrɪk] adj. 偏心的
crank [kræŋk] n. 曲柄
clutch [klʌtʃ] n. 离合器
engage [ɪnˈgeɪdʒ] vi. 啮合
circumference [səˈkʌmfərəns] n. 圆周；周长
mate [meɪt] vi. 紧密配合

crank mechanism 曲柄连杆机构
compression ring 压缩环
oil control ring 机油环
clamping bolt 紧固螺栓
bearing shell 轴瓦
bearing cap 轴承盖
locking plate 防松板
set screw 紧固螺钉
wrist pin 活塞销
rod bushing 连杆衬套
rod nut 连杆螺母
flywheel mounting flange 飞轮安装法兰
main journal 主轴颈

SENTENCES 翻译示例

❶ The crank mechanism is at the heart of the reciprocating piston engine, and its purpose is to translate the linear motion of the pistons into rotary motion for the purpose of extracting useful work.
曲柄连杆机构位于往复式活塞发动机的中心，其目的是将活塞的直线运动转化为旋转运动，以提取有用的功。

❷ A piston is a cylindrical piece of metal that moves up and down inside the cylinder.
活塞是一个圆柱形的金属，在气缸内上下移动。

❸ The connecting rod connects the piston to the crankshaft. It can rotate at both ends so that its angle can change as the piston moves and the crankshaft rotates.
连杆连接活塞和曲轴。它可以在两端旋转，使它的角度可以随着活塞移动和曲轴旋转而改变。

❹ The connecting rod big end is connected to the crank by the means of crank pin.
连杆大头通过曲柄销连接到曲柄上。

❺ The flywheel is a large, heavy metal disk that mounts on the rear of an engine's crankshaft.
飞轮是一个大而重的金属圆盘，安装在发动机曲轴的后部。

ASSIGNMENTS 思考与练习

1. What's the purpose of the crank mechanism?

2. How many sets of piston rings are fitted on the piston? What are they?

3. What's the function of the flywheel?

2.3.2 The Valve Mechanism

The valve mechanism (Figure 2-15) consists of valves, rocker arms, push rods, tappets, and the camshaft. The valve mechanism's only job is that of a traffic cop. It lets air and fuel in and out of the engine at the proper time. The timing is controlled by the camshaft which is synchronized to the crankshaft by a chain or belt.

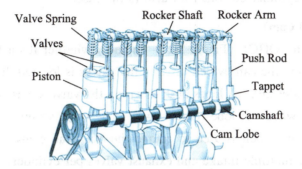

Figure 2-15 The Valve Mechanism

Camshafts

The camshaft is manufactured with precisely machined lobes which control valve opening.

Cam Lobes

Cam lobes are precisely machined into shapes which determine when the valve opens in relation to the piston position, how far the valve is displaced, and the length of time the valve remains open.

Push Rods

Engines designed with the camshaft located in the engine block use push rods, acting on rocker arms, to open valves. Push rods are seated on tappets which ride on the camshaft lobes.

Hydraulic Tappets

Hydraulic tappets are used most often since they can reduce valve train noise by maintaining zero valve clearance (no spacing between valve train components). There are also mechanical tappets and roller tappets.

Valves

Each cylinder has at least one intake valve and one exhaust valve. Some engines are designed with two sets of valves per cylinder. The intake valve has a larger diameter than the exhaust valve, which maximizes air flow to the cylinder. The exhaust valve must withstand higher temperatures than the intake valve since the air flowing past the intake valve keeps the intake valve at a lower temperature.

OHV (Overhead Valve)

An overhead valve engine (OHV engine) (Figure 2-16) is an engine in which the valves are placed in the cylinder head. In overhead valve engines, there is only one cam, nestled in between the V of the opposing cylinder banks. OHV engines almost always have only two valves per cylinder but this isn't always the case.

OHC (Overhead Cam)

In overhead cam (OHC) (Figure 2-17) engines, whether it's a V configuration or a straight configuration, the cam which actuates the valves is located directly on top of said valves. The cam rotates and the lobes push down on the valve stems, causing the valves to open and then close when the lobe rotates away. The valve springs of course provide the return force. A chain or belt is used to couple the overhead cams to the main shaft and quite often there are multiple intake and exhaust valves per cylinder.

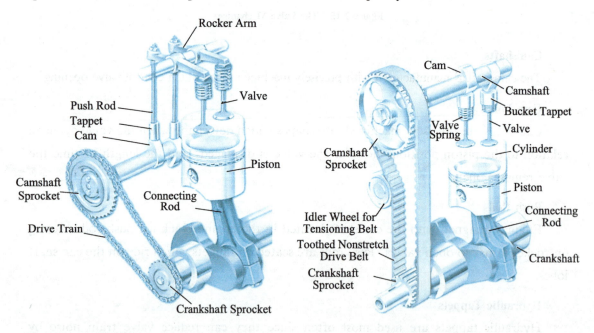

Figure 2-16　OHV Engines, Camshaft with Pushrods　　Figure 2-17　OHC Engines, Engine-with-Overhead-Camshafts

▶ KEY TERMS 关键词

valve [vælv] n. 气门
rocker arm 摇臂

push rod 推杆
tappet [ˈtæpɪt] n. [机] 挺柱

camshaft [ˈkæmʃɑːft] n. [机] 凸轮轴
synchronize [ˈsɪŋkrənaɪz] vi. 同步
chain [tʃeɪn] n. 链
belt [belt] n. 带
lobe [ləʊb] n. 凸角

clearance [ˈklɪərəns] n 间隙
diameter [daɪˈæmɪtə(r)] n. 直径
nestle [ˈnesl] vt. 安置
actuate [ˈæktʃueɪt] vt. 驱动
camshaft sprocket 凸轮轴链轮

SENTENCES 翻译示例

❶ Cam lobes are precisely machined into shapes which determine when the valve opens in relation to the piston position, how far the valve is displaced, and the length of time the valve remains open.
凸轮的凸角被精确地加工成形，它决定了气门开启时与活塞位置的关系，气门的位移距离，以及气门保持开启的时长。

❷ Engines designed with the camshaft located in the engine block use push rods, acting on rocker arms, to open valves.
发动机的凸轮轴位于发动机缸体上，使用推杆作用于摇臂，打开气门。

❸ Each cylinder has at least one intake valve and one exhaust valve. Some engines are designed with two sets of valves per cylinder.
每个气缸至少有一个进气门和一个排气门。有些发动机每个气缸设计有两组气门。

❹ An overhead valve engine (OHV engine) is an engine in which the valves are placed in the cylinder head.
顶置气门发动机是一种气门被置于气缸盖内的发动机。

❺ In overhead cam engines, whether it's a V configuration or a straight configuration, the cam which actuates the valves is located directly on top of said valves.
在顶置凸轮轴发动机中，无论是V形结构还是直列结构，驱动气门的凸轮都直接位于气门的顶部。

ASIGNMENTS 思考与练习

1. List the basic composition of the valve mechanism.
2. What's the job of the valve mechanism?
3. What do OHC and OHV mean?

2.4 Five Systems

2.4.1 The Fuel Supply System

Gasoline must be properly mixed with air before it can be introduced into the cylinder.

The combination of gasoline and air creates a greater explosion. The fuel pump draws the gasoline from the gas **tank** mounted at the **rear** of the car. The gasoline is drawn into a **carburetor** on some cars, while it is fuel-injected on others. Both devices mix the gasoline with air (approximately 14 parts of air to 1 part of gasoline) and **spray** this mixture as a fine mist into the cylinders. Other parts of the fuel supply system (Figure 2-18) include the **air cleaner** (a **filter** to ensure that the air mixed into the fuel is free of **impurities**) and the intake manifold (distributes the fuel mixture to the cylinders).

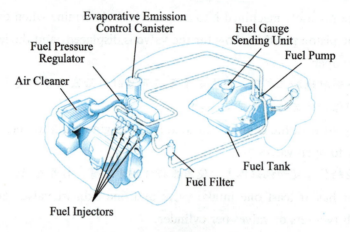

Figure 2-18 The Fuel Supply System

Fuel Tanks

Basically it is a holding tank for your fuel. When you fill up at a gas station the gas travels down the filler tube and into the tank. In the tank, there is a sending unit which tells the gas **gauge** how much gas is in the tank. In recent years, the gas tank has become a little more complicated, as it now often houses the fuel pump and has more emissions controls to prevent **vapors** leaking into the air.

Fuel Pumps

On newer cars the fuel pump (Figure 2-19) is usually **installed** in the fuel tank. Older cars have the fuel pump attached to the engine or on the frame rail between the tank and the engine. If the pump is in the tank or on the frame rail then it is **electric** and is run by your car's **battery**. Fuel pumps **mounted** to the engine use the motion of the engine to

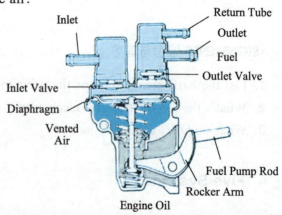

Figure 2-19 The Fuel Pump (SUZUKI RF600 Fuel Pump)

pump the fuel, most often being driven by the camshaft, but sometimes the crankshaft.

Fuel Filters

Clean fuel is critical to engine life and performance. Fuel injectors and carburetors have tiny openings which clog easily, so filtering the fuel is a necessity. Fuel filter (Figure 2-20) can be before or after the fuel pump, sometimes both. They are most often made from a paper element, but can be stainless steel or synthetic material and are designed to be disposable in most cases. Some performance fuel filters will have a washable mesh, which eliminated the need for replacement.

Fuel Injectors

Most domestic cars after 1986 and earlier foreign cars came from the factory with fuel injection. Instead of a carburetor to mix the fuel and air, a computer controls when the fuel injectors open to let fuel into the engine. This has resulted in lower emissions and better fuel economy. The fuel injector is basically a tiny electric valve which opens and closes with an electric signal. In Figure 2-21 below, you can see the injectors towards the outer part of the intake. By injecting the fuel close to the cylinder head, the fuel stays atomized (in tiny particles) so it will burn better when ignited by the spark plug.

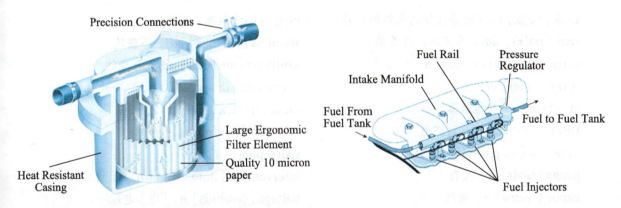

Figure 2-20　Fuel Filters (Toyota Genuine Fuel Filter)　　　Figure 2-21　Fuel Injectors

Carburetors

A carburetor takes the fuel and mixes it with air without computer intervention. While simple in operation, they tend to need frequent tuning and rebuilding. This is why newer cars have done away with carburetors in favor of fuel injection.

EFI (Electronic Fuel Injection)

Electronic fuel injection (EFI) is a type of technology and mechanical structure that supplies fuel to an engine. These systems are most common in automobiles and trucks. Electronic models use a series of circuits and pressure gauges to open and close fuel valves with precision and at high speeds.

Several sensors are included as part of the system, mostly to ensure that the correct amount of fuel is delivered to the injectors and then to the intake valves. These sensors include an engine speed sensor, voltage sensor, coolant temperature sensor, throttle position sensor, oxygen sensor, and airflow sensor. In addition, an intake manifold absolute pressure sensor monitors the air pressure in the intake manifold to determine the amount of power being generated.

In a sequential fuel injection system, the injectors open one at a time, in conjunction with the opening of each cylinder. Some other injection systems may open all injectors simultaneously. The sequential option is advantageous because it allows for faster response when the driver makes a rapid change.

The entire injection system is controlled by an electronic control unit (ECU), which functions as a central exchange for information coming in from all the various sensors. The ECU uses this information to determine the length of pulse, spark advance angle, and other elements.

KEY TERMS 关键词

tank [tæŋk] n. (储存液体或气体的) 箱
rear [rɪə(r)] adj. 后方的；后面的
carburetor [ˌkɑːbjʊˈretə] n. 化油器
spray [spreɪ] vt. 喷射
air cleaner 空气滤清器
filter [ˈfɪltə(r)] n. 过滤器
impurity [ɪmˈpjʊərəti] n. 杂质
gauge [geɪdʒ] n. 仪表
vapor [ˈveɪpə] n. 蒸汽
install [ɪnˈstɔːl] vt. 安装
electric [ɪˈlektrɪk] adj. 电的；电动的
battery [ˈbætəri] n. [电] 电池，蓄电池
mount [maʊnt] vt. 安装
injector [ɪnˈdʒektə] n. 喷油器

clog [klɒg] 阻塞；塞住
stainless [ˈsteɪnləs] adj. 不锈的
synthetic [sɪnˈθetɪk] adj. 合成的
disposable [dɪˈspəʊzəbl] adj. 一次性的
mesh [meʃ] n. 网状物
emission [ɪˈmɪʃn] n. 排放
spark plug 火花塞
intervention [ˌɪntəˈvenʃn] n. 干预
voltage [ˈvəʊltɪdʒ] n. [电] 电压
oxygen [ˈɒksɪdʒən] n. [化学] 氧
sequential [sɪˈkwenʃl] adj. 连续的；相继的
simultaneously [ˌsɪməlˈteɪniəsli] adv. 同时地

SENTENCES 翻译示例

❶ Gasoline must be properly mixed with air before it can be introduced into the cylinder.
汽油在进入气缸之前必须与空气充分混合。

❷ In recent years, the gas tank has become a little more complicated, as it now often houses the fuel pump and has more emissions controls to prevent vapors leaking into the air.

近年来，油箱变得略为复杂，因为它现在通常安装燃油泵，并且具有更多的排放控制，以防止气体泄漏到空气中。

❸ If the pump is in the tank or on the frame rail then it is electric and is run by your car's battery.

如果燃油泵在油箱内或车架轨道上，那么它就是电动的，由汽车蓄电池驱动。

❹ They are most often made from a paper element, but can be stainless steel or synthetic material and are designed to be disposable in most cases.

燃油滤清器通常是由纸质滤芯制成，但也可以是不锈钢或合成材料，并被设计成在大多数情况下是可一次性使用的。

❺ The fuel injector is basically a tiny electric valve which opens and closes with an electric signal.

喷油器基本上是一个微小的电磁阀，利用电信号控制其开启和关闭。

▶ ASIGNMENTS 思考与练习

1. List the main components of the fuel supply system.
2. What is the electronic fuel injection (EFI)?
3. Learn more about EFI after class and make a brief introduction next class.

2.4.2 The Lubrication System

The purpose of the lubrication system (Figure 2-22) is to circulate oil through the engine. An engine must have a good lubrication system. Without it, the friction heat from

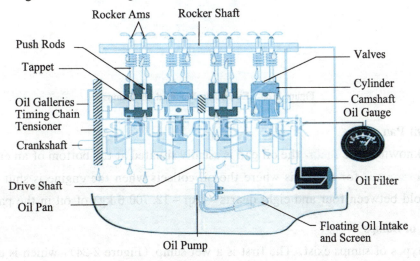

Figure 2-22　The Lubrication System

the contact of moving parts would wear the parts and cause power loss. Oil, when placed between two moving parts, separates them with a film. This oil film prevents the parts from rubbing against between each other. This oil film also cushions the parts, giving quieter and smoother engine operating.

Engine oil serves a vital purpose. It lubricates, cleans and cools the many moving parts in an engine as they cycle thousands of times every minute. It reduces wear on engine components and ensures everything works efficiently at controlled temperatures. Keeping fresh oil moving through the lubrication system reduces the need for repairs and makes your engine last longer.

Engines have dozens of moving parts, and they all need to be well lubricated to provide smooth, consistent performance. Oil travels between the following parts as it flows through your engine.

Oil Pumps

The oil pump pressurizes the oil, pushing it through the engine and keeping the components continuously lubricated. Multi-lobe rotary pumps are the most common type of oil pump. Externally mounted oil pumps (Figure 2-23) usually have the oil filter attached to the pump body.

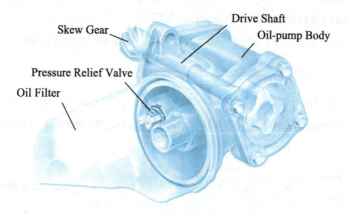

Figure 2-23　Externally Mounted Oil Pumps

The Oil Pan

Also known as the sump, the oil pan is usually situated at the bottom of an engine, and serves as a reservoir for oil. It is where the oil collects when the engine is shut off. Most vehicles hold between four and eight quarts (1 qr = 12.700 6 kg) of oil in the pan.

Types of Sumps

Two types of sumps exist. The first is a wet sump (Figure 2-24), which is used in the majority of vehicles. In this system, the oil pan is located at the bottom of the engine. This design is practical for most vehicles because the pan is located close to where the oil is drawn from, and is relatively inexpensive to manufacture and repair.

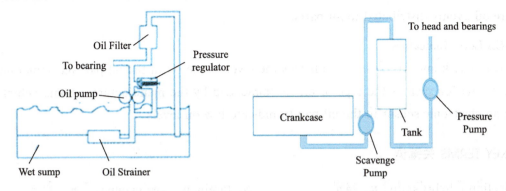

Figure 2-24   Wet Sumps   Figure 2-25   Dry Sumps

The second type of sump is a dry sump (Figure 2-25), which is most often seen on high-performance vehicles. The oil pan is located elsewhere on the engine, specifically not at the bottom. This design allows the vehicle to sit lower to the ground, which lowers the center of gravity and improves handling. It also helps prevent oil starvation if the oil sloshes away from the pickup tube under high cornering loads.

Pickup Tubes

Driven by the oil pump, this tube sucks up oil from the oil pan when the engine is turned on, sending it through the oil filter and throughout the engine.

Pressure Relief Valves

It regulates oil pressure for a consistent flow as load and engine speed changes.

Oil Filters

Oil filter (Figure 2-26) strains the oil to trap debris, dirt, metal particles, and other contaminants that can wear down and cause damage to engine components.

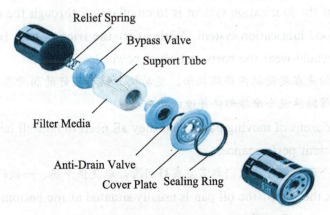

Figure 2-26   Exploded View of a Typical Oil Filters

Spurt Holes and Galleries

Channels and holes that are drilled or cast into the cylinder block and its components ensure oil evenly distributed to all parts.

Oil Level Indicators

It is also known as **dipstick**, indicates the level of the oil in the oil pan and sometimes has information such as the type of oil recommended by the manufacturer. Some vehicles have an electronic sensor in the oil pan to indicate low oil levels.

▶ KEY TERMS 关键词

lubrication [ˌluːbrɪˈkeɪʃn] *n*. 润滑
wear [weə(r)] *n*. 磨损
film [fɪlm] *n*. 油膜
rub [rʌb] *vi*. 摩擦
cushion [ˈkʊʃn] *vt*. 缓冲
sump [sʌmp] *n*. 油底壳
reservoir [ˈrezəvwɑː(r)] *n*. （机器或发动机的）储液器
starvation [stɑːˈveɪʃn] *n*. 匮乏
slosh [slɒʃ] *vi*. 溅出
strain [streɪn] *vi*. 竭力
trap [træp] *vt*. 使……受限制
debris [ˈdebriː] *n*. 残渣

contaminant [kənˈtæmɪnənt] *n*. 杂质
dipstick [ˈdɪpstɪk] *n*. 量油尺
skew gear 斜齿轮
pickup tube 吸入管
pressure relief valve 限压阀
oil filter 机油滤清器
bypass valve 旁通阀
cover plate 盖板
anti-drain valve 止回阀
filter media 过滤介质
spurt holes and galleries 喷油孔道
oil level indicator 油位指示器；机油尺

▶ SENTENCES 翻译示例

❶ The purpose of the lubrication system is to circulate oil through the engine. An engine must have a good lubrication system. Without it, the friction heat from the contact of moving parts would wear the parts and cause power loss.
润滑系统的目的是在发动机内循环机油。发动机必须有良好的润滑系统。没有它，运动部件接触时的摩擦热就会磨损部件并造成功率损耗。

❷ Engines have dozens of moving parts, and they all need to be well lubricated to provide smooth, consistent performance.
发动机有几十个运动部件，它们都需要良好润滑，以提供平稳、一致的性能。

❸ Also known as the sump, the oil pan is usually situated at the bottom of an engine, and serves as a reservoir for oil.

油底壳通常位于发动机的底部，作为储油室，也被称为"sump"。

❹ The oil pump pressurizes the oil, pushing it through the engine and keeping the components continuously lubricated.

机油泵对机油进行加压，使其通过发动机并保持组件持续润滑。

❺ Channels and holes that are drilled or cast into the cylinder block and its components ensure oil evenly distributed to all parts.

钻入或铸入气缸体及其部件的通道和孔，确保机油均匀地分布于各部件。

ASIGNMENTS 思考与练习

1. What components does the engine lubrication system consist of?
2. What is the purpose of engine oil?
3. What are the differences between a wet sump and a dry sump?

2.4.3 The Cooling System

The primary job of the cooling system (Figure 2-27) is to keep the engine from overheating by transferring this heat to the air. Another important job of the cooling system is to allow the engine to heat up as quickly as possible, and then to keep the engine at a constant temperature.

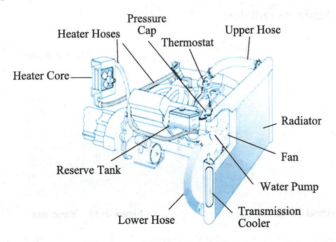

Figure 2-27 The Cooling System

There are two types of cooling systems found on cars: liquid-cooled and air-cooled.

Liquid Cooling

The cooling system on liquid-cooled cars *circulates* a fluid through pipes and passageways in the engine. As this liquid passes through the hot engine, it absorbs heat, cooling the engine. After the fluid leaves the engine, it passes through a heat *exchanger*, or radiator, which transfers the heat from the fluid to the air blowing through the exchanger.

Air Cooling

Some older cars, and very few modern cars, are air-cooled. Instead of circulating fluid through the engine, the engine block is covered in aluminum fins that conduct the heat away from the cylinder. A powerful fan forces air over these fins, which cools the engine by transferring the heat to the air.

Fluid

Water is one of the most effective fluids for holding heat, but water freezes at too high a temperature to be used in car engines. The fluid that most cars use is a mixture of water and ethylene glycol ($C_2H_6O_2$), also known as antifreeze. By adding ethylene glycol to water, the boiling and freezing points are improved significantly.

The Water Pump

The water pump is a simple centrifugal pump (Figure 2-28) driven by a belt connected to the crankshaft of the engine. The pump circulates fluid whenever the engine is running.

Radiators

A radiator (Figure 2-29) is a type of heat exchanger. It is designed to transfer heat from the hot coolant that flows through it to the air blown through it by the fan. Most modern cars use aluminum radiators.

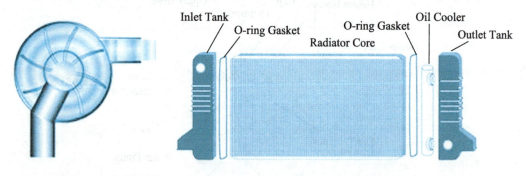

Figure 2-28　Centrifugal Pump　　　　　Figure 2-29　Radiators

The Pressure Cap

The radiator cap (Figure 2-30) actually increases the boiling point of your coolant by about 45 ℉ (25 ℃). The cap is actually a pressure release valve, and on cars it is usually set to 15 psi (1 psi = 6.895 kPa). The boiling point of water increases when the water is placed under pressure.

The Thermostat

The thermostat's (Figure 2-31) main job is to allow the engine to heat up quickly, and then to keep the engine at a constant temperature. It does this by regulating the amount of water that goes through the radiator. At low temperatures, the outlet to the radiator is completely blocked — all of the coolant is recirculated back through the engine.

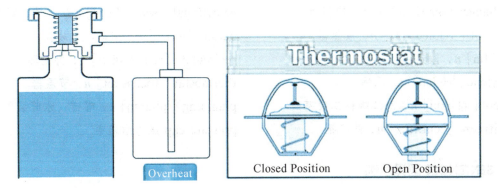

Figure 2-30　The Radiator Cap　　　　　Figure 2-31　The Thermostat

Fans

Like the thermostat, the cooling fan has to be controlled so that it allows the engine to maintain a constant temperature.

Circulation (Figure 2-32)

Since most cars are liquid-cooled, we will focus on that system. The pump sends the fluid into the engine block, where it makes its way through passages in the engine around the cylinders. Then it returns through the cylinder head of the engine. The thermostat is located where the fluid leaves the engine. The plumbing around the thermostat sends the fluid back to the pump directly if the thermostat is closed. If it is open, the fluid goes through the radiator first and then back to the pump.

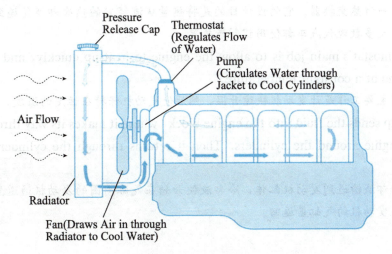

Figure 2-32　Circulation

KEY TERMS 关键词

circulate [ˈsɜːkjəleɪt] vt. 使循环
exchanger [ɪksˈtʃeɪndʒə] n. 交换器
radiator [ˈreɪdieɪtə(r)] n. 散热器
fin [fɪn] n. 散热片
ethylene [ˈeθiliːn] n. 乙烯
glycol [ˈɡlaɪkɒl] n. 乙二醇；二羟基醇
antifreeze [ˈæntɪfriːz] n. 防冻剂

freezing [ˈfriːzɪŋ] adj. 冰冻的
centrifugal [ˌsentrɪˈfjuːɡl] adj. [力] 离心的
outlet [ˈaʊtlet] n. 出口，排放孔
recirculate [riːˈsɜːkjʊleɪt] v. 再循环
thermostat [ˈθɜːməstæt] n. 节温器
plumbing [ˈplʌmɪŋ] n. 管道；水管装置
pressure cap 压力水箱盖

SENTENCES 翻译示例

❶ The primary job of the cooling system is to keep the engine from overheating by transferring this heat to the air. Another important job of the cooling system is to allow the engine to heat up as quickly as possible, and then to keep the engine at a constant temperature.
冷却系统的主要工作是通过将热量传递给空气来防止发动机过热。冷却系统的另一个重要工作是让发动机尽可能快地升温，然后让发动机保持恒定的温度。

❷ The water pump is a simple centrifugal pump driven by a belt connected to the crankshaft of the engine.
水泵是一个简单的离心泵，由连接到发动机曲轴的传动带驱动。

❸ A radiator is a type of heat exchanger. It is designed to transfer heat from the hot coolant that flows through it to the air blown through it by the fan. Most modern cars use aluminum radiators.
散热器是一种热交换器。它的设计目的是将热量从流经它的热冷却液传递到风扇吹过的空气中。大多数现代汽车都使用铝制散热器。

❹ The thermostat's main job is to allow the engine to heat up quickly, and then to keep the engine at a constant temperature.
节温器的主要工作是让发动机快速升温，然后使发动机保持在恒定的温度。

❺ The pump sends the fluid into the engine block, where it makes its way through passages in the engine around the cylinders. Then it returns through the cylinder head of the engine.
水泵将冷却液输送到发动机缸体，冷却液便开始在气缸周围的发动机通道里流动。然后冷却液从发动机的气缸盖返回。

ASIGNMENTS 思考与练习

1. What is the job of the engine cooling system?
2. List the main components of the engine cooling system.
3. What is the job of the thermostat?

2.4.4 The Ignition System

The ignition system (Figure 2-33) has two tasks to perform. First, it must create a voltage high enough (20 000 + V) to arc across the gap of a spark plug, thus creating a spark strong enough to ignite the air/fuel mixture for combustion. Second, it must control the timing of that the spark, so it occurs at the exact right time and send it to the correct cylinder.

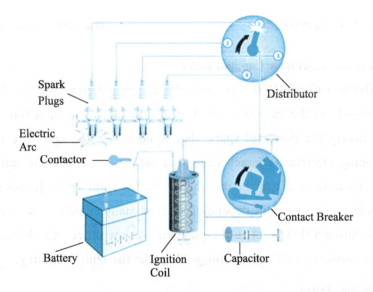

Figure 2-33 The Ignition System

The Ignition Coil

The ignition coil (Figure 2-34) is the unit that takes your relatively weak battery power and turns it into a spark powerful enough to ignite fuel vapor. Inside a traditional ignition coil are two coils of wire on top of each other. These coils are called windings (Figure 2-35). One winding is called the primary winding, the other is the secondary. The primary winding gets the juice together to make a spark and the secondary sends it out the door to the distributor.

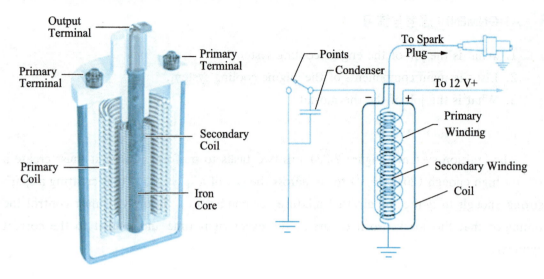

Figure 2-34　Ignition Coils　　　　　　Figure 2-35　Windings

The Distributor, Distributor Cap and Rotor

The distributor (Figure 2-36) is basically a very precise spinner. As it spins, it distributes the sparks to the individual spark plugs at exactly the right time. It distributes the sparks by taking the powerful spark that came in via the coil wire and sending it through a spinning electrical contact known as the rotor. The rotor spins because it's connected directly to the shaft of the distributor. As the rotor spins, it makes contact with a number of points (4, 6, 8 or 12 depending on how many cylinders your engine has) and sends the spark through that point to the plug wire on the other end. Modern distributors have electronic assistance that can do things like alter the ignition timing.

Spark Plugs and Wires

The spark is taken to the spark plug through the spark plug wires. The spark plugs (Figure 2-37) are screwed into the cylinder head, which means that the end of the plug is sitting at the top of the cylinder where the action happens. At just the right time (thanks to the distributor), when the intake valves have let the right amount of fuel vapor and air into the cylinder, the spark plug makes a nice, blue, hot spark that ignites the mixture and creates combustion.

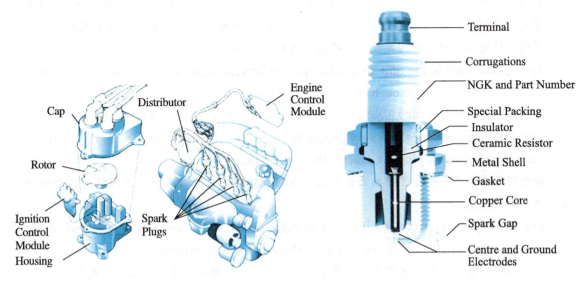

Figure 2-36　The Distributor

Figure 2-37　Spark Plugs

The Ignition Module

In the old days, a distributor relied on a lot of its own "mechanical intuition" to keep the spark timed perfectly. It did this through a setup called a points-and- condenser system. Ignition points were set to a specific gap that created an optimal spark while the condenser regulated. Nowadays this is all handled by computers. The computer that directly regulates your ignition system is called the ignition module, or ignition control module.

▶ KEY TERMS 关键词

voltage ['vəultɪdʒ] n. [电] 电压
arc [ɑːk] vt. 形成电弧
spark plug 火花塞
coil [kɔɪl] n. 线圈
winding ['waɪndɪŋ] n. 绕组
juice [dʒuːs] n. （俚语）电流

distributor [dɪ'strɪbjətə(r)] n. 分电器
spinner ['spɪnə(r)] n. 旋转器
screw [skruː] vt. 旋，拧
condenser [kən'densə] n. [电] 电容器
optimal ['ɒptɪməl] adj. 最佳的
module ['mɒdjuːl] n. 模块

▶ SENTENCES 翻译示例

❶ The ignition system has two tasks to perform. First, it must create a voltage high enough (20 000 + V) to arc across the gap of a spark plug, thus creating a spark strong enough to ignite the air/fuel mixture for combustion. Second, it must control the timing of that the spark so it occurs at the exact right time and send it to the correct cylinder.

点火系统执行两个任务。首先，它必须创造一个足够高的电压（20 000伏特以上），以击穿火花塞间隙，从而产生足够强的火花来点燃空气/燃料混合气。第二，它必须控制点火时间，使它在准确的时间发生，并将其发送到正确的气缸。

❷ The ignition coil is the unit that takes your relatively weak battery power and turns it into a spark powerful enough to ignite fuel vapor.

点火线圈是将相对较弱的电池能量转化成一个足以点燃可燃混合气的电火花的装置。

❸ The distributor is basically a very precise spinner. As it spins, it distributes the sparks to the individual spark plugs at exactly the right time.

分电器基本上是一个非常精确的旋转器。当它旋转时，它会在正确的时间将火花分配到单个的火花塞上。

❹ The spark plugs are screwed into the cylinder head, which means that the end of the plug is sitting at the top of the cylinder where the action happens.

火花塞被拧进气缸盖，这意味着火花塞的顶端位于气缸顶部，在这个位置上点火。

❺ The computer that directly regulates your ignition system is called the ignition module, or ignition control module.

直接调节点火系统的计算机称为点火模块，即点火控制模块。

ASIGNMENTS 思考与练习

1. What are the two tasks of the ignition system?
2. List the main components of the ignition system.
3. What's the function of thc distributor?

2.4.5 The Starting System

Starting the engine is possibly the most important function of the vehicle's electrical system. The starting system (Figure 2-38) performs this function by changing electrical energy from the battery to mechanical energy in the starting motor. This motor then transfers the mechanical energy, through gears, to the flywheel on the engine's crankshaft. During cranking, the flywheel rotates and the air-fuel mixture is drawn into the cylinders, compressed and ignited to start the engine. The starting system is controlled by the ignition switch and protected by a fusible link.

The Starter Motor

A starter is an electric motor that turns over or "cranks" the engine to start it. The starter motor is powered by the car battery. The starter motor has a magnetic switch that shifts a rotating gear (pinion gear) into and out of mesh with the ring gear on the engine flywheel. The gear-reduction starter motor (Figure 2-39) contains the components shown.

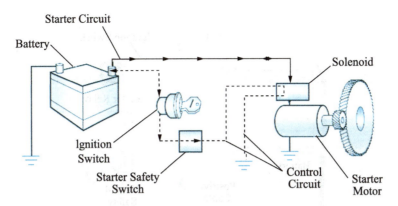

Figure 2-38   The Starting System

This type of starter has a compact, high-speed motor and a set of reduction gears. While the motor is smaller and weighs less than conventional starting motors, it operates at higher speed. The gear-reduction starter is the replacement starter for most conventional starter (Figure 2-40).

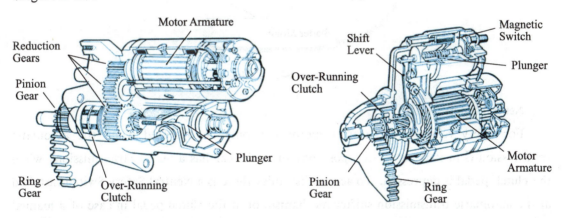

Figure 2-39   The Gear-Reduction Starter   Figure 2-40   The Conventional Starter

The Starter Solenoid

The starter solenoid works as a powerful electric relay. When activated, it closes the electric circuit and sends the battery power to the starter motor. At the same time, the starter solenoid pushes the starter gear forward to mesh it with the engine flywheel (flex plate) ring gear teeth.

Battery Cables

The starter motor requires a very high current to turn over the engine, that's why it's connected to the battery with thick (large gauge) cables (Figure 2-41). The negative (ground) cable connects the "−" battery terminal to the engine cylinder block, close to the starter. The positive cable connects the "+" battery terminal to the starter solenoid.

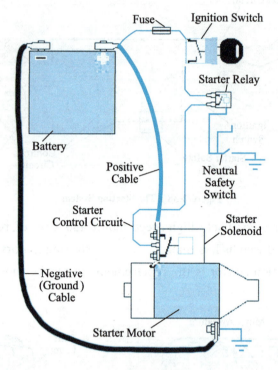

Figure 2-41 Cables

Neutral Safety Switch

For safety reasons, the starter motor can only be operated when the automatic transmission is in Park or Neutral position; or if the car has a manual transmission, when the clutch pedal is depressed. To accomplish this, there is a Neutral Safety Switch installed at the automatic transmission shifter mechanism or at the clutch pedal in case of a manual transmission.

Starter Relay

A relay is a device that allows a small amount of electrical current to control a large amount of current. A starter relay (Figure 2-42) is installed in series between the battery and the starter. Some cars use a starter solenoid to accomplish the same purpose of allowing a small amount of current from the ignition switch to control a high current flow from the battery to the starter.

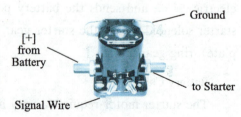

Figure 2-42 Starter Relay

The Ignition Switch

The ignition switch generally has four positions: off, accessories, on and start. Some cars have two off positions, off and lock; one turns off the car, and the other allows the key to be removed from the ignition.

Batteries

The purpose of the battery is to supply current to the starter motor, provide current to the ignition system while cranking, to supply additional current when the demand is higher than the alternator can supply and to act as an electrical reservoir.

KEY TERMS 关键词

gear [gɪə(r)] n. 齿轮；传动装置
fusible [ˈfjuːzəbəl] adj. 易熔的
crank [kræŋk] vt. 用曲轴发动（转动）
magnetic [mægˈnetɪk] adj. 磁性；磁力
mesh [meʃ] vi. 相啮合
conventional [kənˈvenʃnəl] adj. 传统的
solenoid [ˈsɒlənɔɪd] n. 电磁线圈
activate [ˈæktɪveɪt] vi. 激活；启动
circuit [ˈsɜːkɪt] n. [电] 电路
cable [ˈkeɪbl] n. 电缆；连接线
negative [ˈnegətɪv] adj. （电荷或电流）负极的

positive [ˈpɒzətɪv] adj. （电荷或电流）正极的
neutral [ˈnjuːtrəl] n. （汽车或机器的）空挡位置
manual [ˈmænjʊəl] adj. 手动的
relay [ˈriːleɪ] n. [电] 继电器
current [ˈkʌrənt] n. 电流
starter motor 起动机
starter solenoid 起动机电磁线圈
battery cables 蓄电池电缆
neutral safety switch 空挡安全开关
starter relay 起动继电器
ignition switch 点火开关

SENTENCES 翻译示例

❶ Starting the engine is possibly the most important function of the vehicle's electrical system. The starting system performs this function by changing electrical energy from the battery to mechanical energy in the starting motor. This motor then transfers the mechanical energy, through gears, to the flywheel on the engine's crankshaft.
起动发动机可能是汽车电气系统最重要的功能。起动系统通过将蓄电池的电能转化为起动机的机械能来实现这个功能。然后，起动机将机械能通过齿轮传递到发动机曲轴的飞轮上。

❷ The starter motor has a magnetic switch that shifts a rotating gear (pinion gear) into and out of mesh with the ring gear on the engine flywheel.
起动机有一个电磁开关，能移动一个旋转齿轮（驱动齿轮），与发动机飞轮上的环形齿轮相啮合或断开。

❸ The starter motor requires a very high current to turn over the engine, that's why it's connected to the battery with thick (large gauge) cables.

由于起动机需要大电流来起动发动机,所以用粗(大规格)电缆将它与蓄电池连接。

❹ For safety reasons, the starter motor can only be operated when the automatic transmission is in Park or Neutral position; or if the car has a manual transmission, when the clutch pedal is depressed.

出于安全原因,起动机只能在自动变速器处于停车或空挡位置时进行操作;或者,如果汽车有手动变速器,离合器踏板处于踩下状态时进行操作。

❺ A relay is a device that allows a small amount of electrical current to control a large amount of current. A starter relay is installed in series between the battery and the starter.

继电器是一种允许少量电流控制大量电流的装置。起动继电器串联在电池和起动机之间。

ASIGNMENTS 思考与练习

1. List the main components of the starting system.
2. What's the function of the starter motor?
3. What's the function of the neutral safety switch?

2.5 Emission Control Systems

Emission control system (Figure 2-43), in automobiles, means employed to limit the **discharge** of **noxious** gases from the internal-combustion engine and other components. There are three main sources of these gases: the engine exhaust, the crankcase, and the fuel tank and carburetor. The exhaust pipe discharges burned and unburned **hydrocarbons**, **carbon monoxide**, **oxides** of **nitrogen** and **sulfur**, and traces of various **acids**, alcohols, and **phenols**. The crankcase is a secondary source of unburned hydrocarbons and, to a lesser

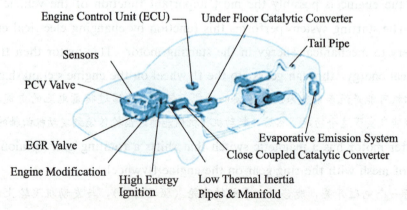

Figure 2-43　Emission Control System

extent, carbon monoxide. In the fuel tank and (in older automobiles) the carburetor, hydrocarbons that are continually evaporating from gasoline constitute a minor but not insignificant contributing factor in pollution. A variety of systems for controlling emissions from all these sources have been developed.

PCV (Positive Crankcase Ventilation) (Figure 2-44)

In the crankcase—the portion of the engine block below the cylinders where the crankshaft is located—leaked combustion gases are combined with ventilating air and returned to the intake manifold for reburning in the combustion chamber. The device that performs this function is known as the positive crankcase ventilation valve, or PCV valve.

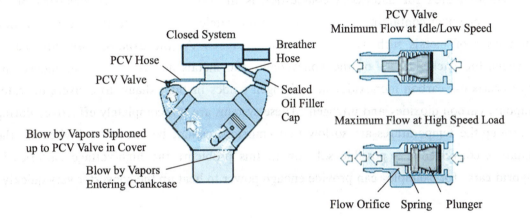

Figure 2-44 Positive Crankcase Ventilation Systems

EGR (Exhaust Gas Recirculation) (Figure 2-45)

To control exhaust emissions, which are responsible for two-thirds of the total engine pollutants, two types of systems are used: the air-injection system and the exhaust gas recirculation (EGR) system. In EGR system, a certain portion of exhaust gases are directed back to the cylinder head, where they are combined with the fuel-air mixture and enter the combustion chamber. The recirculated exhaust gases serve to lower the temperature of combustion, a condition that favours lower production of nitrogen oxides as combustion products (though at some loss of engine efficiency). In a typical air-injection system, an engine-driven pump injects air into the exhaust manifold, where the air combines with unburned hydrocarbons and carbon monoxide at a high temperature and, in effect, continues the combustion process. In this way, a large percentage of the pollutants that were formerly discharged through the exhaust system are burned.

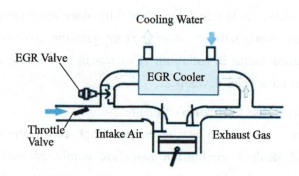

Figure 2-45　Exhaust Gas Recirulation Systems

The Catalytic Converter（Figure 2-46）

Another area for additional combustion is the catalytic converter, consisting of an insulated chamber containing ceramic pellets or a ceramic honeycomb structure coated with a thin layer of metals such as platinum and palladium. As the exhaust gases are passed through the packed beads or the honeycomb, the metals act as catalysts to induce the hydrocarbons, carbon monoxide, and nitrogen oxides in the exhaust to convert to water vapour, carbon dioxide, and nitrogen. These systems are not completely effective: during warm-up the temperatures are so low that emissions cannot be catalyzed. Preheating the catalytic converter is a possible solution to this problem; the high-voltage batteries in hybrid cars, for example, can provide enough power to heat up the converter very quickly.

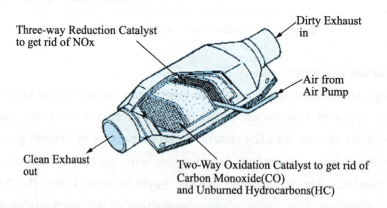

Figure 2-46　The Catalytic Converter

The Canister

In the past, gasoline fumes evaporating from the fuel tank and carburetor were vented directly into the atmosphere. Today those emissions are greatly reduced by sealed fuel-tank caps and the so-called evaporative emission control（EVAP）system（Figure 2-47）, the heart of which is a canister of activated charcoal capable of holding up to 35 percent of its own weight in fuel vapour. In operation, fuel-tank vapours flow from the sealed fuel tank to a vapour separator, which returns raw fuel to the tank and channels fuel vapour through a purge valve to the canister. The canister acts as a storehouse; when the engine is running, the vapours are drawn by the resultant vacuum from the canister, through a filter, and into the combustion chamber, where they are burned.

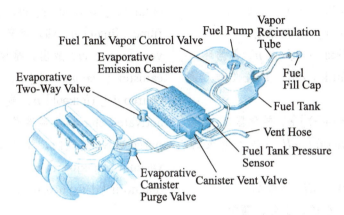

Figure 2-47 Evaporative Emission Control Systems

Improvements in combustion efficiency are effected by computerized control over the whole process of combustion. This control ensures the most efficient operation of the systems described above. In addition, computer-controlled fuel-injection systems ensure more precise air-fuel mixtures, creating greater efficiency in combustion and lower generation of pollutants.

OBD II (The Second-Generation Onboard Diagnosis)

Starting as early as 1994, some U. S. vehicles were equipped with a new government mandated the second-generation onboard diagnosis (OBD II). By model year, 1996, OBD II was required on all new cars and light trucks. OBD II is designed to detect emission problems. When a problem is detected, the "Check Engine" light comes on and a diagnostic trouble code is stored in the powertrain computer (PCM). Later, the code can be read using a scan tool to determine the nature of the problem.

KEY TERMS 关键词

emission [iˈmɪʃn] n. 排放
discharge [dɪsˈtʃɑːdʒ] n. 排放
noxious [ˈnɒkʃəs] adj. 有害的；有毒的
hydrocarbon [ˌhaɪdrəˈkɑːbn] n. [化学] 碳氢化合物

carbon [ˈkɑːbn] n. [化学] 碳
monoxide [mɒˈnɒksaɪd] n. [化学] 一氧化碳；一氧化合物
oxide [ˈɒksaɪd] n. [化学] 氧化物
nitrogen [ˈnaɪtrədʒən] n. [化学] 氮；氮气

sulfur [ˈsʌlfə] n. 硫
acid [ˈæsɪd] n. 酸
phenol [ˈfiːnɒl] n. [化学] 苯酚
evaporate [ɪˈvæpəreɪt] vi. 蒸发，挥发
ventilate [ˈventɪleɪt] vt. 使通风
ventilation [ˌventɪˈleɪʃ(ə)n] n. 通风
pollutant [pəˈluːtənt] n. 污染物
recirculation [riːˌsɜːkjʊˈleɪʃən] n. 再循环
catalytic [ˌkætəˈlɪtɪk] adj. 起催化作用的 n. 催化剂
converter [kənˈvɜːtə(r)] n. 转化器
insulated [ˈɪnsjuleɪtɪd] adj. [电] 绝缘的；隔热的
ceramic [səˈræmɪk] adj. 陶瓷的
pellet [ˈpelɪt] n. 小球，小丸，颗粒

honeycomb [ˈhʌnikəʊm] n. 蜂巢状之物
platinum [ˈplætɪnəm] n. [化学] 铂
palladium [pəˈleɪdiəm] n. [化学] 钯
bead [biːd] n. 珠子，小珠
catalyst [ˈkæt(ə)lɪst] n. [化学] 催化剂
catalyze [ˈkætəlaɪzər] vt. 催化
fume [fjuːm] n. 烟，烟雾
vent [vent] vi. 放出，排放
canister [ˈkænɪstə(r)] n. 活性炭罐
charcoal [ˈtʃɑːkəʊl] n. 炭
activated charcoal 活性炭
purge valve 放气阀，放水阀，清洗阀
vacuum [ˈvækjʊəm] n. 真空
diagnosis [daɪəɡˈnəʊsɪs] n. 诊断

SENTENCES 翻译示例

❶ Emission control system, in automobiles, means employed to limit the discharge of noxious gases from the internal-combustion engine and other components.
在汽车中，排放控制系统是用来限制从内燃机和其他部件排放有害气体的。

❷ In the crankcase—the portion of the engine block below the cylinders where the crankshaft is located—leaked combustion gases are combined with ventilating air and returned to the intake manifold for reburning in the combustion chamber. The device that performs this function is known as the positive crankcase ventilation valve, or PCV valve.
在曲轴箱中，气缸下部放置曲轴的发动机缸体部分泄漏的燃烧气体与通风空气相结合，回到进气歧管，在燃烧室中重新燃烧。执行此功能的装置称为曲轴箱强制通风阀，或PCV阀。

❸ To control exhaust emissions, which are responsible for two-thirds of the total engine pollutants, two types of systems are used: the air-injection system and the exhaust gas recirculation (EGR) system.
为了控制占发动机总污染物三分之二的废气排放，使用了两种类型的系统：空气喷射系统和废气再循环系统。

❹ Another area for additional combustion is the catalytic converter, consisting of an insulated chamber containing ceramic pellets or a ceramic honeycomb structure coated with a thin layer of metals such as platinum and palladium.

另一个额外燃烧的地方是催化转化器。由包含陶瓷颗粒的绝热室或涂有金属如铂和钯的薄层的陶瓷峰窝结构组成。

❺ Today those emissions are greatly reduced by sealed fuel-tank caps and the so-called evaporative control system, the heart of which is a canister of activated charcoal capable of holding up to 35 percent of its own weight in fuel vapour.

今天，由于密封油箱盖和燃油蒸发排放控制系统的使用，这些排放物已经大大减少了。燃油蒸发排放控制系统的核心是一个活性炭罐，能吸咐高达其自重35%的燃料蒸汽。

ASIGNMENTS 思考与练习

1. What is the function of PCV?
2. What is the function of EGR?
3. What is the function of catalytic converter?

2.6 Turbochargers

A turbocharger (Figure 2-48) is an exhaust-driven device that **boosts** an engine's power output. Normally, the downward motion of the pistons pulls air into the engine; this air is mixed with fuel, which is ignited to make power. Stepping on the accelerator increases the amount of air that can be drawn in. (So you're not really stepping on the gas, you're stepping on the air!)

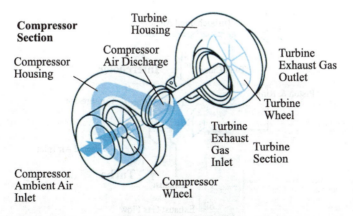

Figure 2-48 Turbochargers

A turbocharger uses a pair of fan-like castings mounted on a common shaft. One (called the turbine) is piped to the exhaust, while the other (the **compressor**) is piped to the intake. The flow of exhaust spins the turbine, which causes the compressor to turn. The compressor blows air into the engine at a greater rate than it can pull in. The greater volume of air can be mixed with a greater volume of fuel, increasing power output. The turbocharger structure is shown in Figure 2-49.

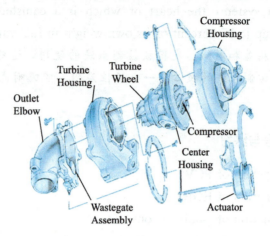

Figure 2-49　The Turbocharger Structure

The turbocharger is bolted to the exhaust manifold of the engine. The exhaust from the cylinders spins the **turbine**, which works like a gas turbine engine. The turbine is connected by a shaft to the compressor, which is located between the air filter and the intake manifold. The compressor **pressurizes** the air going into the pistons. The exhaust from the cylinders passes through the turbine **blades**, causing the turbine to spin. The more exhaust that goes through the blades, the faster they **spin**. See turbocharger working diagram (Figure 2-50) below.

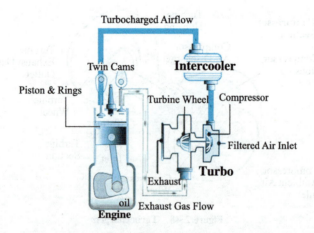

Figure 2-50　The Turbocharger Working Diagram

On the other end of the shaft that the turbine is attached to, the compressor pumps air into the cylinders. The compressor is a type of centrifugal pump — it draws air in at the center of its blades and flings it outward as it spins.

　　In order for the turbocharger to work, there needs to be enough exhaust pressure to spin ("spool up") the turbines. This may not happen until the speed of the engine reaches 2 000~3 000 revolutions per minute (RPM). This is called turbo lag. Once the turbo spools up, look out — the result is usually a strong surge of power, sometimes accompanied by a jet-engine-like whistle.

▶ KEY TERMS 关键词

boost [buːst] *vt*. 增加；提高
compressor [kəmˈpresə(r)] *n*. 压缩机
turbine [ˈtɜːbaɪn] *n*. 涡轮
pressurize [ˈpreʃəraɪz] *vt*. 加压；增压
blade [bleɪd] *n*. 叶片
spin [spɪn] *vi*. 旋转
turbo [ˈtɜːbəʊ] *n*. 涡轮增压机
lag [læg] *n*. 滞后；延迟

spool up 加速
surge [sɜːdʒ] *n*.（数量的）急剧增加，激增
turbine wheel 涡轮
compressor wheel 压缩机轮
compressor ambient air inlet 压缩机进气口
turbine exhaust gas outlet 涡轮废气出口
wastegate assembly 排气泄压阀总成

▶ SENTENCES 翻译示例

❶ A turbocharger is an exhaust-driven device that boosts an engine's power output. Normally, the downward motion of the pistons pulls air into the engine; this air is mixed with fuel, which is ignited to make power.
涡轮增压器是一种排气驱动装置，可以提高发动机的输出功率。通常，活塞的向下运动将空气吸入发动机，空气与燃料混合在一起，燃烧产生动力。

❷ A turbocharger uses a pair of fan-like castings mounted on a common shaft. One (called the turbine) is piped to the exhaust, while the other (the compressor) is piped to the intake.
涡轮增压器使用一对安装在共用轴上的扇形铸件。一台（称为涡轮机）通过管道连接至排气口，而另一台（压缩机）通过管道连接到进气口。

❸ The turbocharger is bolted to the exhaust manifold of the engine. The exhaust from the cylinders spins the turbine, which works like a gas turbine engine.
涡轮增压器用螺栓固定在发动机的排气歧管上。气缸里排出的废气使涡轮旋转，这就像燃气涡轮发动机。

❹ The compressor is a type of centrifugal pump — it draws air in at the center of its blades and flings it outward as it spins.
压缩机是一种离心泵，它将空气吸进其叶片的中心，并在旋转时向外甩出。

❺ In order for the turbocharger to work, there needs to be enough exhaust pressure to spin ("spool up") the turbines. This may not happen until the speed of the engine reaches 2 000~3 000 revolutions per minute (RPM). This is called turbo lag.

为了使涡轮增压器工作，需要有足够的排气压力来旋转（"加速"）涡轮机。直到发动机的速度达到每分钟 2 000~3 000 转时才可能发生这种情况。这叫作涡轮迟滞。

ASIGNMENTS 思考与练习

1. What's the function of a turbocharger?
2. What is the working process of a turbocharger?
3. What is turbo lag?

Case Study 实车案例

BMW's New V12 Engine　宝马新 V12 发动机

With TwinPower Turbo technology incorporated for the first time, this new M Performance engine produces 600 hp and 590 lb-ft of torque. It's harnessed by a highly sophisticated chassis specifically tailored to the model, and deployed to the road via BMW's xDrive all-wheel-drive system with a rear-bias for more dynamic handling.

The 12-cylinder engine layout traditionally enjoys an exclusive status above all others, and in the new M760Li xDrive V12 provides a superb blend of performance and refinement. The 6 592cc M Performance TwinPower Turbo 12-cylinder engine develops an output of 600 hp at 5 500 rpm and generates its peak torque of 590 lb-ft from as low down as 1 500 rpm. This enables the car to accelerate from zero to 62 mph in just 3.9 seconds and on to a governed top speed of 155mph. It now also links up with the Auto Start-Stop function, which is just one measure that contributes to an impressive official combined fuel consumption figure of 22.4 mpg.

For the construction of the all-aluminum block, BMW engineers focused on maximising rigidity while also minimizing weight. Using a closed-deck structure, combined with bolts holding the cylinder head down on the floor plate of the crankcase, has ensured the stability of the cylinder liners. Double bolts on the main bearings, with an additional connection to the side panels through threaded support bushes and bolts, reduce the influence of lateral forces from the crankdrive on the crankcase. Further components that serve to reduce vibrations and noise to an absolute minimum are iron-coated aluminum pistons; forged connecting rods assembled using the cracking process, and likewise, a forged crankshaft.

Two key features have elevated the performance and efficiency of the new V12 onto an even higher level: M Performance TwinPower Turbo technology and High Precision Injection. Together they enable sharp responses to even the slightest movement of the accelerator, a linear torque curve and exceptionally low fuel consumption and CO_2 emissions for a car in this performance class.

Under an engine cover bearing "M Performance" lettering are two mono-scroll turbochargers, located — thanks to the small 60-degree cylinder angle — in a compact arrangement on the outside of the two rows of cylinders. Each turbocharger supplies six cylinders with compressed air. Their positioning allows for short, straight and therefore flow-efficient pipe connections between the exhaust system and the turbochargers. A sophisticated indirect intercooler, minimising the overall volume of air required and reducing lag, cools the air from each turbocharger. An additional water pump feeds the separate coolant circuit required for this purpose, whose air-to-water heat exchangers are positioned directly on the intake manifold.

The engine's catalytic converters are equipped with advanced exhaust gas sensors and quickly reach their optimum operating temperature thanks to their positioning close to the engine, assisting the M760Li xDrive V12 in meeting the EU6c exhaust standard. In order to reduce backpressure, the M sports exhaust system features mostly straight pipes of the largest possible diameter. The evolution of the rear silencers and Flap Activation system allows everything from maximum refinement to a full-bodied 12-cylinder soundtrack.

The adoption of high precision fuel injection optimises the combustion process. Injectors positioned centrally in the cylinder head measure out the fuel precisely and spray it into the combustion chambers in finely atomized form and at up to 200 bar of pressure. The mixture cooling brought about by the directly injected fuel also allows a higher compression ratio than that achieved by a turbocharged engine with manifold injection.

The M Performance 12-cylinder engine also features, in customary BMW fashion, Double-VANOS continuously variable camshaft timing. This allows the engine to run under part loads with a high level of residual gas and reduced throttle losses, maximizing fuel efficiency. Double-VANOS also contributes to the engine's rapid responses.

Another optimization with the new engine is the Oil Supply system. Its volume flow-controlled pump operates only when required and is therefore extremely efficient.

An eight-speed Steptronic Sport transmission is fitted as standard in the new M760Li xDrive V12. M Performance-specific tuning of the shift programs delivers sportier gear changes and more instantaneous downshifts throughout the rev range; Launch Control function is also included. The transmission can also be operated via the gearshift paddles on the steering wheel: in manual mode, the transmission holds the selected gear even when the engine hits the rev limiter. At the same time, its compact construction, low weight, optimized efficiency and flawless interaction with the Auto Start-Stop function allows it to play a significant role in reducing fuel consumptions and emissions.

汽车专业英语词汇特点和翻译

1. 转化、派生、合成等构词法

汽车专业英语中大量词汇是通过转化、派生、合成等构词法构成的。

转化是指由一个词类转化为另一类，如：crank (crank the engine) 名词"曲柄"转化为动词"用曲柄发动"，arc (arc across the gap of a spark plug) 名词"电弧"转化为动词"用电弧击穿"等等。

英语中前缀和后缀种类繁多，在处理派生词时，需要熟悉前缀和后缀的意义和功能，如：antifreeze 防冻剂，disengage 脱离，coaxial 同轴的，deformation 变形，unsprung 未装弹簧的，dismantle 拆卸等等。

合成指由两个或更多的词合成一个词，如 electromagnet 电磁铁，horsepower 马力，driveshaft 传动轴，crankcase 曲轴箱，snowmobile 摩托雪橇。翻译合成词时可以根据构成他们的单词的意义进行猜测，但是应尽量予以核实，杜绝想当然的现象。

2. 缩写词

汽车专业英语里还含有大量的缩写词。缩写词主要由词组中的首字母构成，也可能由词组中的第一个字母或前两、三个字母构成，或者由音节中的首字母构成。其优点是书写简便，但是也给不熟悉它的人们带来了阅读和理解上的困难。

比如：EFI（electronic fuel injection）电子燃油喷射，ICE（internal combustion engine）内燃机，MT（manual transmission）手动变速器，SS（steering system）转向系统，TL（tubeless）无内胎，ALT（alternator）交流发电机，ABS（anti-lock brake system）防抱死制动系统，EPB（electronic parking brake）电动停车制动，AV（autonomous vehicle）自动驾驶汽车，PHEV（plug-in hybrid electric vehicle）插电式混合动力汽车等等。

汽车专业英语虽然大量使用专业词汇和术语，但是它的基本词汇仍然是普通的常用词汇。翻译时，需要根据上下文综合考虑，使译文得体。

Chapter 3
Chassis

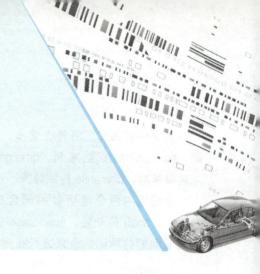

━━━━ ▪ 基本要求 ▪ ━━━━

1. 掌握汽车底盘四大部分基本构造的英文表达。
2. 翻译汽车底盘各部分工作过程的英文表达。

━━━━ ▪ 重点和难点 ▪ ━━━━

1. 翻译汽车传动系统的英文描述。
2. 翻译汽车行驶系统的英文描述。
3. 翻译汽车转向系统的英文描述。
4. 翻译汽车制动系统的英文描述。

━━━━ ▪ 导入新课 ▪ ━━━━

The automotive chassis provides the strength necessary to support a vehicle's components and the load placed upon it. The components which make up the chassis are held together in proper relation to each other by the frame. In this chapter we will discuss the operational characteristics and components of the automotive chassis.

3.1 The Transmission System

3.1.1 Clutches

The **clutch** is located between the back of the engine and the front of the transmission. It exists to provide the operator with the ability to **engage** and **disengage** the engine flywheel from the transmission.

The clutch (Figure 3-1) consists of a cover, a **pressure plate**, and a disc with friction facings. The cover is **bolt**ed to the engine flywheel.

Figure 3-1 Clutches

Thus, it rotates with the engine at all times. Inside the cover is a pressure plate, which also rotates with the cover and the flywheel. Sandwiched between the pressure plate and the flywheel is the clutch disc. This disc is connected to the transmission input shaft by means of splines.

1. Structure

The basic parts of a clutch are shown in Figure 3-2.

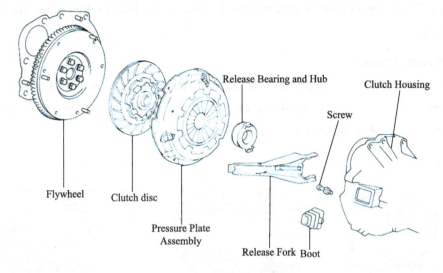

Figure 3-2   Parts of a Clutch

Flywheels

As a large steel or aluminum "disc", the flywheel (Figure 3-3) is bolted to the crankshaft of the engine. The flywheel does many things — acts as balancer for the engine, dampens engine vibrations caused by the firing of each cylinder, and provides a smooth-machined "friction" surface that the clutch can contact. But its main function is to transfer engine torque from the engine to the transmission. The flywheel also has teeth along the circumference, allowing the starter motor to contact when turning the engine over.

Figure 3-3   Flywheels

Pressure Plates

The pressure plate (Figure 3-4) is a spring-loaded device that can either engage or disengage the clutch disc and the flywheel. The clutch disc fits between the flywheel and the pressure plate. The springs used in most pressure plates are of diaphragm-type springs, however a few use multiple coil springs.

Clutch Disc

The clutch disc (Figure 3-5) is basically a steel plate, covered with a frictional material that goes between the flywheel and the pressure plate. In the center of the disc is the hub, which is designed to fit over the spines of the input shaft of the transmission. When the clutch is engaged, the disc is "squeezed" between the flywheel and pressure plate, and power from the engine is transmitted by the disc's hub to the input shaft of the transmission.

Diaphragm Springs

The diaphragm spring (Figure 3-6) is made of spring steel. It is riveted or bolted to the clutch cover. A pivot ring is located at each side of the diaphragm spring and functions as a pivot while the diaphragm spring is operating.

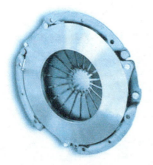 

Figure 3-4   Pressure Plates   Figure 3-5   Clutch Disc   Figure 3-6   Diaphragm Springs

Clutch Release Mechanisms

A clutch release mechanism allows the operator to operate the clutch. Generally, it consists of the clutch pedal assembly, a mechanical linkage, cable or hydraulic circuit, the release bearing, and the clutch fork.

Manual (Cable): The clutch cable mechanism (Figure 3-7) uses a steel cable inside a flexible housing to transfer pedal movement to the clutch fork. The cable is usually fastened to the upper end of the clutch pedal, with the other end of the cable connecting to the clutch fork. The cable housing is mounted in a stationary position. This allows the cable to slide inside the housing whenever the clutch pedal is moved. One end of the clutch cable housing has a threaded sleeve for clutch adjustment.

Hydraulic: A hydraulic clutch release mechanism (Figure 3-8) uses a simple hydraulic circuit to transfer clutch pedal action to the clutch fork. It has three basic parts — master cylinder, hydraulic lines, and a slave cylinder. Movement of the clutch pedal creates hydraulic

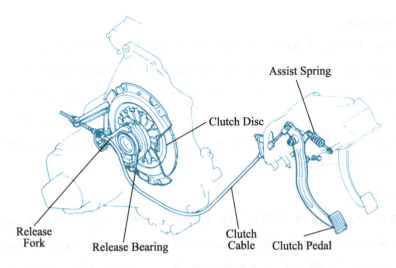

Figure 3-7 Clutch Cable Mechanisms

pressure in the master cylinder, which actuates the slave cylinder. The slave cylinder then moves the clutch fork.

The master cylinder is the controlling cylinder that develops the hydraulic pressure. The slave cylinder is the operating cylinder that is actuated by the pressure created by the master cylinder.

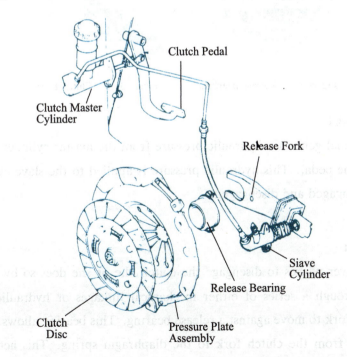

Figure 3-8 Hydraulic Clutch Release Mechanisms

Release Bearings

The release bearing (Figure 3-9), also called the throw-out bearing, is a ball bearing. It is located between the clutch fork and the pressure plate diaphragm. The bearing only operates when the clutch is disengaged. It reduces friction between the pressure plate lever and the release fork. The release bearing is a sealed unit pack with lubricant. It slides on a hub sleeve extending out from the front of the manual transmission and is moved by either hydraulic or manual pressure.

Clutch Forks

The clutch fork (Figure 3-10), also called a clutch arm or release arm, transfers motion from the release mechanism to the release bearing and pressure plate. When the clutch fork is moved by the release mechanism, it pries on the release bearing to disengage the clutch.

Figure 3-9   Release Bearings   Figure 3-10   Clutch Forks

The Clutch Pedal

The clutch pedal generates hydraulic pressure from the master cylinder with the force from depressing the pedal. This hydraulic pressure is applied to the slave cylinder and the clutch is finally engaged and disengaged.

2. Principle

Disengagement

When the driver wishes to disengage the clutch, he or she does so by depressing the clutch pedal. Through a series of either mechanical linkages or hydraulics, this action causes the clutch fork to move against a release bearing. This bearing allows the axial force to be transmitted from the clutch fork to the diaphragm spring. This action causes the diaphragm spring to pull the pressure plate away from the friction disc. At this point, no torque can be transmitted to the transmission shaft, and the clutch is disengaged.

Engagement

When the operator releases the clutch pedal, spring pressure inside the pressure plate pushes forward on the clutch disc. This action locks the flywheel, the clutch disc and the pressure plate together. The engine rotates the transmission input shaft again. The principle is shown in Figure 3-11.

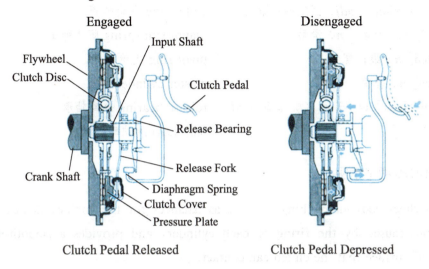

Figure 3-11　Principle

There are many different types and designs of vehicle clutches, yet they all work to achieve the same thing. That is to help convert the turning motion produced in the car's engine into the turning motion of the wheels. Most designs are based around one or two friction plates pressed tightly together or against the flywheel. The clutch can be engaged and disengaged using the clutch pedal, which will always be found to the left of the brake pedal.

▶ KEY TERMS 关键词

clutch [klʌtʃ] n. 离合器
engage [ɪnˈɡeɪdʒ] vi. 啮合
disengage [ˌdɪsɪnˈɡeɪdʒ] vt. 使脱离；解开
bolt [bəʊlt] n. 螺栓，螺钉；vi. 闩上，拴住
spline [splaɪn] n. 花键 vt. 开键槽；用花键联接
balancer [ˈbælənsə] n. 平衡器
dampen [ˈdæmpən] vt. 使潮湿，阻尼，减振

circumference [səˈkʌmfərəns] n. 圆周；周长
hub [hʌb] n. 中心；毂
squeeze [skwiːz] vt. 挤；紧握
rivet [ˈrɪvɪt] n. 铆钉 vt. 铆接；固定
release [rɪˈliːs] vt. 释放；发射
mechanism [ˈmekənɪzəm] n. 机制；原理

cable [ˈkeɪbəl] n. 缆绳；电缆
hydraulic [haɪˈdrɔːlɪk] adj. 液压的
fork [fɔːk] n. 叉
flexible [ˈfleksəbl] adj. 柔韧的；易弯曲的
mount [maʊnt] vt. 安装，架置
stationary [ˈsteɪʃənri] adj. 固定的；静止的
slide [slaɪd] vi. 滑动；n. 滑动
thread [θred] n. 线；螺纹
sleeve [sliːv] n. 套筒
actuate [ˈæktʃueɪt] vt. 开动（机器等）；促使，驱使

seal [siːl] n. 密封 vt. 密封
transfer [trænsˈfɜː(r)] vt. 传递
pry [praɪ] vt. 撬动
depress [dɪˈpres] v. 推下，拉下
pressure plate 压盘
coil spring 螺旋弹簧
diaphragm spring 膜片弹簧
pivot ring 支承环
master cylinder 主缸
release bearing 分离轴承
ball bearing 球轴承

SENTENCES 翻译示例

❶ The flywheel does many things — acts as balancer for the engine, dampens engine vibrations caused by the firing of each cylinder, and provides a smooth-machined "friction" surface that the clutch can contact.
作为发动机的平衡器，飞轮有许多作用，减轻每个气缸的燃烧引起的发动机振动，并提供一个光滑加工的"摩擦"表面用以和离合器接触。

❷ When the clutch is engaged, the disc is "squeezed" between the flywheel and pressure plate, and power from the engine is transmitted by the disc's hub to the input shaft of the transmission.
当离合器接合时，离合器从动盘在飞轮和压盘之间被"挤压"，发动机的动力通过盘毂传送到变速器的输入轴上。

❸ The clutch can be engaged and disengaged using the clutch pedal, which will always be found to the left of the brake pedal.
离合器可以使用离合器踏板进行接合和分离，离合器踏板始终位于制动踏板的左侧。

ASIGNMENTS 思考与练习

1. List the main components of a clutch.
2. What's the function of a clutch?
3. Try to explain the principle of a clutch.

3.1.2 The Manual Transmission

A manual transmission (MT) (Figure 3-12) is designed with two purposes in mind. One purpose of the transmission is to provide the operator with the option of maneuvering the vehicle in either the forward or reverse direction. This is a basic requirement of all automotive vehicles. Almost all vehicles have multiple forward gear ratios, but in most cases, only one ratio is provided for reverse. Another purpose of the transmission is to provide the operator with a selection of gear ratios between engine and wheel so that the vehicle can operate at the best efficiency under a variety of operating conditions and loads.

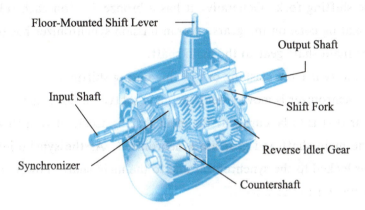

Figure 3-12 The Manual Transmission

1. Structure

Transmission Cases

The transmission case provides support for the bearings and shafts, as well as an enclosure for lubricating oil. A manual transmission case is cast from either iron or aluminum. Because they are lighter in weight, aluminum cases are preferred. A drain plug and fill plug are provided for servicing. The drain plug is located on the bottom of the case.

Transmission Shafts

A manual transmission usually has three steel shafts mounted inside the transmission case. These shafts are the input shaft, the countershaft and the main shaft (output shaft).

Input Shafts: The input shaft, also known as the clutch shaft, transfers rotation from the clutch disc to the countershaft gears. The outer end of the shaft is splined. The inner end has a machined gear that meshes with the countershaft. A bearing in the transmission case supports the input shaft in the case. When the clutch disc turns, the input shaft gear and gears on the countershaft turn.

Countershafts: The countershaft, also known as the cluster gear shaft, holds the countershaft gear into mesh with the input shaft gear and other gears in the transmission. It is located slightly below and to one side of the clutch shaft.

Output Shafts: The output shaft holds the output gears and synchronizers. The rear of the shaft extends to the extension housing where it connects to the drive shaft to turn the wheel of the vehicle. Gears on the shaft are free to rotate, but the synchronizers are locked on the shaft. The synchronizers will only turn when the shaft itself turns.

The Synchronizer

The synchronizer (Figure 3-13) is a sleeve that slides back and forth on the main shaft by means of the shifting fork. Generally, it has a bronze cone on each side that engages with a tapered mating cone on the gears. A transmission synchronizer has two functions.

- Lock the main shaft gear to the main shaft.
- Prevent the gear from clashing or grinding during shifting.

When the synchronizer is moved along the main shaft, the cones act as a clutch. Upon touching the gear that is to be engaged, the main shaft is accelerated or slowed down until the speeds of the main shaft and gear are synchronized. As the synchronizer is slid to a gear, the gear is locked to the synchronizer and to the main shaft. Power can then be sent out of the transmission to the wheels.

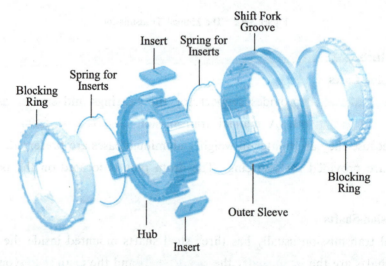

Figure 3-13 The Synchronizer

Shift Forks

Shift fork fits around the synchronizer sleeves to transfer movement to the sleeves from the shift linkage. The shift fork sits in a groove cutting into the synchronizer sleeve. The linkage rod or shifting rail connects the shift fork to the operator's shift lever.

2. Power Flow

Now that you understand the basic parts and structure of a manual transmission, we will cover the flow of power through a four-speed manual transmission. The power flow is shown in Figure 3-14.

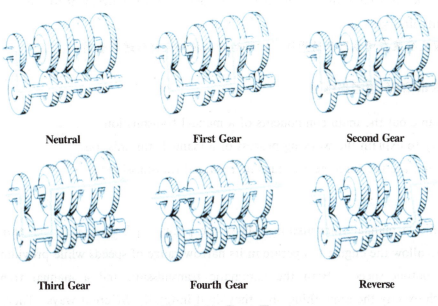

Neutral　　　　　　　　First Gear　　　　　　　　Second Gear

Third Gear　　　　　　　Fourth Gear　　　　　　　Reverse

Figure 3-14　Power Flow

▶ KEY TERMS 关键词

manual [ˈmænjʊəl] *adj*. 手工的；体力的
maneuver [məˈnuːvə] *vt*. 操纵
reverse [rɪˈvɜːs] *adj*. 反面的；颠倒的
lubricating [ˈluːbrɪkeɪtɪŋ] *adj*. 润滑的
aluminum [əˈluːmɪnəm] *n*. 铝
countershaft [ˈkaʊntəʃɑːft] *n*. 中间轴
mesh [meʃ] *vt*. 啮合
synchronizer [ˈsɪŋkrənaɪzə] *n*. 同步器

cone [kəʊn] *n*. 圆锥体
grind [graɪnd] *n*./*vt*. 磨
gear ratio 传动比
transmission case 变速器壳体
drain plug 放油塞
input shaft 输入轴
main shaft 主轴
shift fork 拨叉

▶ SENTENCES 翻译示例

❶ One purpose of the transmission is to provide the operator with the option of maneuvering the vehicle in either the forward or reverse direction.
变速器的一个作用是为驾驶员提供操纵车辆前后行驶的选择。

❷ The countershaft, also known as the cluster gear shaft, holds the countershaft gear into mesh with the input shaft gear and other gears in the transmission.

中间轴也称为集束齿轮轴,为中间轴齿轮与变速器内的输入轴齿轮和其他齿轮啮合提供支撑。

❸ Shift fork fits around the synchronizer sleeves to transfer movement to the sleeves from the shift linkage.

换挡拨叉安装在同步器套筒周围,以将运动从换挡连杆传递到套筒上。

▶ ASIGNMENTS 思考与练习

1. Name out the main components of a manual transmission.
2. Try to explain the working process of a manual transmission.
3. What are the three gear groups in a manual transmission?

3.1.3 The Automatic Transmission

Just like a manual transmission (MT), the primary job of a automatic transmission (AT) is to allow the engine to operate in its narrow range of speeds while providing a wide range of output speeds. Both the automatic transmission and a manual transmission accomplish exactly the same thing, but they do it in totally different ways. There are two big differences between an automatic transmission and a manual transmission.

- There is no clutch pedal in an automatic transmission car.
- Once you put the transmission into drive, everything else is automatic.

The key difference between a manual and an automatic transmission is that the manual transmission locks and unlocks different sets of gears to the output shaft to achieve the various gear ratios, while in an automatic transmission, the same set of gears produces all of the different gear ratios. The planetary gearset is the device that makes this possible in an automatic transmission.

1. Structure

The main components that make up an automatic transmission include:

Planetary Gear Sets

The basic planetary gear set (Figure 3-15) consists of a sun gear in the center, a planet carrier with the planetary pinions (or planets) mounted to it, and a ring gear with internal teeth, all remaining in

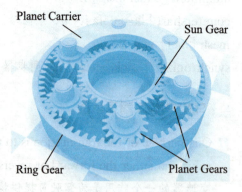

Figure 3-15 The Planetary Gear Set

constant mesh. While the planets spin as they rotate around the sun gear, the planets and the carrier act as a single unit. Any member of the gear set can be fixed or can spin. To transmit torque, one of the elements must be fixed. If all elements are allowed to rotate, no torque can be transmitted, and the gear set is in neutral.

Torque Converters

On automatic transmissions, the torque converter takes the place of the clutch found on standard shift vehicles. A torque converter is a device that is mounted between the engine and the transmission. It is there to allow the engine to continue running when the vehicle comes to a stop. As shown in Figure 3-16, the principle behind a torque converter is like taking a fan that is plugged into the wall and blowing air into another fan which is unplugged. If you grab the blade on the unplugged fan, you are able to hold it from turning, but as soon as you let go, it will begin to speed up until it comes close to the speed of the powered fan. The difference with it is that instead of using air, a torque converter uses oil or transmission fluid, to be more precise.

A torque converter (Figure 3-17) consists of three internal elements that work together to transmit power to the transmission. The three elements of the torque converter are the pump, the turbine and the stator. The pump is mounted directly to the converter housing which in turn is bolted directly to the engine's crankshaft and turns at engine speed. The turbine is inside the housing and is connected directly to the input shaft of the transmission providing power to move the vehicle. The stator is mounted to a one-way clutch so that it can spin freely in one direction but not in the other. Each of the three elements has fins mounted in them to precisely direct the flow of oil through the converter.

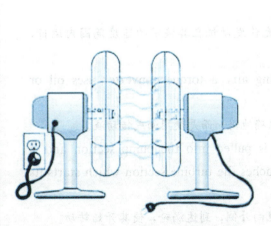

Figure 3-16 Two Fans Form a Simple Coupling

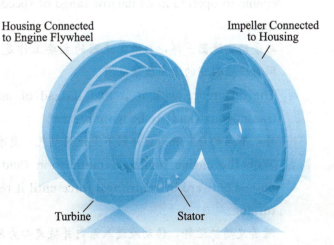

Figure 3-17 Torque Converters

2. Principle

With the engine running, transmission fluid is pulled into the pump section and is pushed outward by centrifugal force until it reaches the turbine section which starts its turning. The fluid continues in a circular motion back towards the center of the turbine where it enters the stator. If the turbine is moving considerably slower than the pump, the fluid will make contact with the front of the stator fins which push the stator into the one way clutch and prevent it from turning. With the stator stopped, the fluid is directed by the stator fins to re-enter the pump at a "helping" angle providing a torque increase. As the speed of the turbine catches up with the pump, the fluid starts hitting the stator blades on the back-side causing the stator to turn in the same direction as the pump and turbine. As the speed increases, all three elements begin to turn at approximately the same speed.

▶ KEY TERMS 关键词

automatic [ˌɔːtəˈmætɪk] *adj*. 自动的
sun gear 太阳轮
ring gear 齿圈
carrier [ˈkærɪə(r)] *n*. 托架，支持物
pinion [ˈpɪnjən] *n*. 小齿轮

torque converter 液力变矩器
turbine [ˈtɜːbaɪn] *n*. 涡轮
stator [ˈsteɪtə] *n*. 导轮
centrifugal force 离心力

▶ SENTENCES 翻译示例

❶ Just like a manual transmission, the automatic transmission's primary job is to allow the engine to operate in its narrow range of speeds while providing a wide range of output speeds.

与手动变速器一样，自动变速器的主要工作是允许发动机在其狭窄的速度范围内运行，同时提供较宽的输出速度范围。

❷ The difference with it is that instead of using air, a torque converter uses oil or transmission fluid, to be more precise.

与之不同的是，液力变矩器不是使用空气，更准确地说，而是使用油或传动液。

❸ With the engine running, transmission fluid is pulled into the pump section and is pushed outward by centrifugal force until it reaches the turbine section which starts its turning.

随着发动机运转，传动液进入泵内并被离心力甩向外侧，到达涡轮，使其开始转动。

ASIGNMENTS 思考与练习

1. What's the difference between a AT and a MT?
2. Name out the main components of a AT.
3. List the main components of a torque converter.

3.1.4 The Continuously Variable Transmission

Unlike traditional automatic transmissions, continuously variable transmissions (CVTs) don't have a gearbox with a set number of gears, which means they don't have interlocking toothed wheels. The most common type of CVT operates on an ingenious pulley system that allows an infinite variability between highest and lowest gears with no discrete steps or shifts.

Pulley-Based CVTs

Most CVTs only have three basic components: a high-power metal or rubber belt, a variable-input "driving" pulley and an output "driven" pulley.

CVTs also have various microprocessors and sensors, but the three components described above are the key elements that enable the technology to work.

The variable-diameter pulleys (Figure 3-18) are the heart of a CVT. Each pulley is made of two cones facing each other. A belt rides in the groove between the two cones. V-belts are preferred from the fact that the belts bear a V-shaped cross section, which increases the frictional grip of the belt.

The Steel Belt

The introduction of new materials makes CVTs even more reliable and efficient. One of the most important advances has been the design and development of metal belts to connect the pulleys. These flexible belts are composed of several thin bands of steel that hold together high-strength, bow-tie-shaped pieces of metal. The steel belt is shown in Figure 3-19.

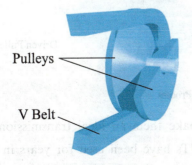

Figure 3-18　Variable-Diameter Pulleys

Figure 3-19　The Steel Belt

Metal belts don't slip and are highly durable, enabling CVTs to handle more engine torque. They are also quieter than rubber-belt-driven CVTs.

Working Process

When one pulley increases its radius, the other decreases its radius to keep the belt tight. As the two pulleys change their radius relative to one another, they create an infinite number of gear ratios — from low to high and everything in between. For example, when the pitch radius is small on the driving pulley and large on the driven pulley, then the rotational speed of the driven pulley decreases, resulting in a lower "gear". When the pitch radius is large on the driving pulley and small on the driven pulley, then the rotational speed of the driven pulley increases, resulting in a higher "gear". Thus, in theory, a CVT has an infinite number of "gears" that it can run through at any time, at any engine or vehicle speed. CVTs may use hydraulic pressure, centrifugal force or spring tension to create the force necessary to adjust the pulley. The working process is shown in Figure 3-20.

Variable-diameter pulleys must always come in pairs. One of the pulleys, known as the drive pulley (or driving pulley), is connected to the crankshaft of the engine. The driving pulley is also called the input pulley because it's where the energy from the engine enters the transmission. The second pulley is called the driven pulley because the first pulley is turning it. As an output pulley, the driven pulley transfers energy to the driveshaft.

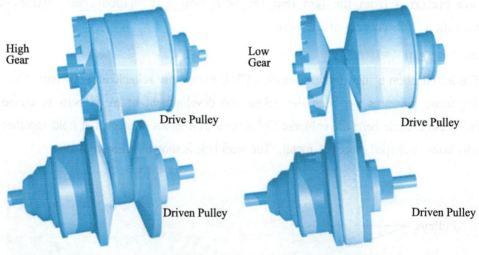

Figure 3-20 Working Process

The simplicity and stepless nature of CVTs make them an ideal transmission for a variety of machines and devices, not just cars. CVTs have been used for years in power tools and drill presses. They've also been used in a variety of vehicles, including tractors and snowmobiles. In all of these applications, the transmissions have relied on high-density rubber belts, which can slip and stretch, thereby reducing their efficiency.

▶ KEY TERMS 关键词

continuously variable transmission 无级变速器
ingenious [ɪnˈdʒiːnɪəs] adj. 有独创性的；精制的
discrete [dɪˈskriːt] adj. 离散的，不连续的
microprocessor [ˌmaɪkrəʊˈprəʊsesə(r)] n. 微处理器
diameter [daɪˈæmɪtə(r)] n. 直径
pitch radius 节圆半径

▶ SENTENCES 翻译示例

❶ Unlike traditional automatic transmissions, continuously variable transmissions don't have a gearbox with a set number of gears, which means they don't have interlocking toothed wheels.
与传统的自动变速器不同，无级变速器没有带有一套齿轮的变速器，这意味着它们没有联锁的齿轮。

❷ Metal belts don't slip and are highly durable, enabling CVTs to handle more engine torque.
金属带不易滑动，并且高度耐用，使无极变速器可以传递更大的发动机转矩。

❸ As the two pulleys change their radius relative to one another, they create an infinite number of gear ratios — from low to high and everything in between.
随着两个带轮改变它们相互的半径，会实现无数个传动比——从低到高的所有值。

▶ ASIGNMENTS 思考与练习

1. List the main components of a CVT.
2. What are the advantages of CVTs?
3. Describe the working process of CVTs.

3.1.5 Propeller Shafts & Universal Joints

In a conventional longitudinally mounted Front Engine, Rear Drive (FR) vehicle, a driveshaft is used to transfer the torque from the engine, through the transmission output shaft, to the differential in the axle, which in turn transmits torque to the wheels. The drive line assembly is shown in Figure 3-21.

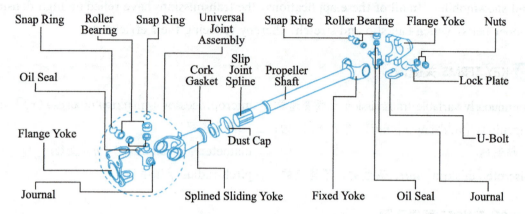

Figure 3-21   The Drive Line Assembly

Propeller Shafts

The propeller shaft（Figure 3-22）can be made out of steel or aluminum and can be either solid or hollow. The propeller shaft can move up and down in response to the road conditions and absorb the change of length by the spline.

Figure 3-22   Propeller Shafts

Most vehicles use a single, one-piece drive shaft. However, many trucks have a two-piece drive shaft. This cuts the length of each shaft to avoid drive line vibration. Since a drive shaft spins at full engine speed in high gear, it must be straight and perfectly balanced. If not balanced, the shaft can vibrate violently. To prevent this vibration, drive shaft balancing weights are welded to the shaft. Small metal weights are attached to the light side to counteract the heavy side for smooth operation.

The Universal Joint

A universal joint（Figure 3-23）is also called a U-joint. The purpose of the universal joint is to absorb the angular changes brought about by changes in relative positions of the

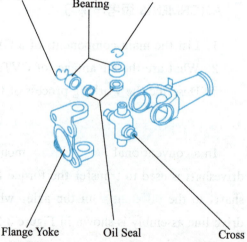

Figure 3-23   The Universal Joint Assembly

differential in relation to the transmission, and in this way to smoothly transmit power from the transmission to the differential. Hooke's joints are commonly used because of their simple construction and functional accuracy. A simple universal joint is composed of three fundamental units consisting of a cross and two yokes.

Center Support Bearings

The center support bearing (Figure 3-24) bolts to the frame or underbody of the vehicle. It supports the center of the drive shaft where the two shafts come together. A sealed ball bearing allows the drive shaft to spin freely. The outside of the ball bearing is held by a thick, rubber support. The rubber mount prevents vibration and noise from transferring into the operator's compartment.

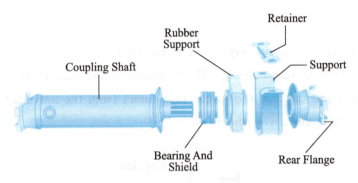

Figure 3-24　Center Support Bearings

▶ KEY TERMS 关键词

longitudinally [ˌlɒndʒɪˈtjuːdɪnəli] *adv*. 纵向地
differential [ˌdɪfəˈrenʃl] *n*. 差速器
absorb [əbˈsɔːb] *vt*. 吸收；吸引；承受
balancing weight 配重；平衡块
weld [weld] *vt*. 焊接；使结合；使成整体
counteract [ˌkaʊntərˈækt] *vt*. 抵消；中和

universal joint 万向节
angular [ˈæŋɡjələ(r)] *adj*. 有角（度）的
cross [krɒs] *n*. 十字接头，十字轴
yoke [jəʊk] *n*. 万向节叉
center support bearing 中间支架轴承

▶ SENTENCES 翻译示例

❶ The propeller shaft can move up and down in response to the road conditions and absorb the change of length by the spline.
传动轴可随路面条件升降，并用花键吸收长度变化。

❷ The purpose of the universal joint is to absorb the angular changes brought about by changes in relative positions of the differential in relation to the transmission.

万向节的作用是吸收由差速器相对于变速器的相对位置变化所引起的角度变化。

❸ Hooke's joints are commonly used because of their simple construction and functional accuracy.

胡克（十字轴）式万向节通常因其结构简单和功能准确而被普遍使用。

ASIGNMENTS 思考与练习

1. What's the purpose of the propeller shaft?
2. Name out the main components of a universal joint.
3. What's the purpose of the universal joint?

3.1.6 The Driving Axle Assembly

The driving axle assembly (Figure 3-25) encloses the final drive gears, differential gears and axle shafts in one housing. The function of the driving axle assemblies is to decrease the speed and increase the torque that comes from the universal joint, and then distribute the power to the drive wheels.

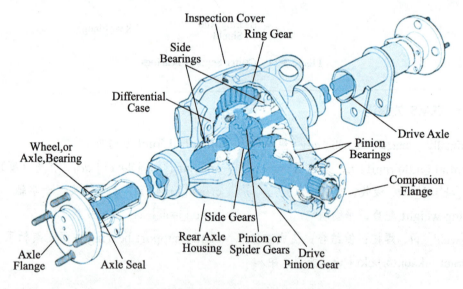

Figure 3-25 The Driving Axle Assembly

1. The Final Drive

A final drive is that part of a power transmission system between the drive shaft and the differential. Its function is to change the direction of the power transmitted by the drive shaft through 90 degrees to the driving axles. At the same time, it provides a fixed reduction between the speed of the drive shaft and the axle driving the wheels. The reduction or gear ratio of the final drive is determined by dividing the number of teeth on the ring gear and by the number of teeth on the pinion gear. In passenger vehicles, this gear ratio varies from about 3∶1 to 5∶1. In trucks it varies from about 5∶1 to 11∶1.

The major components of the final drive include the pinion gear, connected to the drive shaft, and a bevel gear or ring gear that is bolted or riveted to the differential carrier.

Pinion Gears

The pinion gear (Figure 3-26) turns the ring gear when the drive shaft is rotating. The outer end of the pinion gear is splined to the rear U-joint yoke. The inner end of the pinion gear meshes with the teeth on the ring gear.

Ring Gears

The pinion gear drives the ring gear (Figure 3-27). It is bolted securely to the differential case and has more teeth than the pinion gear. The ring gear transfers rotating power through a 90-degree angle change.

Figure 3-26 Pinion Gears

Figure 3-27 Ring Gears

2. Differentials

Another important unit in the power train is the differential (Figure 3-28), which is driven by the final drive. The differential is located between the axles and permits one axle to turn at a different speed from that of the other. The variations in axle speed are necessary when a vehicle rounds a corner or travels over uneven ground. At the same time, the differential transmits engine torque to the drive axles.

A differential assembly uses drive shaft rotation to transfer power to the axle shafts. The term differential can be remembered by thinking of the words "different" and "axle". The differential must be capable of providing torque to both axles, even when they are turning at different speeds. The differential assembly is constructed from the following: the differential case, the spider gears.

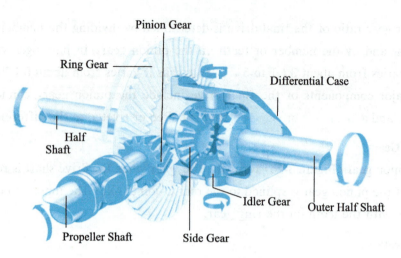

Figure 3-28 The Differential

The Differential Case

The differential case holds the ring gear, the spider gears, and the inner ends of the axles.

Spider Gears

The spider gears are a set of small bevel gears that include two axle gears (differential side gears) and two pinion gears (differential idler gears). The spider gears mount inside the differential case. A pinion shaft passes through the two side gears and case. The two side gears mesh with the inner ends of the axles.

Limited Slip Differentials

The conventional differential delivers the same amount of torque to each rear wheel when both wheels have equal traction. When one wheel has less traction than the other, for example, when one wheel slips on ice, the other wheel cannot deliver torque. All turning effort goes to the slipping wheel. To provide good, even traction, even though one wheel is slipping, a limited slip differential is used in many vehicles. It is very similar to the standard unit but has some means of preventing wheel spin and loss of traction. The standard differential delivers maximum torque to the wheel with minimum traction. The limited slip differential delivers maximum torque to the wheel with maximum traction.

KEY TERMS 关键词

final drive 主减速器
distribute [dɪˈstrɪbjuːt] vt. 分配；散布
bevel gear 锥齿轮

ring gear 内齿圈；环形齿轮
spider gear 星形齿轮
limited slip differential 限滑差速器

▶ SENTENCES 翻译示例

① The function of the driving axle assemblies is to decrease the speed and increase the torque that comes from the universal joint, and then distribute the power to the drive wheels.

驱动桥总成的作用是降低来自万向节的速度并且增加转矩，然后将动力分配给驱动轮。

② A final drive is that part of a power transmission system between the drive shaft and the differential.

主减速器是动力传动系统的一部分，位于传动轴和差速器之间。

③ The differential is located between the axles and permits one axle to turn at a different speed from that of the other.

差速器位于两根半轴之间，允许两轴以不同的速度转动。

▶ ASIGNMENTS 思考与练习

1. List the main parts of the driving axle assembly.
2. What's the function of the final drive?
3. What's the function of the differential?

3.2 The Running System

3.2.1 Frames

The frame is the main part of the chassis on which remaining parts of chassis are mounted. The frame should be extremely **rigid** and strong so that it can **withstand** shocks, **twist**s, stresses and vibrations to which it is subjected while vehicle is moving on road. It is also called underbody. The frame is supported on the wheels and tire assemblies. The frame is narrow in the front for providing short turning radius to front wheels. It widens out at the rear side to provide larger space in the body.

1. Types of Frames

There have been a few different frame designs over the years. Two basic frame construction types are body-on-frame and **unibody**.

Body-On-Frame

The body is made of sheet panels and isolated frame by inserting rubber mountings in between. The separate frame and body type of vehicle construction is the most common technique used when producing most full-sized and cargo vehicles. In this type of construction, the frame and the vehicle body are made separately, and each is a complete unit by itself. The frame is designed to support the weight of the body and absorb all of the loads. The body merely contains and, in some cases, protects the cargo.

The body generally is bolted to the frame at a few points to allow for *flexure* of the frame and to *distribute* the loads to the intended load-carrying members. The components of this type of frame are the *side members*, the *cross members* and the *gusset* plates. The typical frame design is shown in Figure 3-29.

The side members, or rails, are the heaviest part of the frame. The side members are shaped to *accommodate* the body and support the weight. They are narrow toward the front of the vehicle to permit a shorter turning radius for the wheels, and then widen under the main part of the body where the body is secured to the frame. The cross members are fixed to the side members to prevent weaving and twisting of the frame. The number, size, and arrangement of the cross members depend on the type of vehicle for which the frame was designed. Usually, a front cross member supports the *radiator* and the front of the engine; the rear cross members support for the fuel tanks and rear trunk on passenger cars. Body-on-frame is shown in Figure 3-30.

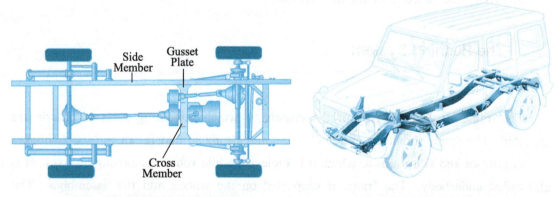

Figure 3-29 Typical Frame Design   Figure 3-30 Body-On-Frame

Unibody

The term "unibody" (Figure 3-31) or "unit body" is short for unitized body. In this type of construction, there is no frame. This single body and frame unit is made up of many different stamped sheet metal pieces welded together. The underbody is made of floor plates, channel and box sections welded into single unit. Such a design is generally lighter and more rigid than a vehicle having a separate body and frame. This assembly replaces the frame. This decreases the overall weight compared to conventional separate frame and body construction. Traditional body-on-frame architecture has shifted to the lighter body structure that is now used on most cars.

2. Subframes

Reduction of Noise, Vibration and Harshness (NVH) is a very important issue for modern cars. Conventional suspensions are mounted directly to the chassis (though via rubber bushing) so that NVH can be easily transmitted to the cabin. One of the popular solutions is to mount the suspension onto a sub-frame (Figure 3-32) (still via bushing), which is usually made of aluminium alloy to minimize the weight. The sub-frame itself can absorb some of the NVH. It is in turn mounted to the body by more bushings, thus reduce NVH further.

Figure 3-31　The Unibody　　　　　Figure 3-32　Subframes

▶ KEY TERMS 关键词

rigid ['rɪdʒɪd] *adj*. 刚性的，刚硬的
withstand [wɪð'stænd] *vt*. 抵挡
twist [twɪst] *n*. 扭曲 *vi*. 扭动；弯曲
unibody ['juːnɪ'bɒdɪ] *n*. 承载式车身
flexure ['flekʃə] *n*. 弯曲
distribute [dɪ'strɪbjuːt] *vt*. 分配；散布
side members 侧梁，纵梁

cross members 横梁
gusset ['gʌsɪt] *n*. 角撑板
accommodate [ə'kɒmədeɪt] *vt*. 调节，适应
radiator ['reɪdɪeɪtə(r)] *n*. 散热器
harshness ['hɑʃnɪs] *n*. 严肃；刺耳；粗糙的事物
bushing ['buʃɪŋ] *n*. 衬套

▶ SENTENCES 翻译示例

❶ The frame should be extremely rigid and strong so that it can withstand shocks, twists, stresses and vibrations to which it is subjected while vehicle is moving on road.
车架必须具有足够的强度和刚度，以承受车辆在道路上行驶时受到的冲击、扭转、应力和振动。

❷ The frame is designed to support the weight of the body and absorb all of the loads.

车架的设计是为了支撑车身的重量和吸收所有的负荷。

❸ One of the popular solutions is to mount the suspension onto a sub-frame (still via bushing), which is usually made of aluminium alloy to minimize the weight.

其中一种常用的解决方案是将悬架安装到一个由铝合金制成的副车架上(仍然通过衬套),以减轻重量。

> **ASIGNMENTS 思考与练习**
>
> 1. Name out the two basic frame construction types.
> 2. What are the differences between body-on-frame and unibody?
> 3. Why is subframe important for modern cars?

3.2.2 Suspensions

A system of mechanical linkages, springs, dampers that are used to connect the wheels to the chassis is known as suspension system. It has usually done two works — controlling the vehicle's handling and braking for safety and keeping the passengers comfortable from bumps, vibrations etc. It also helps to maintain correct vehicle height. The design of front and rear suspension of a car may be different. Typical suspension system on a rear-wheel-drive car is shown in Figure 3-33.

Figure 3-33　Typical Suspension Systems on a Rear-Wheel-Drive Car

1. Structure

Springs

It is a mechanical device which is typically used to store energy and subsequently release it, to absorb shock, or to maintain a force between contacting surfaces. Today's springing systems are based on one of four basic designs.

Leaf Springs: The leaf Springs (Figure 3-34) is the oldest and simplest spring of suspension. Several long, thin steel leaves are bound together in a pack by clamps. A leaf spring is fixed to the axle by U-bolts that clamp the center of the stack of steel strips. One end of the pack is connected to the vehicle's frame via a bushing. The other end uses a shackle. Combined with the flexing of the leaf pack itself, it provides the suspension movement and cushions the ride. They are still used today on most trucks and heavy-duty vehicles.

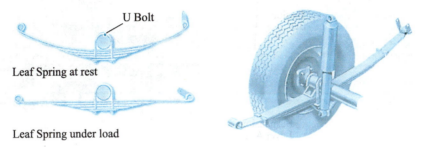

Figure 3-34　Leaf Springs

Coil Springs: A coil spring (Figure 3-35) is also known as a helical spring. It's made of an elastic material formed into the shape of a helix. Coil springs compress and expand to absorb the motion of the wheels.

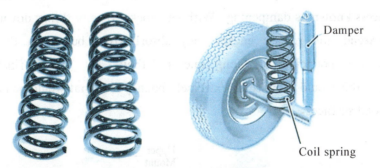

Figure 3-35　Coil Springs

Torsion Bars: Torsion bar (Figure 3-36) uses the twisting properties of a steel bar to provide coil-spring-like performance. Instead of compressing, a torsion bar twists. Due to pre-stressing, they are directional. This is how they work: One end of a bar is anchored to the vehicle frame. The other end is attached to a wishbone, which acts like a lever that moves perpendicular to the torsion bar. When the wheel hits a bump, vertical motion is transferred to the wishbone and then, through the levering action, to the torsion bar. The torsion bar then twists along its axis to provide the spring force.

Air Springs: Air springs (Figure 3-37), which consists of a cylindrical chamber of air positioned between the wheel and the car's body, use the compressive qualities of air to absorb wheel vibrations. The concept is actually more than a century old and could be found on horse-drawn buggies. Air springs from this era were made from air-filled, leather diaphragms, much like a bellows. They were replaced with molded-rubber air springs in the 1930s.

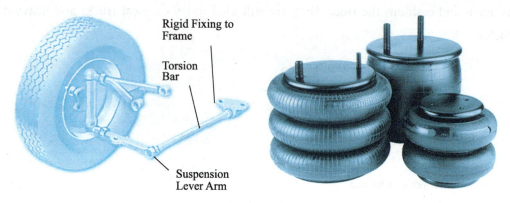

Figure 3-36　Torsion Bars　　　　　　　　Figure 3-37　Air Springs

Shock Absorbers

Shock absorbers (Figure 3-38) (also known as "shocks") are the suspension components which slow, then stop the up-and-down bouncing movement of your vehicle's springs through a process known as dampening. Without shocks to calm things down, springs will continue to extend and release energy they absorb from bumps in the road at an uncontrolled rate — bouncing for a long time until their kinetic energy finally dissipates. Needless to say, this would produce an extremely bouncy ride that would be hard to control over uneven road surfaces.

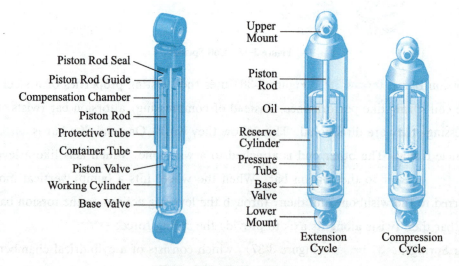

Figure 3-38　Shock Absorbers

Essentially, shock absorbers control unwanted spring motion by turning kinetic energy of suspension travel into heat energy that's channeled away using hydraulic fluid. Most standard shock absorbers will produce greater resistance during their extension cycle (getting longer) compared to their compression cycle (getting shorter). Shock absorbers bolt between the vehicle's frame and suspension members near each wheel. Each mounting point is typicaly described as "eye" (round bushing which bolt passes through). Inside the shock absorber is a metal rod attached to a piston that moves up and down inside a cylinder filled with hydraulic oil. Most modern shocks also contain nitrogen gas to reduce shock absorber fade that happens if oil becomes aerated and bubbly due to heat buildup.

Control Arms

Control arms (Figure 3-39) are one of the most boring, yet mechanically impressive parts on a car. In the most basic of terms, the control arms allow up and down movement of the suspension while holding the knuckles, spindles and axles firmly onto the car. They have been an integral part of suspension systems for nearly a century. Over this time, they have come in a variety of shapes, sizes and materials but they have always served the same exact function — to hold everything together!

Figure 3-39   Control Arms

Now, you can't talk about control arms without talking about ball joints and rubber control arm bushings, because they are all "best friends". The vast majority of control arms will have a rubber bushing or ball joint mounted securely to them. These allow the control arm to rotate up and down without binding up.

The oldest versions of control arms were most commonly made from stamped steel because it was cheap, fast and easy. Over the years, many control arms have evolved from their humble stamped steel beginnings to elaborate cast aluminum pieces that are stronger and lighter than ever before.

2. Types of Suspension Systems

Classification of suspension types can be done by position (front or rear) or type (solid or independent). The solid axle front suspension has practically disappeared from the passenger car. Thus, this work will group suspensions by type, with the understanding that the solid axle types generally are found only at the rear of the vehicle. There are three major types of suspensions. They are dependent, independent and semi-independent system.

(1) **Independent Suspension Systems**

This system means that the suspension is set-up in such a way that allows the wheel on the left and right side of the vehicle to move vertically independent up and down while driving on uneven surface. Force acting on the single wheel does not affect the other as there is no mechanical linkage between the two hubs of the same vehicle. In most of the vehicle, it is employed in front wheels. Independent suspension is shown in Figure 3-40.

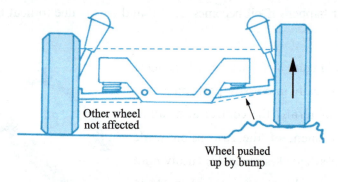

Figure 3-40 The Independent Suspension

This type of suspension usually offers better ride quality and handling due to less unsprung weight. The main advantages of independent suspension are that they require less space, they provide easier steer ability, low weight, etc. Examples of independent suspension are:

The McPherson Strut Suspension

The McPherson strut suspension (Figure 3-41, Figure 3-42) was invented in the 1940s by Earl S. McPherson of Ford. It was introduced on the 1950 English Ford and has since become one of the dominating suspensions systems of the world because of its compactness and low cost.

The McPherson strut combines a shock absorber and a coil spring into a single unit. This provides a more compact and lighter suspension system that can be used for front-wheel drive vehicles. Unlike other suspension designs, in McPherson strut suspension, the shock absorber also serves as a link to control the position of the wheel. Therefore it saves the upper control arm. Besides, since the strut is vertically positioned, the whole suspension is very compact. To front-wheel drive cars, whose engine and transmission are all located inside the front compartment, they need front suspensions which engage very little width of the car. Undoubtedly, McPherson strut suspension is the most suitable one.

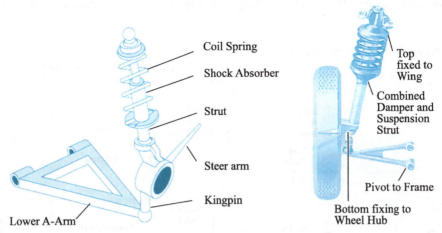

Figure 3-41 The McPherson Strut Suspension

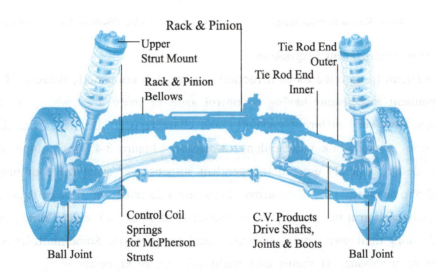

Figure 3-42 The McPherson Strut Suspensions on a Vehicle

Double Wishbone Suspensions

Double wishbone (or "A-arms") suspension (Figure 3-43, Figure 3- 44) are the most ideal suspension. It can be used in front and rear wheels. Notice that the control arms are of unequal length, with the upper arm shorter than the lower arm. This design is known as the short-arm/long-arm, or the parallel arm design. While there are several different possible configurations, this design typically uses two wishbone-shaped arms to locate the wheel. Each wishbone, which has two mounting positions to the frame and one at the wheel, bears a shock absorber and a coil spring to absorb vibrations. Double-wishbone suspensions allow for more control over the camber angle of the wheel. It is more costly than McPherson strut and torsion beam because it involves more components and more suspension pick up points in the car body. Owing to these reasons, very few small cars adopt it.

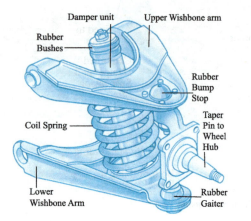

Figure 3-43 The Double Wishbone Suspension

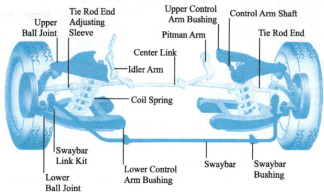

Figure 3-44 Double Wishbone Suspensions on a Vehicle

Multi-Link Independent Suspensions

It is difficult to describe its construction because it is not strictly defined. In theory, any independent suspensions having 3 control arms or more are multi-links. Different designs may have very different geometry and characteristic. Derived from the double wishbone one, a multi-link independent suspension (Figure 3-45) is a type of vehicle suspension design typically used in independent suspensions, using three or more lateral arms, and one or more longitudinal arms. These arms do not have to be of equal length.

Typically each arm has a ball joint or rubber bushing at each end. Consequently they react loads along their own length, in tension and compression. Some multi-links do use a swing arm or wishbone. It seems that multi-link can offer better compromise between handling and space efficiency.

Figure 3-45 Multi-link Suspensions on a Vehicle

(2) The Dependent Suspension System

There is a rigid linkage between the two wheels of the same axle. Force acting on one wheel will affect the opposite wheel. For each motion of the wheel caused by road irregularities affects the coupled wheel as well. Dependent suspension is shown in Figure 3-46.

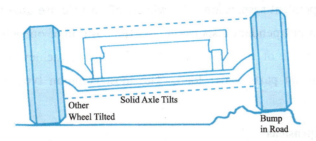

Figure 3-46 The Dependent Suspension

A solid axle has wheels mounted to each end of a rigid beam. Such systems are generally used when high load-carrying capability is required because they are very robust assemblies. Examples of this system are:

Hotchkiss Suspensions

A solid axle or beam axle called Hotchkiss Suspension (Figure 3-47, Figure 3-48) is a dependent type suspension. It is mostly used in rear wheels in which the rear axle is supported and located by two leaf springs. The vertical movement of one wheel influences the other. Hotchkiss Suspensions are simple and economical to manufacture. They are so rigid that there is no change in track width and toe-in on a full bump which helps in low wearing of tires. The main disadvantage is that the mass of the beam is included in unsprung weight of the vehicle which results in low ride quality.

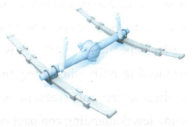

Figure 3-47 Hotchkiss Suspensions

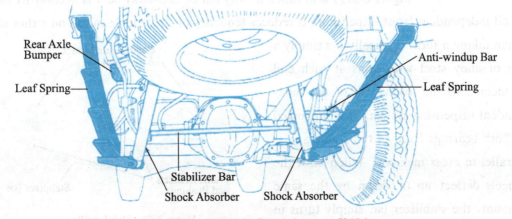

Figure 3-48 Hotchkiss Suspensions on a Vehicle

(3) The Semi-Independent Suspension

In a semi-independent suspension, the wheels of an axle are able to move relative to one another as in an independent suspension, but the position of one wheel has an effect on the position and attitude of the other wheel. This effect is achieved via the twisting or deflecting of suspension parts under load. The most common type of semi-independent suspension is the twist beam.

Twist-Beam Suspensions

Most modern mini cars up to C-segment (for instance, VW Golf) employ torsion beam as the rear suspension. Why? Compared with double wishbones and multi-link suspensions, it engages little width of the car, thus enable greater rear seat room. It is mostly used in the rear wheel of the cars. It is very favorable due to its low cost and it is very durable. It is simple in design and is very light in weight. In fact, twist-beam suspension (Figure 3-49) is only half-independent — there is a torsion beam connecting both wheels together, which allows limited degree of freedom when forced. For some less demanding compact cars, this saves the anti-roll bars. On the contrary, it doesn't provide the same level of ride and handling as double wishbones or multi-link suspensions.

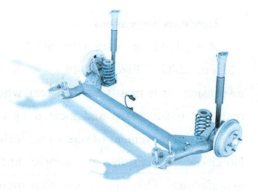

Figure 3-49　Twist-Beam Suspensions on a Vehicle

3. Stabilizer Bar

Stabilizer bar (Figure 3-50), also called a sway bar or anti-sway bar, is necessarily used in all independent front suspension. It reduces tendency of the vehicle to roll on either side when taking a turn. Typically it's simply a bar of alloy steel with arms at each end connected to the lower arm of the independent suspension system. It is supported in bush bearings fixed in the frame and is parallel to cross member. When both the wheels deflect up or down by the same amount, the stabilizer bar simply turns in the bush bearings.

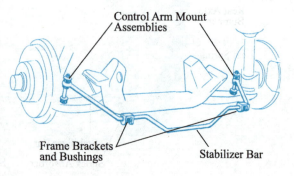

Figure 3-50　Stabilizer Bars

KEY TERMS 关键词

damper [ˈdæmpə(r)] *n.* 减振器
suspension [səˈspenʃn] *n.* 悬挂,悬吊
leaf spring 钢板弹簧
clamp [klæmp] *n.* 夹子
shackle [ˈʃækl] *n.* 钩环,锁扣
coil spring 螺旋弹簧
helical [ˈhelɪkl] *adj.* 螺旋形的
elastic [ɪˈlæstɪk] *adj.* 有弹性的
torsion bar 扭杆弹簧
anchor [ˈæŋkə(r)] *vt.* 使固定
perpendicular [ˌpɜːpənˈdɪkjələ(r)] *adj.* 垂直的
air spring 气体弹簧
bellows [ˈbeləʊz] *n.* 风箱
calm [kɑːm] *vt.* 使平静;使镇定
shock absorber 减振器
kinetic [kɪˈnetɪk] *adj.* 运动的
dissipate [ˈdɪsɪpeɪt] *vt.* 消耗
nitrogen [ˈnaɪtrədʒən] *n.* 氮
aerated [ˈeəreɪtɪd] *adj.* 充气的
bubbly [ˈbʌbli] *adj.* 起泡的
knuckle [ˈnʌkl] *n.* 关节
spindle [ˈspɪndl] *n.* 轴,主轴

ball joint 球形接头
elaborate [ɪˈlæbəreɪt] *adj.* 精心制作的
cast [kɑːst] *vt. / n.* 浇铸
solid [ˈsɒlɪd] *adj.* 固体的
unsprung weight 簧下质量
McPherson strut suspension 麦弗逊式悬架
strut [strʌt] *n.* 支柱
compactness [kəmˈpæktnɪs] *n.* 简洁;紧密
wishbone [ˈwɪʃbəʊn] *n.* 叉骨
configuration [kənˌfɪɡəˈreɪʃn] *n.* 配置;结构
multi-link 多连杆
lateral [ˈlætərəl] *adj.* 横的,侧面
longitudinal [ˌlɒŋɡɪˈtjuːdɪnl] *adj.* 长度的,
    纵向的
compromise [ˈkɒmprəmaɪz] *n.* 妥协,和解;
    折中
irregularities [ɪˌreɡjʊˈlærɪtɪz] *n.* 不规则性
Hotchkiss [ˈhɒtʃkɪs] *n.* 霍奇基斯
Hotchkiss suspension 霍奇基斯悬架
twist beam 扭力梁
stabilizer bar 稳定杆

SENTENCES 翻译示例

❶ It has usually done two works-controlling the vehicle's handling and braking for safety and keeping the passengers comfortable from bumps, vibrations etc.
它通常有两个作用,分别是控制车辆的操作和制动的安全,并保持乘客的舒适性、避免颠簸、振动等。

❷ It is a mechanical device which is typically used to store energy and subsequently release it, to absorb shock, or to maintain a force between contacting surfaces.
它是一种机械装置,通常用于储存能量并随后释放它,用以吸收冲击或保持接触面之间的力。

❸ On the contrary, it doesn't provide the same level of ride and handling as double wishbones or multi-link suspensions.
相反,它不能提供与双叉臂或多连杆悬架相同的行驶和操控水平。

> **ASIGNMENTS 思考与练习**
>
> 1. List three types of springs used in automobile suspension.
> 2. What does a stabilizer bar do?
> 3. List the differences between the dependent and the independent suspension system.

3.2.3 Wheels and Tires

1. Wheels

Wheels must have enough strength to carry the weight of the vehicle and withstand a wide range of speed and road conditions. Wheel construction is shown in Figure 3-51.

Drop Center Wheels

The drop center wheel (Figure 3-52) is made in one piece and is commonly used on passenger vehicles because it allows for easier installation and removal of the tire.

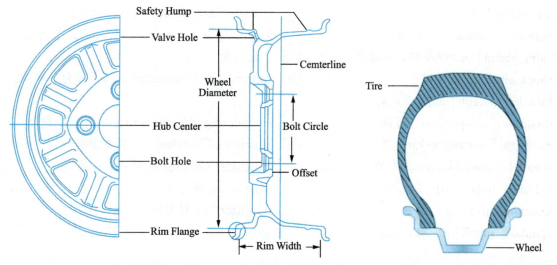

Figure 3-51　Wheels Construction　　　　Figure 3-52　Drop Center Wheels

2. Tires

Tires are mounted on the **rim**s of wheels. They enclose a tube between rim and itself. Air is filled at a designated pressure inside the tube. The tire remains inflated due to air pressure inside tube. The tire carries the vehicle load and provides cushioning effect. It absorbs some of the vibrations generated due to vehicle's movement on uneven surfaces. It also resists the vehicle's tendency to oversteer or turn during cornering. Tire must generate minimum noise when vehicle takes turn on the road. It should provide good grip with the road surface under all conditions.

(1) Types of Tires

Two types of tubeless tires are used in vehicles.

Bias-Ply Tires

A bias-ply tire (Figure 3-53) is one of the oldest designs. The position of the cords in a bias-ply tire allows the body of the tire to flex easily. This design improves the cushioning action, which provides a smooth ride on rough roads. A bias-ply tire has the plies running at an angle from bead to bead. The cord angle is also reversed from ply to ply, forming a crisscross pattern. The tread is bonded directly to the top ply. A major disadvantage of a bias-ply tire is that the weakness of the plies and tread reduce traction at high speeds and increase rolling resistance.

Radial Ply Tires

The radial ply tire (Figure 3-54) has a very flexible sidewall, but a stiff tread. This design provides for a very stable footprint (shape and amount of tread touching the road surface) which improves safety, cornering, braking, and wear. The radial ply tire has plies running straight across from bead to bead with stabilizer belts directly beneath the tread. The belts can be made of steel, fiberglass, or other materials. A major disadvantage of the radial ply tire is that it produces a harder ride at low speeds. The stiff tread does not flex as much on rough road surfaces.

(2) Structure

Tire Structure is shown in Figure 3-55.

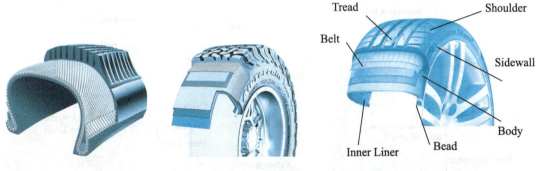

Figure 3-53 Bias-Ply Tires   Figure 3-54 Radial Ply Tires   Figure 3-55 Tire Structure

Body: The body, also known as the "carcass" or "casing", is the core of the tire. The carcass is the framework of the tire. The carcass refers to all layers made up of tire cord. It absorbs the tire's internal air pressure, weight and shock.

Tread: It's made from a compound of many natural and synthetic rubbers and other components. The tread consists of a thick layer of rubber which comes into direct contact with the road surface.

Shoulder: Located between the tread and sidewall, the shoulder is the thickest part in a tire. Because of this, the shoulder is designed to quickly and easily dissipate heat that accumulates inside the tire while driving.

Sidewall: Located between the tire's shoulder and bead, the sidewall protects the carcass on the inside and provides a comfortable riding experience due to its flexibility during driving. Also, the type of tire, size, structure, tread pattern, manufacturer, brand name, and other detailed information are marked on the sidewall.

Bead: The bead wraps around the end of the cord and fixes the tire to the rim. It is high-strength, rubber-coated, steel cable that clamps the tire to the rim. In general, the rim is slightly tightened, so in the case of sudden reduction of air pressure while driving, the tire will not become unfastened from the rim.

Belt: The belt is a cord layer placed in between the tread and carcass in a tire to protect the carcass. It absorbs external shock and prevents injury to the tread from coming into direct contact with the carcass. The belt is a strong reinforcement layer located in the circumference in between the tread and carcass in radial tires.

Inner Liner: The inner liner substitute for the tube in the tire's interior and consists of rubber layer with low air permeability. The rubber layer generally consists of butyl and synthetic rubber. The main function of the inner liner is to hold high-pressure air inside.

Dimensions

There are some important tire dimensions (Figure 3-56) that we must know. These are illustrated and described below.

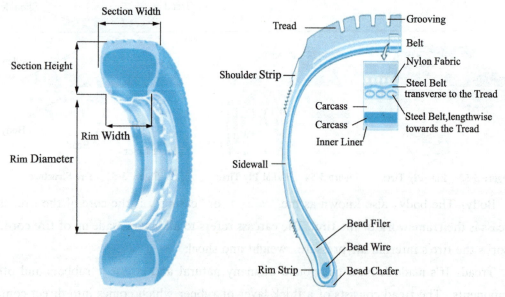

Figure 3-56　Tire Dimensions

Tire Sidewall Markings

Tire Sidewall Markings (Figure 3-57) contain some information we need to know.

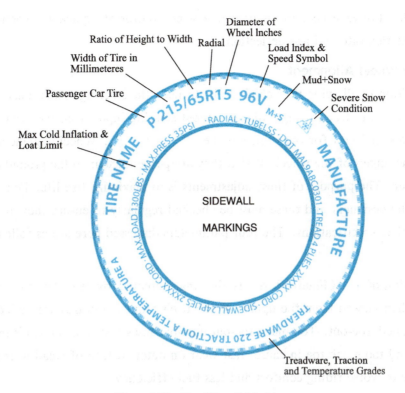

Figure 3-57 Tire Sidewall Markings

Aspect Ratio

There is another dimension of a tire that is useful to know — though strictly speaking, it's a calculation rather than a true dimension. It's known as the tire's aspect ratio (Figure 3-58). Aspect Ratio is the relationship of a tire's height to width when mounted and inflated on a rim of correct size.

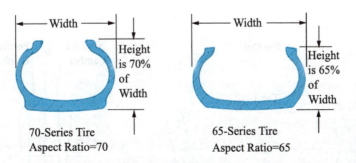

Figure 3-58 Aspect Ratio

Why do we care about a tire's aspect ratio? Because the height to width relationship determines the shape of the tire on the rim, and more importantly, the performance characteristics of the tire. If the sidewall height of a tire is reduced slightly, the sidewall stiffness is increased greatly. Higher aspect ratios deliver greater deflection under load and a softer ride. Lower aspect ratios deliver a wider footprint, quicker response, less slip angle, lower flex rate and less deflection.

3. The Wheel Alignment

In addition to allowing the vehicle to be turned, the steering system must be set up to allow the vehicle to track straight ahead without steering input from the driver. Thus, an important design factor for the vehicle is the wheel alignment. Wheel alignment consists of adjusting the angles of the wheels so that they are perpendicular to the ground and parallel to each other. The purpose of these adjustments is to maximize tire life. Four parameters are set by the designer, and these must be checked regularly to ensure they are within the original vehicle specifications. The four parameters discussed here are as follows.

Toe

Definition of toe (Figure 3-59) is the angle created by tire direction and vehicle direction when viewed from the upper. If the tire's front is inward, it's called Toe-in; if outward, called Toe-out. Too much toe-out usually causes fast wear on tire's inner surface of tread. And too much toe-in causes fast wear on outer surface of tread in reverse. Both cases results in worse riding comfort and less fuel efficiency.

Camber

Definition of Camber (Figure 3-60) is the angle, measured in degrees, created by steering axis and vertical line to the ground when viewed from the front or rear. If the top of the wheel is leaning out from the center of the car, then the camber is positive; if it's leaning in, then the camber is negative; if the tire stands perfectly vertical, it is called neutral camber; if the camber is out of adjustment, it will cause tire wear on one side of the tire's tread.

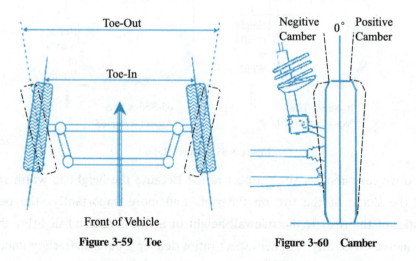

Figure 3-59 Toe   Figure 3-60 Camber

With the development of suspension and vehicle technology, most vehicles today have negative camber, which increases outer tire's contact area and provides stable cornering performance. On many front-wheel-drive vehicles, camber is not adjustable. If the camber is out on these cars, it indicates that something is worn or bent, possibly from an accident and must be repaired or replaced.

Steering Axis Inclination (SAI)

Steering Axis Inclination (SAI) (Figure 3-61) is the measurement in degrees of the steering pivot line when viewed from the front of the vehicle. This angle causes the vehicle to lift slightly when you turn the wheel away from a straight ahead position. This action uses the weight of the vehicle to cause the steering wheel to return to the center when you let go of it after making a turn.

Caster

Definition of Caster (Figure 3-62) is the angle created by steering axis and vertical line to the ground when viewed from the side. Caster is positive if the axis is angled backward, and negative if forward. Typically, positive caster will make the vehicle more stable at high speeds.

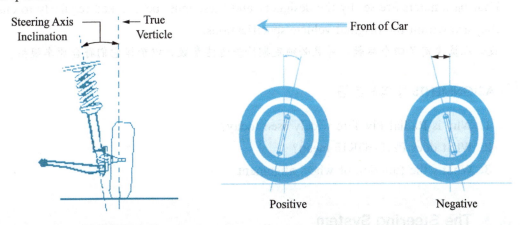

Figure 3-61　Steering Axis Inclination (SAI)　　　　Figure 3-62　Caster

Incorrect alignment settings will usually result in more rapid tire wear. Therefore, alignment should be checked whenever new tires or suspension components are installed, and any time unusual tire wear patterns appear. Alignment should also be checked after the vehicle has encountered a major road hazard or curb.

▶ KEY TERMS 关键词

rim [rɪm] n. 边，边缘；轮辋　　　　　　ply [plaɪ] n. (pl. plies) 层
bias-ply tire 斜交胎　　　　　　　　　　bead [biːd] n. 胎圈

cord [kɔːd] n. 绳索
tread [tred] n. 胎面
radial ply tire 子午线轮胎
sidewall ['saɪdwɔːl] n. 轮胎侧壁
carcass ['kɑːkəs] n. 构架，外胎身
synthetic [sɪn'θetɪk] adj. 合成的
accumulate [ə'kjuːmjəleɪt] vi. 累积；积聚

aspect ratio 压缩比
wheel alignment 车轮定位
toe [təʊ] n. 前束
camber ['kæmbə(r)] n. 主销外倾
Steering Axis Inclination 主销内倾
caster ['kɑːstə(r)] n. 主销后倾

◉ SENTENCES 翻译示例

❶ It absorbs some of the vibrations generated due to vehicle's movement on uneven surfaces.
它吸收了由于车辆在不平路面上行驶而产生的一些振动。

❷ A major disadvantage of a bias-ply tire is that the weakness of the plies and tread reduce traction at high speeds and increase rolling resistance.
斜交轮胎的一个主要缺点是帘布层和胎面薄弱性降低了高速行驶时的牵引力，增加了滚动阻力。

❸ Four parameters are set by the designer, and these must be checked regularly to ensure they are within the original vehicle specifications.
设计人员设定了四个参数，并且必须定期检查这些参数，以确保它们符合原车规格。

◉ ASIGNMENTS 思考与练习

1. Why is Radial Ply Tire widely used today?
2. What does P215/65R15 mean?
3. What's the function of wheel alignment?

3.3 The Steering System

The steering system (Figure 3-63) allows the operator to guide the vehicle along the road and turn left or right as desired. The gears in the steering gear assembly not only steer the front wheels, but at the same time, they act as reduction gears, reducing steering wheel turning effort by increasing the output torque. At first most systems were manual, and then power steering became popular. It is now installed in

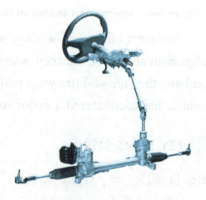

Figure 3-63 The Steering System

most vehicles manufactured today.

3.3.1 Manual Steering Systems

Steering Wheels

The steering wheel is the critical interface between driver and car. Handle the steering operation.

Steering Columns

The steering column consists of the steering main shaft which transmits the steering wheel rotation to the steering gear, and the column tube which fixes the steering main shaft to the body. The steering wheel is fitted to the top end of the steering main shaft by a nut. The steering column incorporates an impact-absorbing mechanism that absorbs the thrust force that would otherwise be applied to the driver at the time of a collision. The bottom end of the steering main shaft is connected to the steering gear, generally by way of a flexible joint or universal joint to minimize the transmission of road shock from the steering gear to the steering wheel.

Steering Gears

Convert the steering torque and rotational deflection from the steering wheel, transmit them to the wheel through the steering linkage, and make the vehicle turn.

There are a couple different types of steering gears. The most common are rack-and-pinion and recirculating ball.

(1) The Rack-and-Pinion Type (Figure 3-64)

A rack and pinion is a pair of gears which convert rotational motion into linear motion. The manual rack-and-pinion steering gear basically consists of a steering gear shaft, pinion gear, rack, thrust spring, bearings, seals, and gear housing. In the rack-and-pinion steering system, the end of the steering gear shaft contains a pinion gear which meshes with a long rack. The rack is connected to the steering arms by tie rods, which are adjustable for maintaining proper toe angle. As the steering wheel is rotated, the pinion gear on the end of the steering shaft rotates. The pinion gear moves the rack from one side to the other. This action pushes or pulls on the tie rods. This turns the wheels to one side or the other so the vehicle can be steered.

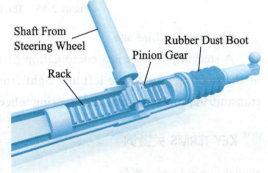

Figure 3-64 The Rack-and-Pinion Type

(2) The Recirculating-Ball Type

Recirculating-ball type is shown in Figure 3-65. In the recirculating ball gears, the input shaft of this type of steering gear is also connected to a worm gear, but the worm gear in a recirculating ball type unit is straight. Mounted on the worm gear is a ball nut. The ball nut has interior spiral grooves that mate with the threads of the worm gear. The ball nut also has exterior gear teeth on one side. These teeth mesh with teeth on a sector gear and shaft.

In the grooves between the ball nut and the worm gear are ball bearings. The ball bearings allow the worm gear and ball nut to mesh and move with little friction. When the steering wheel is turned, the input shaft will rotate the worm gear. The ball bearing will transmit the turning force form the worm gear to the ball nut, causing the ball nut to move up and down the worm gear. Ball return guides are connected to each end of the ball nut grooves. These allow the ball bearing to circulate in a continuous loop.

As the ball nut moves up or down on the worm gear, it causes the sector gear to rotate which, in turn, causes the pitman arm to swivel back and forth. This motion is transferred to the steering arm and knuckle to turn the wheel.

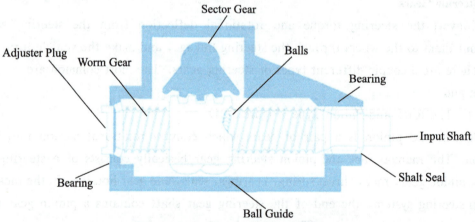

Figure 3-65   The Recirculating-Ball Type

The Steering Linkage

A steering linkage is a combination of the rods and arms that transmit the movement of the steering gear to the left and right front wheels. The steering linkage must accurately transmit the movement of the steering wheel to the front wheels.

▶ KEY TERMS 关键词

swivel ['swɪvl] vi. 旋转
steering system 转向系统
steering wheel 转向盘

interface ['ɪntəfeɪs] n. 界面
steering column 转向柱
incorporate [ɪn'kɔːpəreɪt] vt. 包含

thrust force 推力
rack [ræk] n. 齿条
recirculating ball 循环球
sector gear 扇形齿轮

SENTENCES 翻译示例

❶ The steering system allows the operator to guide the vehicle along the road and turn left or right as desired
转向系统允许驾驶员沿着道路行驶，并根据需要左转或右转。

❷ The gears in the steering gear assembly not only steer the front wheels, but at the same time, they act as reduction gears, reducing steering wheel turning effort by increasing the output torque.
转向器总成中的齿轮不仅可以转动前轮，同时还可以作为减速齿轮，通过增加输出转矩来减少转向盘的转向力度。

❸ The steering linkage must accurately transmit the movement of the steering wheel to the front wheels.
转向连杆必须准确地将转向盘的运动传递给前轮。

ASIGNMENTS 思考与练习

1. Please list types of the steering gears used in cars today.
2. How does a rack-and-pinion steering system work?
3. Name out the main components of a steering system.

3.3.2 Power Steering Systems

To improve driving comfort, most modern automobiles have wide, low pressure tires which increase the tire-to-road surface contact area. As a result of this, more steering effort is required. Steering effort can be decreased by increasing the gear ratio of the steering gear. However, this will cause a larger rotary motion of the steering wheel when the vehicle is turning, making sharp turns impossible. Therefore, to keep the steering fast and, at the same time the steering effort small, some sort of a steering assist device became necessary. In other words, power steering, which had been chiefly used on larger vehicles, is now also used on compact passenger cars. Power steering allows manual steering to always be available, even if the engine is not running or the power-assist system fails.

There are hydraulic type, electro-hydraulic type and electric type power steering.

1. Hydraulic Power Steering (HPS)

Hydraulic power steering (Figure 3-66) utilizes a hydraulic pump driven by the engine; this pump enables a small amount of fluid to be under pressure. This pressure in turn assists the steering mechanism in directing the tires as you turn the steering wheel. This kind of power steering system typically includes a pump, power steering fluid, a pressure hose assembly, a control valve and a return line.

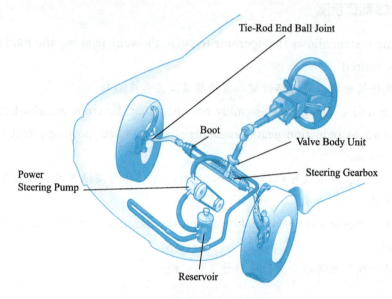

Figure 3-66 Hydraulic Power Steering

Pumps

The pump (Figure 3-67) is driven by the engine crank pulley and drive belt, and sends fluid, under pressure, to the gear housing. The discharge volume of the pump is in proportion to the engine speed, but the amount of fluid sent to the gear housing is regulated by a flow control valve, with excess fluid being returned to the suction side.

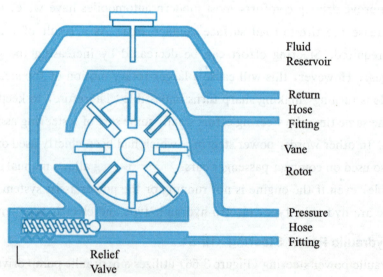

Figure 3-67 Pumps

Reservoir Tanks

The reservoir tank supplies the power with steering fluid. It is installed either directly to the pump body or separately. If not installed to the pump body, it is connected to it by two hoses. Normally, the reservoir tank cap has a level gauge for checking the fluid level.

Flow Control Valves

The flow control valve controls the flow volume of the fluid from the pump to the gear housing, maintaining a constant flow regardless of the pump speed.

Rotary Valves

A power-steering system should assist the driver only when he is exerting force on the steering wheel (such as when starting a turn). When the driver is not exerting force (such as when driving in a straight line), the system shouldn't provide any assist. The device that senses the force on the steering wheel is called the rotary valve (Figure 3-68).

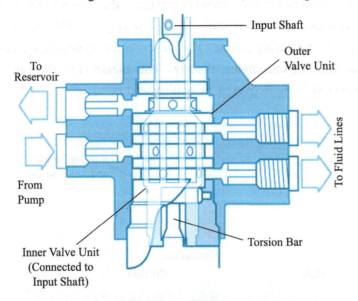

Figure 3-68 Rotary Valves

The key to the rotary valve is a torsion bar. The torsion bar is a thin rod of metal that twists when torque is applied to it. The top of the bar is connected to the steering wheel, and the bottom of the bar is connected to the pinion or worm gear (which turns the wheels), so the amount of torque in the torsion bar is equal to the amount of torque the driver is using to turn the wheels. The more torque the driver uses to turn the wheels, the more the bar twists.

As the torsion bar twists, it rotates the inside of the spool valve relative to the outside. Because the inner part of the spool valve is also connected to the steering shaft (and therefore to the steering wheel), the amount of rotation between the inner and outer parts of the spool valve depends on how much torque the driver applies to the steering wheel.

When the steering wheel is not being turned, both hydraulic lines provide the same amount of pressure to the steering gear. However, if the spool valve is turned one way or the other, ports open up to provide high-pressure fluid to the appropriate line.

Energy savings is one of the most significant concerns in the development of new vehicles, particularly power-steering systems, as over 70% of the fuel consumed by conventional hydraulic power steering (HPS) systems is unnecessary and can be avoided. Therefore, the application of a more advanced power steering systems like electric power steering (EPS) and electro-hydraulic power steering (EHPS) could save a lot of energy. New types of power steering systems are particularly needed for commercial vehicles.

2. Electro-Hydraulic Power Steering (EHPS)

The electro-hydraulic power steering (Figure 3-69) is just like any other hydraulic power steering system, but a major difference is that in conventional hydraulic system, the hydraulic system will extract power from the engine, which lowers the total power output of the car and decreases the fuel mileage of the car slightly. On the other hand, in this electro-hydraulic power steering system, the power to the hydraulic system is delivered by an electric motor and not the engine directly. This means that the engine load does not change as the power is being delivered by battery and motor.

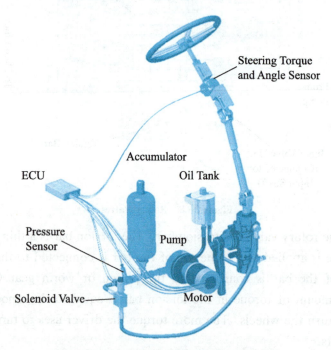

Figure 3-69　Electro-hydraulic Power Steering

3. Electric Power Steering (EPS)

Electric power steering (EPS) (Figure 3-70) is all electronic. It's designed to use an electric motor to provide directional control to the driver of a vehicle. Electric power steering systems do not require engine power to operate. Thus, a vehicle equipped with an EPS system may achieve an estimated three percent greater fuel economy than the same vehicle with conventional hydraulic power steering. As an added benefit, more of the engine's power is transmitted to its intended location — the wheels. The EPS system is replacing the hydraulic steering system and is destined to soon become mainstream among automotive manufacturers.

The EPS system consists of four major components.

- The EPS control module which collects data from the EPS components and sends out the required information;
- The EPS motor, its speed strength and direction are controlled by the EPS Control Unit;
- The reduction gear, which inputs the power assist to the steering rack assembly;
- The torque sensor which monitors the driver's input and the EPS system's mechanical output.

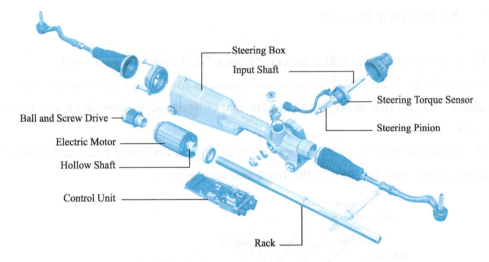

Figure 3-70　Electric Power Steering

KEY TERMS 关键词

power steering 动力转向
reservoir tank 油罐
flow control valve 流量控制阀

rotary valve 转阀
spool [spuːl] n. 线轴
spool valve 滑阀

SENTENCES 翻译示例

❶ Therefore, to keep the steering fast and, at the same time the steering effort small, some sort of a steering assist device became necessary.

因此，要保持转向速度快，同时转向的力度小，需要使用某种转向辅助装置。

❷ The pump is driven by the engine crank pulley and drive belt, and sends fluid, under pressure, to the gear housing.

液压泵由发动机曲轴带轮和传动带驱动，并在压力下将液压油输送到齿轮箱。

❸ The EPS system is replacing the hydraulic steering system and is destined to soon become mainstream among automotive manufacturers.

电动助力转向系统正在取代液压转向系统，并将很快成为汽车制造商中的主流。

◉ ASIGNMENTS 思考与练习

1. What are the parts of a car steering system?
2. Please list types of the power steering system used in cars today.
3. When the power steering system fails, whether the driver can steer the car? Why?

3.4　The Braking System

There are two types of brake systems (Figure 3-71): **parking brake** and **service brake**. The parking brake, also called "emergency" brake, is the brake that is designed to "hold" the vehicle. The service brake is the system that is designed to slow down the vehicle or bring it to a stop.

The service brake is activated every time you step on the brake pedal and it distributes the braking force hydraulically to the front and rear wheels.

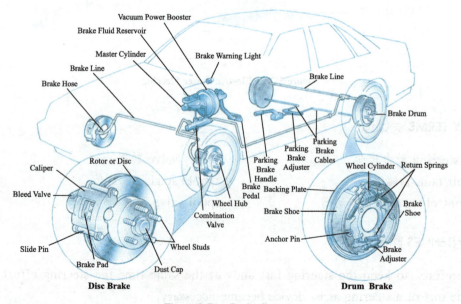

Figure 3-71　Brake Systems

The parking brake is typically cable operated and applies force to either dedicated brake shoes inside the rear rotor or, through the piston in the caliper. It can be operated by a separate pedal or a hand lever, usually located between the front seats.

3.4.1 The Hydraulic Braking System

Hydraulic operation of the brake systems has been the universal design for more than 60 years. The complete components of oil or hydraulic braking system consists of master cylinder, steel lines, rubber hoses, booster and brake apply devices at each wheel.

1. Structure

The Vacuum Booster

The vacuum booster (Figure 3-72) is located between the brake pedal linkage and the master cylinder. The brake booster is a device that utilizes the different pressure between the engine vacuum and the atmosphere to amplify the force of your foot to operate the brakes. When the operator depresses the brake pedal, the power booster increases the amount of pressure applied to the piston within the master cylinder without the operator having to greatly increase brake pedal pressure. When a vehicle is powered by a diesel engine, the absence of intake manifold vacuum requires the use of an auxiliary vacuum pump. This pump may be driven by the engine or by an electric motor.

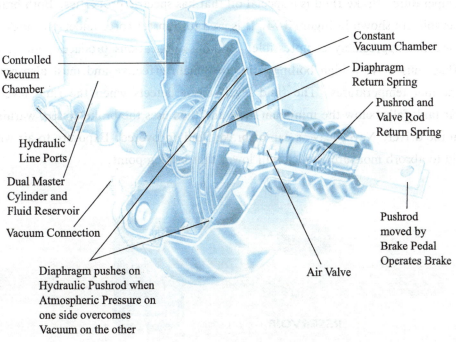

Figure 3-72　The Vacuum Booster

The Master Cylinder

The master cylinder (Figure 3-73) is located in front of the booster. The master cylinder is a device that converts the operation force applied by the brake pedal into hydraulic pressure. Currently, the master cylinder which includes two pistons, generates hydraulic pressure in brake lines of two-line braking system. The hydraulic pressure is then applied to the disc brake calipers or the wheel cylinders of the drum brakes.

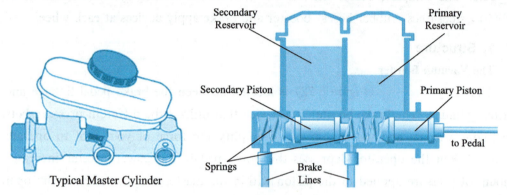

Figure 3-73　The Master Cylinder

Brake Fluid & Reservoir

The reservoir serves to absorb changes in the brake fluid volume caused by changes in fluid temperature. Brake fluid is a special oil that has specific properties. Both brake fluid and reservoir are shown in Figure 3-74. It is used to transfer force under pressure, because liquids are not appreciably compressible. Braking applications produce a lot of heat so brake fluid must have a high boiling point to remain effective and must also not freeze under normal temperatures. The fluid level sensor detects when the fluid level in the reservoir tank falls below the minimum level and then uses the brake system warning light to warn the driver. Never leave a can of brake fluid uncovered. Exposure to air will cause the fluid to absorb moisture, which will lower that boiling point.

Figure 3-74　Brake Fluid & Reservoir

Brake Lines and Hoses

The rigid lines or pipes of a brake hydraulic system made of steel tubing for system safety. Rubber hoses are used only in places that require flexibility, such as at the front wheels, which move up and down as well as steer. The rest of the system uses non-corrosive seamless steel tubing with special fittings at all attachment points. Brake lines and hoses (Figure 3-75) contain the high-pressure fluid, and the fluid acts like a solid rod to transfer force to the wheel cylinders and caliper pistons.

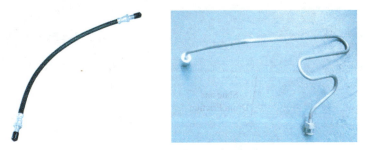

Figure 3-75　Brake Lines and Hoses

Drum Brakes

Early automotive brake systems used a drum design at all four wheels. They were called drum brakes (Figure 3-76) because the components were housed in a round drum that rotated along with the wheel. The drum brake, when released (Figure 3-77), leaves an air gap between the shoes and drum. The drum brake, when it is working (Figure 3-78), would force the shoes against the drum and slow the wheel. Fluid was used to transfer the movement of the brake pedal into the movement of the brake shoes, while the shoes themselves were made of a heat-resistant friction material similar to that used on clutch plates.

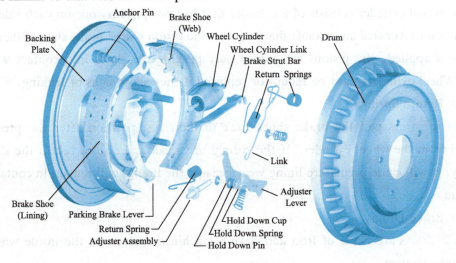

Figure 3-76　Drum Brakes

This basic design proved capable under most circumstances, but it had one major flaw. When the drums are heated by hard braking, the diameter of the drum increases due to the expansion of the material and the brakes must be further depressed to obtain effective braking action. This increase of pedal motion is known as brake fade and can lead to brake failure in extreme circumstances. Usually this fading was the result of too much heat build-up within the drum. For this reason, drum brakes have been replaced in most modern automobiles, but drum brakes are still used in some modern cars owing to weight and cost advantages.

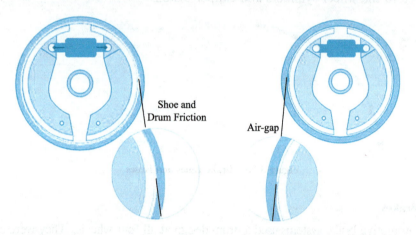

Figure 3-77　Drum Brake Released　　　Figure 3-78　Drum Brake Working

(1) Backing Plates

The backing plate is what holds everything together. It attaches to the axle and forms a solid surface for the wheel cylinder, brake shoes and assorted hardware. It rarely causes any problems.

(2) Wheel Cylinders

The wheel cylinder consists of a cylinder that has two pistons, one on each side. Each piston has a rubber seal and a shaft that connects the piston with a brake shoe. When brake pressure is applied, the pistons are forced out, pushing the shoes into contact with the drum. Wheel cylinders must be rebuilt or replaced if they show signs of leaking.

(3) Return Springs

Return springs pull the brake shoes back to their rest position after the pressure is released from the wheel cylinder. If the springs are weak and do not return the shoes all the way, it will cause premature lining wear because the linings will remain in contact with the drum.

(4) Brake Drums

Brake drums are made of iron and have a machined surface on the inside where the shoes make contact.

(5) Brake Shoes

Like the disk pads, brake shoes consist of a steel shoe with the friction material or lining riveted or bonded to it. Also like disk pads, the linings eventually wear out and must be replaced.

(6) Self-Adjusting Systems

The parts of a self-adjusting system should be clean and move freely to insure that the brakes maintain their adjustment over the life of the linings. If the self-adjusters stop working, you will notice that you will have to step down further and further on the brake pedal before you feel the brakes begin to engage. Disk brakes are self-adjusting by nature and do not require any type of mechanism.

Disc Brakes

Though disc brakes (Figure 3-79) rely on the same basic principles to slow a vehicle, their design is far superior to that of drum brakes. Instead of housing the major components within a metal drum, disc brakes use a slim rotor and small caliper to halt wheel movement. Within the caliper are two brake pads, one on each side of the rotor, that clamp together when the brake pedal is pressed. Fluid is used to transfer the movement of the brake pedal into the movement of the brake pads.

But unlike drum brakes, which allow heat to build up inside the drum during heavy braking, the rotor used in disc brakes is fully exposed to outside air. This exposure works to constantly cool the rotor, greatly reducing its tendency to overheat or cause fading.

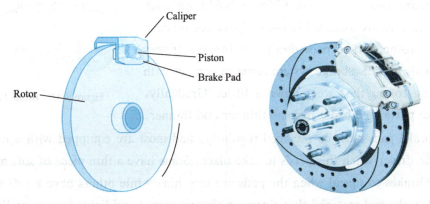

Figure 3-79　Disc Brakes

(1) Discs/Rotors

The design of the disc/rotor (Figure 3-80) varies somewhat. Many are hollowed out with fins joining together the disc's two contact surfaces. This "ventilated" disc design helps to dissipate the generated heat. Some motorcycle and sports car brakes instead have many small holes drilled through them for the same purpose. Additionally, the holes aid the pads in wiping water from the braking surface. Other designs include "slots" — shallow channels machined into the disc to aid in removing used brake material from the brake pads. Slotted discs are generally not used on road cars because they quickly wear down brake pads. However, this removal of material is beneficial to race cars since it keeps the pads soft.

(2) Caliper

The brake caliper (Figure 3-81) is the assembly which houses the brake pads and pistons. The pistons are usually made of aluminum or chrome plated iron.

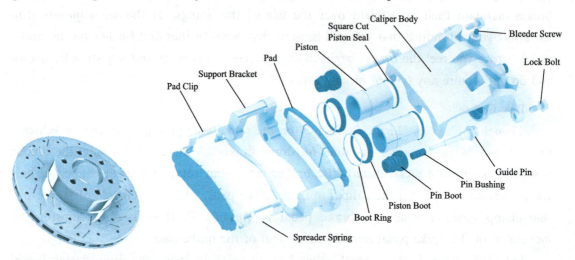

Figure 3-80 Discs/Rotors   Figure 3-81 Calipers

(3) Brake Pads

There are two brake pads (Figure 3-82) on each caliper. The pads are mounted in the caliper, one on each side of the rotor. Brake pads don't last forever. Every time the pads in a disc brake system come in contact with the spinning rotor, they wear down a little. Gradually, these brake parts (the pads) become thinner and thinner.

Figure 3-82 Brake Pads

The brake pads must be replaced regularly, and most are equipped with a method of alerting the driver when this needs to take place. Some have a thin piece of soft metal that causes the brakes to squeal when the pads are too thin, while others have a soft metal tab embedded in the pad material that closes an electric circuit and lights a warning light when the brake pad gets thin. More expensive cars may use an electronic sensor.

2. Types of Calipers

There are two types of calipers: floating and fixed.

(1) Floating Calipers

Single Piston Floating Caliper (Figure 3-83) is the most popular and also least costly to manufacture and service. A floating caliper "floats" or moves in a track in its support so that it can center itself over the rotor. As you apply brake pressure, the hydraulic fluid forces the piston against the inner pad, which in turn pushes against the rotor. It also pushes the caliper in the opposite direction against the outer pad, pressing it against the other side of the rotor.

(2) Fixed Calipers

The entire caliper is solidly mounted and there is a piston or pistons on both sides of the disc. The pistons push the two brake pads to both sides of the disc. The fixed caliper (Figure 3-84) use multiple pistons sorted in pairs with two, four or six pistons. The fixed caliper can apply more squeezing power and apply that power more evenly during braking. Fixed calipers also provide a better feel through the brake pedal whenever the driver applies the brake which is preferable for luxury and performance vehicles.

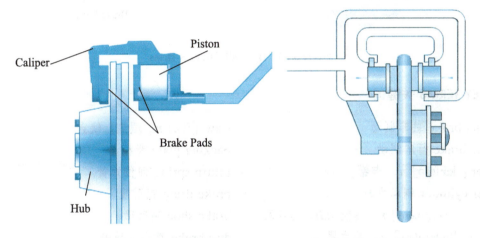

Figure 3-83 Floating Calipers   Figure 3-84 Fixed Calipers

Both types of disc brakes are effective as part of an efficient braking system and this is evident by the fact that the less powerful floating caliper is used much more than the fixed caliper.

The floating or sliding caliper is good enough for most vehicles and since it is lighter and cheaper. The fixed caliper is only required when a vehicle is built with tremendous amounts of speed or is a heavy vehicle with a reasonable amount of speed then more powerful braking would become priority over low cost and weight.

3. Principle

Hydraulic brake system is shown in Figure 3-85. When the brake pedal is depressed, the pressure on the brake pedal moves a piston in the master cylinder, forcing the brake fluid from the master cylinder through the brake lines and flexible hoses to the calipers and wheel cylinders. The force applied to the brake pedal produces a proportional force on each of the pistons. The calipers and wheel cylinders contain pistons, which are connected to a disc brake pad or brake shoe. Each output piston pushes the attached friction material against the surface of the rotor or wall of the brake drum, thus slowing down the rotation of the wheel. When pressure on the pedal is released, the pads and shoes return to their released positions.

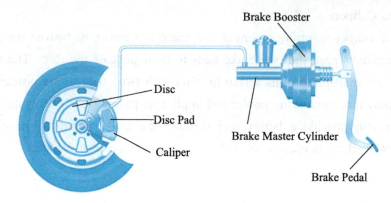

Figure 3-85 Hydraulic Brake Systems

KEY TERMS 关键词

parking brake 驻车制动
service brake 行车制动
caliper ['kælɪpə] n. 卡钳
master cylinder 制动主缸
vacuum ['vækjuːəm] n. 真空 adj. 真空的
booster ['buːstə(r)] n. 助力器
atmosphere ['ætməsfɪə(r)] n. 大气；空气
auxiliary [ɔːɡ'zɪliəri] adj. 辅助的
wheel cylinder 制动轮缸
brake fluid 制动液
corrosive [kə'rəʊsɪv] adj. 腐蚀的；侵蚀性的
drum brake 鼓式制动器

flaw [flɔː] n. 瑕疵，缺点
backing plate 背板
return spring 回位弹簧
brake drum 制动鼓
brake shoe 制动蹄
disc brake 盘式制动器
self-adjusting [ˌselfə'dʒʌstɪŋ] adj. 自动调节的
brake pad 制动衬块
disc [dɪsk] n. 圆盘
tab [tæb] n. 片，薄片
floating ['fləʊtɪŋ] adj. 漂浮的
luxury ['lʌkʃəri] adj. 奢侈的

SENTENCES 翻译示例

❶ The brake booster is a device that utilizes the different pressure between the engine vacuum and the atmosphere to amplify the force of your foot to operate the brakes.
制动助力器是一种利用发动机真空与大气之间的压力差来增强制动推力的装置。

❷ The master cylinder is a device that converts the operation force applied by the brake pedal into hydraulic pressure.

主缸是一种将制动踏板施加的操作力转换为液压的装置。

❸ Though disc brakes rely on the same basic principles to slow a vehicle, their design is far superior to that of drum brakes.

尽管盘式制动器依靠相同的基本原理来减缓车辆的速度,但其设计远远优于鼓式制动器。

ASIGNMENTS 思考与练习

1. To stop a vehicle, the driver exerts a force on the brake pedal, how is this force transferred to each wheel?

2. Explain how Disc Brakes operate?

3. How does the power brake booster work?

3.4.2 The Parking Brake & Anti-Lock Brake System (ABS)

1. Parking Brakes

The parking brake (Figure 3-86) does not rely on the hydraulic system, but on a cable or electric servo system. Pulling on the hand lever, depressing the parking brake pedal, or engaging the electronic parking brake system will pull the cable, mechanically engaging the brakes. On cars with rear drum brakes, the cable engages the brake shoes using a lever. On cars with rear disc brakes, the parking brake may be a set of brake shoes inside, used only for the parking brake system.

Sometimes, the parking brake system is referred to as the "emergency brake system," because in case of a loss of hydraulic fluid or other brake problem, you may be able to slow your vehicle by using the parking brake system.

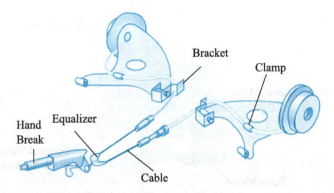

Figure 3-86　Parking Brakes

2. Anti-lock Brake Systems

Anti-lock brake systems (ABS) are one of the greatest advancements in automotive safety. Before ABS, a driver in a panic often slammed on the brakes and locked them up, causing a skid. That's why driving schools would teach students to pump the brake pedal rapidly. ABS uses an on board computer, hydraulic pump and valves and sensors to keep the brakes from locking up. So when the driver pushes the pedal to the floor, ABS essentially pumps the brakes for you, and far quicker than you could ever do on your own.

(1) Structure

The system mainly consists of an electronic control unit (ECU), a hydraulic actuator, and wheel speed sensors at each wheel.

ABS Computers

The ABS computer uses the signals from the wheel speed sensor to control the operation of the hydraulic actuator. If a wheel-locking tendency is detected, the computer will command appropriate wheel cylinder valve positions to modulate brake fluid pressure in some or all of the hydraulic circuits to prevent wheel lockup and provide optimum braking.

Hydraulic Actuators

The hydraulic actuator (Figure 3-87) located in the engine compartment contains valves and a pump motor. The valves have 3 positions.

- In position one, the valve is open; pressure from the master cylinder is passed right through to the brake.
- In position two, the valve blocks the line, isolating that brake from the master cylinder. This prevents the pressure from rising further.
- In position three, the valve releases some of the pressure from the brake.

Since the valve is able to release pressure from the brakes, there has to be some way to put that pressure back. That is what the pump motor does. When a valve reduces the pressure in a line, the pump is there to get the pressure back up.

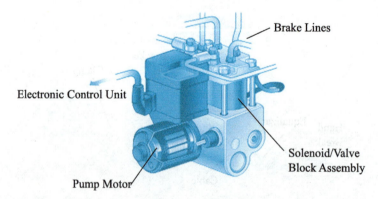

Figure 3-87 Actuators

Under most conditions, ABS results in a decreased stopping distance by keeping the tire — road at the maximum coefficient of friction. However, its primary benefit is that vehicle control is maintained throughout the stop by inhibiting lockup of any wheel.

Wheel Speed Sensors

The anti-lock braking system needs some way of knowing when a wheel is about to lock up. The ABS wheel speed sensors (Figure 3-88), which are located at each wheel, provide this information.

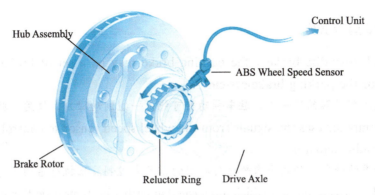

Figure 3-88 ABS Wheel Speed Sensors

(2) Principle

A typical ABS includes a central electronic control unit (ECU), four wheel speed sensors, and hydraulic valves within the brake hydraulics. Anti-lock Brake Working System is shown in Figure 3-89. The ECU constantly monitors the rotational speed of each wheel. If it detects a wheel rotating significantly slower than the others, a condition indicative of impending wheel lock, it actuates the valves to reduce hydraulic pressure to the brake at the affected wheel, thus reducing the braking force on that wheel, the wheel then turns faster. Conversely, if the ECU detects a wheel turning significantly faster than the others, brake hydraulic pressure to the wheel is increased so the braking force is reapplied, slowing down the wheel. This process is repeated continuously and can be detected by the driver via brake pedal pulsation.

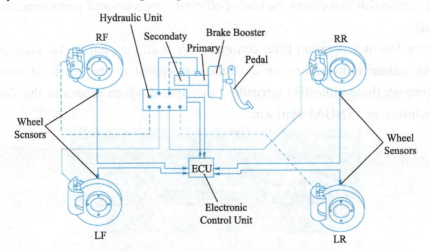

Figure 3-89 Anti-lock Brake Working Systems

KEY TERMS 关键词

emergency [i'mɜːdʒənsi] n. 紧急情况
anti-lock brake system 防抱死制动系统
actuator ['æktʃueɪtə] n. 执行机构

SENTENCES 翻译示例

1. On cars with rear disc brakes, the parking brake may be a set of brake shoes inside, used only for the parking brake system.
在装有后盘式制动器的汽车上，驻车制动器可能是一组制动蹄片，仅用于驻车制动系统。
2. The ABS computer uses the signals from the wheel speed sensor to control the operation of the hydraulic actuator.
防抱死制动系统计算机使用来自轮速传感器的信号来控制液压执行器的操作。
3. The ABS wheel speed sensors, which are located at each wheel, provide this information.
位于每个车轮上的防抱死制动系统轮速传感器提供了这一信息。

ASIGNMENTS 思考与练习

1. Explain how the Antilock Brake System prevents wheels from locking.
2. What kind of energy does kinetic energy change into when a vehicle is stopping?
3. What are the benefits for a vehicle equipped with ABS?

Case Study 实车案例

Pillars of the 2016 Prius 2016 年普锐斯的支柱

Each generation of the Toyota Prius has benefited from the latest advancements in hybrid technology, credentials that deliver the kind of efficient, environmental performance that appeals to the head.

The new fourth-generation Prius continues this tradition, but it also takes aim at the fun-seeking enthusiast by embracing qualities that appeal to the heart. It realises these qualities through three pillar-like attributes, the first of which relates to the Toyota New Global Architecture (TNGA) platform.

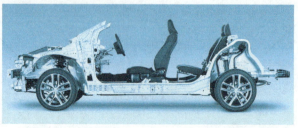

Prius: Toyota's First TNGA Platform

The new Toyota Prius is the first model to be based on the Toyota New Global Architecture platform. Its specific version, known as GA-C, will be shared with forthcoming models and joined by further variations to suit applications from compact sports cars to SUVs.

This modular platform plays a defining role in the car's essential fun-to-drive quality, offering a lower centre of gravity, precise and responsive handling, and an engaging driving position. What's more, extensive use of high-strength steel and additional reinforcements means the body is 60 percent more rigid than before.

The quality of the chassis has a direct bearing on handling, because body control is not reliant on firmer suspension settings, which can compromise ride and comfort. Further suspension enhancement can be seen in the revised caster angle of the McPherson front struts for more direct response and the adoption of double wishbone rear suspension (see image below), which produces one-third the level of shock when driving on uneven roads.

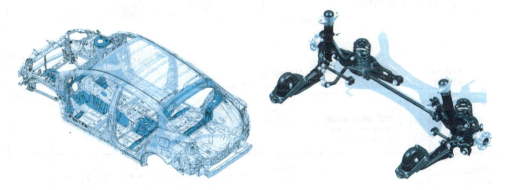

On winding roads, new Prius holds to the driver's intended line and there is outstanding straight-line stability when driving at speed. In fact, the chassis is able to fully harness the more responsive character of the new full hybrid system.

TNGA and Improved Vehicle Packaging

A particular advantage of TNGA is the way it defines the position of key components, simplifying the overall design but without detracting from the styling qualities that give each vehicle its individual character and appeal.

For example, driving components such as the pedals, steering column and driver's seat now conform to one of five different but ergonomically ideal layouts according to vehicle type and platform. Refinements can still be made in the angles of these components but time no longer has to be wasted fine-tuning the origination points for individual models.

TNGA also brings a new approach to the layout of the engine compartment, focusing on placing components lower down within the chassis and organised in a clean and tidy manner. This improved packaging results in a more attractive bonnet line, which, in turn, improves safety by giving the driver a clearer forward view.

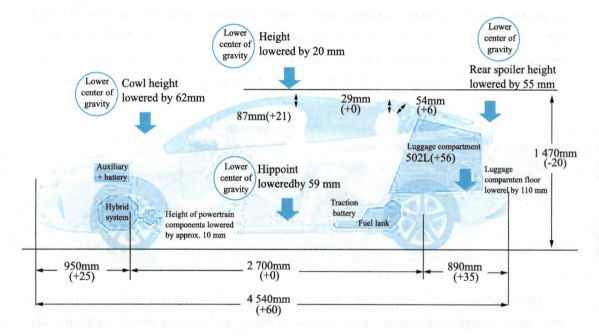

TNGA and Improved Safety Performance

The new TNGA platform is designed to meet the exacting standards of independent crash testing programmes worldwide and provide the highest levels of active and preventative safety through the functions and systems of Toyota Safety Sense.

······ 汽车专业英语句法特点和翻译 ······

为了准确无误、全面客观地传递信息，汽车专业英语使用了很多结构复杂的长句子以及大量的被动结构。因此翻译汽车专业英语时必须对原文理解透彻，熟悉语法知识，才能对原文句子进行准确的剖析。

被动结构与主动结构

　　汽车专业英语客观，严谨，大量使用被动结构，而汉语中被动句的应用没有英语广泛，在译成汉语时可以考虑使用主动结构进行翻译。例如：

1) The clutch can be engaged and disengaged using the clutch pedal, which will always be found to the left of the brake pedal.

　　离合器可以使用离合器踏板进行接合和分离，离合器踏板始终位于制动踏板的左侧。

2) The frame is designed to support the weight of the body and absorb all of the loads.

　　车架的设计是为了支撑车身的重量和吸收所有的负荷。

3) Four parameters are set by the designer, and these must be checked regularly to ensure they are within the original vehicle specifications.

　　设计人员设定了四个参数，并且必须定期检查这些参数，以确保它们符合原车规格。

Chapter 4
Electrical & Electronic Systems

──── 基本要求 ────

1. 掌握汽车电气与电子系统构成的英文表达。
2. 翻译汽车电气与电子系统的工作原理的英文表达。

──── 重点和难点 ────

1. 翻译汽车蓄电池和交流发电机的英文描述。
2. 翻译汽车照明、信号系统及仪表盘的英文描述。
3. 翻译汽车安全及舒适辅助设备的英文描述。
4. 翻译汽车常用诊断设备的英文描述。

──── 导入新课 ────

The electrical and electronic systems of the motor become increasingly more complex and fundamental to the workings of modern vehicles. The advances in microcomputing and associated technology have now made control of all vehicle functions possible by electrical means. The complex circuits and systems now in use have developed in a very interesting way. More electronics, more functions, more software—the car is turning into a smartphone on wheels.

4.1 Power Supply Systems

4.1.1 Lead-Acid Batteries

Lead-acid **battery** is commonly used in most of the automobiles. A lead-acid battery is an electrochemical device that stores and provides electrical energy and is mostly **rechargeable**.

A battery supplies power to the starter and ignition system to start the engine. They also supply **current** necessary when the electrical demands exceed the output of the **charging** system.

Structure

The lead acid battery (Figure 4-1) is made up of various parts, the main parts are plates, electrolyte, container, etc.

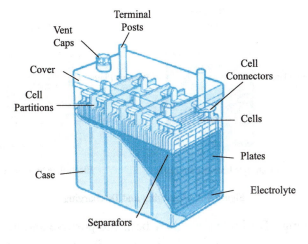

Figure 4-1 Lead-Acid Batteries

Battery case is made of glass, hard rubber or plastic. Usually it is divided into some individual compartments that consist of one cell. The basic construction of a nominal 12V lead-acid battery consists of six cells connected in series, and each battery cell is 2 volts.

The active material is held in grids to form the positive and negative plates. The arrangement of plates in one cell is shown in Figure 4-2. The first and last plates are negative plates.

The positive plates are made of lead peroxide, are cast metallic frame.

The negative plates are made of spongy lead, are cast metallic frame.

A wood or paper made separator is placed between every positive and negative plate to prevent short circuit, and must be able to permit free circulation of electrolyte.

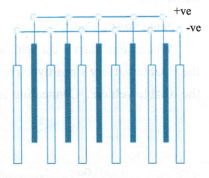

Figure 4-2 Arrangement of Plates

The electrolyte is a 35% sulfuric acid and 65% distilled water solution, which causes a chemical reaction that produces electrons. When mixing, you always pour acid to distilled water.

Charging and Discharging (Figure 4-3)

Battery charging: During charging, the chemical reaction is reversed. The sulphate will leave the plates and return to the electrolyte in the form of sulphuric acid and the plates will change back to lead peroxide and spongy lead.

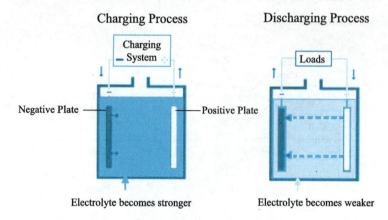

Figure 4-3 Charging and Discharging

Battery discharging: During **discharging**, both the positive and negative plates become lead sulfate, and the electrolyte loses much of its dissolved sulfuric acid and becomes primarily water.

Charging Methods

Normal charging (slow charge) —The selected charging current is about 1/10 of the battery's **capacity** for over 8 ~ 12 hours.

Quick charging (fast charge) —The charging current is very large over a short period of time. The safe limit should never exceed the battery's capacity values even in emergency.

Jump Start a Car

When jump start a car with a discharged battery, connect the positive jumper cable to the disable battery's positive **terminal**, connect the negative cable to an engine ground on the disable vehicle. Connection for jump start a car is shown in Figure 4-4.

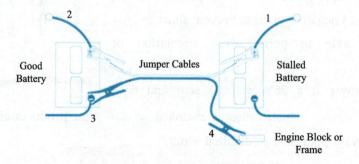

Figure 4-4 Connection for Jump Start a Car

KEY TERMS 关键词

battery [ˈbætərɪ] n. [电]电池，蓄电池
rechargeable [riːˈtʃɑːdʒəbl] adj. 可再充电的
current [ˈkʌrənt] n. 电流
charge [tʃɑːdʒ] vt. 使充电 vi. 充电
electrolyte [ɪˈlektrəlaɪt] n. 电解液，电解质
compartment [kəmˈpɑːtmənt] n. 隔间；隔层
cell [sel] n. 电池；小室
positive [ˈpɒzətɪv] adj. 正的，阳性的
negative [ˈneɡətɪv] adj. 负的；阴性的

peroxide [pəˈrɒksaɪd] n. 过氧化物
spongy [ˈspʌndʒi] adj. 海绵状的
separator [ˈsepəreɪtə(r)] n. 分离器；隔板
circuit [ˈsɜːkɪt] n. 电路，回路
solution [səˈluːʃn] n. 溶液
sulfuric [sʌlˈfjuːrɪk] adj. 硫黄的
distilled [dɪsˈtɪld] adj. 由蒸馏得来的
discharge [dɪsˈtʃɑːdʒ] vt. 放电
capacity [kəˈpæsəti] n. 容量
terminal [ˈtɜːmɪnl] n. 端子

SENTENCES 翻译示例

❶ A lead-acid battery is an electrochemical device that stores and provides electrical energy and is mostly rechargeable.

铅酸蓄电池是一种电化学装置，它储存和提供电能，并且大部分可以反复充电。

❷ The electrolyte is a 35% sulfuric acid and 65% distilled water solution, which causes a chemical reaction that produces electrons.

电解液是一种由35%的硫酸和65%的蒸馏水混合而成，通过内部化学反应形成电流的溶液。

❸ The sulphate will leave the plates and return to the electrolyte in the form of sulphuric acid and the plates will change back to lead peroxide and spongy lead.

极板上的硫酸盐将以硫酸的形式回到电解液中，极板材质也恢复为过氧化铅和海绵状铅。

ASIGNMENTS 思考与练习

1. Describe the purpose of a "lead-acid" battery.
2. Make a clearly labeled sketch to show how a 12V battery is constructed.
3. Describe the processes of battery charging and discharging.

4.1.2 Charging Systems

During cranking, the battery supplies all of the vehicle's electrical power. However, once the engine is running, the charging system (Figure 4-5) is responsible for producing enough energy to meet the demands of all of the loads in the electrical system, while recharging the battery.

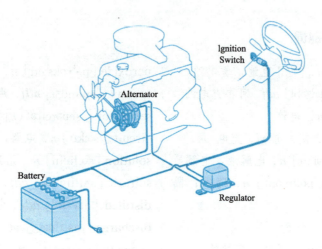

Figure 4-5　Charging Systems

The charging system consists of the alternator, regulator and the interconnecting wiring. The main component is the alternator, which generates direct current for recharging the battery and powering vehicle electrical loads.

Operation of Alternators

The alternator (Figure 4-6) is made up of four main parts: stator, rotor, diode rectifier and voltage regulator.

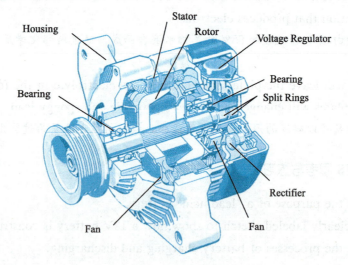

Figure 4-6　Alternators

The alternator uses the principle of electromagnetism to produce current. Typical alternator circuit is shown in Figure 4-7. The rotor is basically a magnet or group of magnets that spin, with all that speed, inside a nest of copper wires, which are called the stator.

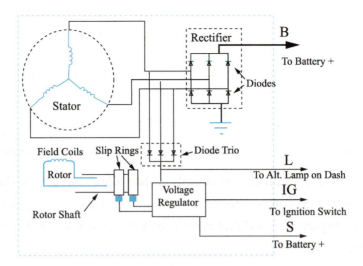

Figure 4-7　Typical Alternator Circuit

The rotor is a rotating magnet that rotates around the stator, which a core of iron **wrapped** in copper wires. These rotor-stator pair rotates within each other and create an alternating current which would be converted by the diode packs into direct current that can be used to charge the battery and power up other electrical components of the vehicle. The voltage regulator controls and maintains the amount of electricity that is made by the alternator.

As the car battery is drained, current is allowed to flow back into it from the alternator and the cycle goes on and on.

Main Components

The rotor (Figure 4-8) assembly consists of a drive shaft, coil and two **pole** pieces. A pulley mounted on one end of the shaft allows the rotor to be spun by a belt driven by the crankshaft pulley at a high speed. A rotor has two **interlocking** sections of electromagnets like fingers of alternating north and south poles, which are evenly distributed on the outside of the rotor.

Figure 4-8　Rotors

The stator (Figure4-9) is mounted to the body of the alternator and remains **stationary**. There is just enough room in the center for the rotor to fit and be able to spin without making any contact. It contains three sets of wires and is spaced inside the alternator 120 degrees apart to form a three phase system. The wires have two forms of connection, Delta connection and Y (star) connection (Figure 4-10).

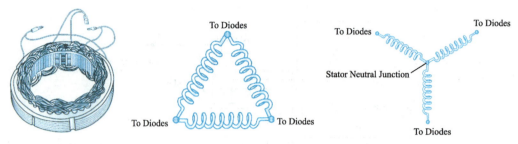

Figure 4-9　Stators　　　　Figure 4-10　Delta Connection and Y Connection

Diodes are one way electrical check valves that allow current to flow only in one direction. All the voltage coming from the alternator is aligned in one direction, thereby converting alternating current to direct current by using a series of 6 diodes mounted in a rectifier assembly.

A voltage regulator regulates the charging voltage that the alternator produces, keeping it between 13.5 and 14.5 volts to protect the electrical components throughout the vehicle.

The voltage regulator can be mounted inside or outside of the alternator housing. Most modern voltage regulators are built-in component on modern alternators.

Troubleshoot the Charging System

The process of checking the charging system operation is as follows.

- Hand and eye checks—belt at correct tension, all connections clean and tight.
- Check battery—must be 70% charged.
- Measure supply voltages to alternator—battery volts.
- Maximum output current—ammeter reading within about 10% of rated maximum output.
- Regulated voltage (ammeter reading 10 A or less)—14.2 V±0.2 V.
- Circuit volt drop—0.5 V maximum.

▶ KEY TERMS 关键词

alternator [ˈɔːltəneɪtə(r)] n. [电] 交流发电机
regulator [ˈregjuleɪtə(r)] n. 调节器
generate [ˈdʒenəreɪt] vt. 产生
stator [ˈsteɪtə] n. 定子
rotor [ˈrəʊtə(r)] n. 转子
diode [ˈdaɪəʊd] n. 二极管
rectifier [ˈrektɪfaɪə] n. 整流器
voltage [ˈvəʊltɪdʒ] n. 电压

electromagnetism [ɪˌlektrəʊˈmæɡnɪtɪzəm] n. 电磁；电磁学
magnet [ˈmæɡnət] n. 磁铁
wrap [ræp] vt. 缠绕
pole [pəʊl] n. 电极
interlock [ˌɪntəˈlɒk] v. 互锁
stationary [ˈsteɪʃənri] adj. 固定的；静止的

▶ SENTENCES 翻译示例

❶ The main component of the charging system is the alternator. The alternator generates direct current for recharging the battery and for powering vehicle electrical loads.

充电系统的主要部件就是交流发电机。它产生直流电给蓄电池充电,并为车辆电气负载供电。

❷ These rotor-stator pair rotates within each other and create an alternating current which would be converted by the diode packs into direct current that can be used to charge the battery and power up other electrical components of the vehicle.

这些转子、定子相对彼此旋转并产生交流电,通过二极管组整流为直流电,用于为蓄电池充电并为车辆的其他电气部件供电。

❸ Diodes are one way electrical check valves that allow current to flow only in one direction.

二极管是电流的单向止回阀,只允许电流单向流动。

▶ ASIGNMENTS 思考与练习

1. State the operation of an alternator.
2. List the main components of an alternator.
3. List two forms of stator winding's connection.

4.2 Lighting, Signal and Dashboard Instruments

4.2.1 Lighting Systems

1. Introduction

The lighting system of an automobile has multiple uses and functions, which are:

- Firstly, it provides **illumination** for the driver of a vehicle to drive safely in dark.
- Secondly, automobile lights enhance the **visibility** of an automobile.
- Thirdly, automobile lights act as the warning signals. They showcase information about the presence, position, size, speed and direction of an automotive.

The lighting system comprises of various lighting and signaling devices or components fixed to the front, sides, rear, and inside of the vehicle. Lights fixed to a vehicle are shown in Figure 4-11.

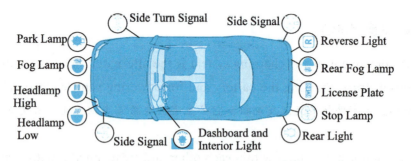

Figure 4-11 Lights Fixed to a Vehicle

According to the lights' location and function, we classified them into exterior lights, interior lights, signal lights, and indicator on dashboard, etc.

Types of light sources used for automotive exterior lighting are incandescent bulbs, tungsten halogen bulbs, HID subsystem, Neon light source, LED source, etc.

2. Exterior Lights

Headlamps

A headlamp is attached to the front of a vehicle to light the road ahead. Headlamps are generally required to produce white light. Modern headlamps are electrically operated, positioned in pairs, one or two on each side of a vehicle, and each one is about 40~60 W.

Side Lamps

Two lights each less than 7 W should be equipped at the front side of an automobile. They are enclosed in a plastic shell. They can be incorporated in the headlight assembly.

Rear Lights

Rear lights, also called tail lamp or rear position lamps, produce only red light. Two must be fitted each with wattage not less than 5 W. The lights may be combined with the vehicle's stop lamps or separate from them.

Reversing Lamps (Backup Lights)

No more than two lights are fitted, a maximum wattage of each is 24 W. They produce white light. When the transmission is placed in reverse gear, backup lights are turned on to illuminate the area behind the vehicle and alarm others.

License Plate Lights

License plate lights are a necessity according to laws, but lighting requirements aren't specified. Rear license plate must be clearly visible, and it is not permitted to obscure the plate.

Stop Lamp (Brake Lights)

There two lights are often combined, and with 15 W and 36 W each. Red steady-burning rear lights, are brighter than the rear lamps, are activated when the driver brakes.

Parking Lights

Parking lights or front position lamps may emit white or amber light. Parking lights are additional dimmer lamps on the outer side of the car's headlights, which improve the parked car's visibility.

Fog Lamps

Fog lamps provide a wide, bar-shaped beam of light, are used in heavy fog, rain, or snow to improve visibility at very low speeds. Front fog lamps produce yellow light, and rear fog lamps produce white light.

3. Beams and Optical Systems of a Headlamp

Beams

A headlamp system is required to produce a low and a high beam, either by an individual lamp for each function or by a single multi-function lamp. Low beam and high beam illumination of road are shown in Figure 4-12.

Low beam headlamps provide a distribution of light to provide adequate forward and lateral illumination, with limits on light directed towards the eyes of other road users to control glare.

High beam headlamps provide a bright, center-weighted distribution of light with no particular control of light directed towards other road users' eyes.

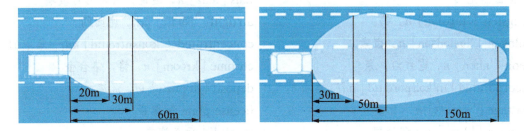

Figure 4-12　Low Beam and High Beam Illumination

Optical Systems of Headlamps

A headlamp (Figure 4-13) comprise of three basic components: reflectors, filament, and special lens that are melded closely in an airtight unit.

The headlight reflector directs the random light rays of the light bulb into a concentrated beam of light. It is consisted of a layer of silver, chrome, or aluminum deposited on a smooth and polished brass or glass surface.

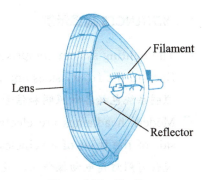

Figure 4-13　Headlamps

The lens also redistribute the reflected light beam and stray rays to certain extent due to which a better overall road illumination is obtained with least glare.

Filament is important to a headlamp. Halogen bulbs, gas-discharge lamp and LED are now widely used in headlamps. But the light patterns are different.

4. Interior Lights

Interior Lights comprises of different types of powerful lighting devices used in the interior portion of a vehicle, such as key light, engine compartment light, glove box light, luggage compartment light, trunk lid light, driving compartment light, instrument display, etc.

Key lights are very powerful mini flashlights that are installed inside the head of a bow or door lock.

Instrument display comprises of small mechanical devices like dual tachometer, altimeter, air speed, vertical speed indicator, ammeter, engine instrument cluster, etc.

▶ KEY TERMS 关键词

illumination [ˌɪluːmɪˈneɪʃn] n. 照明
visibility [ˌvɪzəˈbɪləti] n. 能见度，可见性
exterior [ɪkˈstɪəriə(r)] adj. 外部的
interior [ɪnˈtɪəriə(r)] adj. 内部的
incandescent [ˌɪnkænˈdesnt] adj. 炽热的；发白热光的
tungsten [ˈtʌŋstən] n. 钨
halogen [ˈhælədʒən] n. 卤素
neon [ˈniːɒn] n. 霓虹灯；氖
incorporated [ɪnˈkɔːrpəreɪtɪd] adj. 合并的
wattage [ˈwɒtɪdʒ] n. 瓦数
dimmer [ˈdɪmə] n. 调光器

beam [biːm] n. 光线
lateral [ˈlætərəl] adj. 侧面的，横向的
glare [gleə(r)] n. 刺眼；炫光
reflector [rɪˈflektə(r)] n. 反射物，反射镜
filament [ˈfɪləmənt] n. 灯丝
lens [lenz] n. 透镜；汽车的灯玻璃
airtight [ˈeətaɪt] adj. 密闭的
concentrated [ˈkɒnsntreɪtɪd] adj. 集中的
chrome [krəʊm] n. 铬，铬合金
deposit [dɪˈpɒzɪt] vi. 沉淀
license plate 车牌照
trunk lid 行李箱盖

▶ SENTENCES 翻译示例

❶ The lighting system comprises of various lighting and signaling devices or components fixed to the front, sides and rear, and inside of the vehicle.
照明系统包括各种照明和信号装置或部件，固定安装在车辆的前部、侧部、后部和内部。

❷ Modern headlamps are electrically operated, positioned in pairs, one or two on each side of the front of a vehicle, and each one is about 40～60 W.
现代前照灯是电动操作的，成对安装在汽车头部的一侧或两侧，每个灯炮功率约为 40～60 W。

❸ When the transmission is placed in reverse gear, backup lights are turned on to illuminate the area behind the vehicle and alarm others.

当变速器挂在倒挡时,倒车灯打开以照亮汽车后方区域并警告其他行人或车辆。

ASIGNMENTS 思考与练习

1. What are the main functions of vehicle lights?
2. Name out the exterior lamps.
3. What are the main components of a headlamp?

4.2.2 Signal Systems

Turn Signals

Turn signals, formally called "direction indicators", are blinking lamps mounted near the left and right of the front and rear corners of a vehicle, and sometimes on the sides or on the side mirrors of a vehicle, activated by the driver on one side of the vehicle at a time to advertise intent to turn or change lanes towards that side.

Turn signals are required to blink on and off, or "flash", at a steady rate of between 60 and 120 blinks per minute (1~2Hz). Figure 4-14 shows the ISO symbol for turn signal. An audio and/or visual tell-tale indicator is required, to advise the driver when the turn signals are activated and operating. The indicator lights are on the vehicle's instrument cluster, and a cyclical "tick-tock" noise generated electromechanically.

Figure 4-14　ISO Symbol for Turn Signal

Reversing Signal Devices

The rear blind spot is a huge problem. For safety reason, some warning devices are equipped with reversing light, buzzer and voice alarming, and automatic controlled by the reversing switch installed in the transmission.

Reversing lamp (Figure 4-15) (backup light) is to warn adjacent vehicle operators and pedestrians of a vehicle's rearward motion, and to provide illumination to the rear when backing up.

Figure 4-15　Reversing Lamps

Back-up beeper is a device originally intended to warn passers-by of a vehicle moving in reverse. Now these alarms are used in a situation whereby no-one is ever likely to be a passer-by.

Voice alarming enables the listener to instantly locate where and what direction the sound is coming from.

Horns

A horn is a legal requirement on automotive vehicles in most countries. The purpose of the horn is to alert or warn approaching pedestrians or motorists. Again, these horns can be either single, or arranged in pairs.

Generally, there are three types of horn: high frequency horn, wind-tone horn, air horn.

With the exception of the air horn, vibratory motion of a diaphragm to create sound is produced by a form of electric bell mechanism.

Car horns are usually electric, driven by a flat circular steel diaphragm that has electromagnet acting on it and is attached to a contactor that repeatedly interrupts the current to that electromagnet. Modern electric horns are shown in Figure 4-16.

Figure 4-16 Modern Electric Horns

KEY TERMS 关键词

blink [blɪŋk] *vi*. 闪烁
activate [ˈæktɪveɪt] *vi*. 激活
audio [ˈɔːdiəʊ] *adj*. 声音的
visual [ˈvɪʒuəl] *adj*. 视觉的
adjacent [əˈdʒeɪsnt] *adj*. 邻近的
pedestrian [pəˈdestriən] *n*. 行人

legal [ˈliːgl] *adj*. 法定的
alert [əˈlɜːt] *vt*. 使警觉，使意识到
frequency [ˈfriːkwənsi] *n*. 频率；频繁
vibratory [ˈvaɪbrətəri] *adj*. 振动性的；震动的
diaphragm [ˈdaɪəfræm] *n*. 膜片

SENTENCES 翻译示例

❶ Turn signals are required to blink on and off, or "flash", at a steady rate of between 60 and 120 blinks per minute (1~2 Hz).

汽车转向信号灯开启后，会反复闪烁，闪烁频率稳定保持在每分钟60~120 次（1~2 Hz）。

❷ For safety reason, some warning devices are equipped with reversing light, buzzer and voice alarming, and automatic controlled by the reversing switch installed in the transmission.

出于安全原因，一些报警装置配备倒车灯、蜂鸣器和语音报警，由安装在变速器中的换向开关自动控制。

❸ The purpose of the horn is to alert or warn approaching pedestrians or motorists.
喇叭的目的是警告或提醒接近的行人或驾驶员。

ASIGNMENTS 思考与练习

1. Describe the function of turn signals.
2. Name out the reversing signal devices.
3. List three types of horn.

4.2.3 Dashboard Instruments

A dashboard（Figure 4-17）also called instrument panel，is a control panel located directly ahead of a vehicle's driver，displaying instrumentation and controls for the vehicle's operation.

Modern cars are equipped with a wide range of sensors and sophisticated on-board electronics，which monitor vehicle performance and caution the driver about special conditions by display，sound and lights.

Figure 4-17　The Dashboard

1. Instrument Gauges

Gauges provide the driver with a scaled indication of the condition of a system，for example，that the fuel tank is half full. There are basically two types of instrument displays：analogue and digital.

Fuel Gauges

Magnetic type fuel gauge consists of two balancing coils and an armature. Difference in magnetic attraction of coils causes armature to move pointer across scale.

Current flow through heating coil is controlled by variable resistance in sending unit. Heating coil heats up bi-metallic arm causing it to bend and deflect gauge unit pointer.

Temperature Gauges

The magnetic type and thermal type of gauges are similar to the fuel gauge as previously discussed.

Oil Pressure Gauges

The variable resistance type sender unit is commonly a rheostat (which is a wire wound coil with a wiper arm). The movement of the diaphragm changes the resistance which causes the circuit voltage to change.

Speedometers

In the past, the speedometer was driven by a drive cable attached to the gear in the transmission. However, electric speedometers are used in nearly all late-model vehicles.

2. Dashboard Lights and Warning Devices

An indicator light comes on to inform the driver that something has been turned on, Such as the rear window defogger. Warning lights notify the driver that something in the system is not functioning properly or that a situation exists that must be corrected. Common warning lights are shown in Figure 4-18.

	Rear Foglight Activated and remains on once the driver turns on the fog beams.		**Seat Belt Reminder** Active as long as the vehicle is moving and the belt remains unfastened.
	Brake System Alert To show low brake fluid level.		**Temperature Warning Light** Engine overheating and the driver should stop the vehicle.
	Front Airbag Informs that a passenger air bag has been switched off manually.		**Battery Warning** Seek professional help to resolve the issue.
	Open Doors Indicator One or more doors are closed incorrectly when the vehicle is driving.		**Hazard Warning Lights** Activated by the driver to indicate a problem with their car to other motorists.
	Oil Pressure Warning Low oil pressure, the engine should be switched off immediately.		**Tyre Pressure Monitor** Inform discorrect tyre pressure and reset light if required to extinguish.
	Child Safety Lock Informs that the child safety lock has been activated.		**Low Fuel Notification** Low fuel level, Refuelling is urgently required.
	Turn Signal Activated once the driver changes direction.		**High Beam Light** Turned on once the driver activates the high beam mode.

Figure 4-18 Common Warning Lights

3. Warning Circuits

Indicator lights and warning devices are generally activated by the closing of a switch. Various types of tone generators, including buzzers, chimes and voice synthesizers are used to remind drivers of vehicle conditions. Figure 4-19 shows a circuit that will warn of "Low Oil" or "Generator not Charging", also sound if lights are left "On" with engine not running.

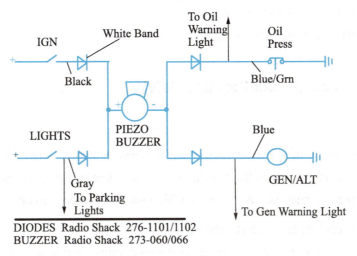

Figure 4-19　A Warning Circuit

▶ KEY TERMS 关键词

panel ['pænl] *n*. 仪表板
sophisticated [sə'fɪstɪkeɪtɪd] *adj*. 复杂的
monitor ['mɒnɪtə(r)] *vt*. 监控
performance [pə'fɔːməns] *n*. 性能
scale [skeɪl] *vt*. 测量；依比例决定

analogue ['ænəlɒg] *adj*. 模拟的；指针的
armature ['ɑːmətʃə(r)] *n*. 电枢
deflect [dɪ'flekt] *vt*. 使转向；使偏斜
rheostat ['riːəˌstæt] *n*. 变阻器
notify ['nəʊtɪfaɪ] *vt*. 通知

▶ SENTENCES 翻译示例

❶ Modern cars are equipped with a wide range of sensors and sophisticated on-board electronics, which monitor vehicle performance and caution the driver about special conditions by display, sound and lights.
现代汽车配备了各种传感器和复杂的车载电子设备，可监控车辆性能，并通过显示器、声音和指示灯警告驾驶员注意汽车的特殊状况。

❷ Difference in magnetic attraction of coils causes armature to move pointer across scale.
线圈磁力之间的差值使得电枢带动指针在表盘内转动。

❸ An indicator light comes on to inform the driver that something has been turned on, such as the rear window defogger.

指示灯是用来告知驾驶员某个系统被启动了，例如后窗除雾器开始工作时灯亮了。

ASIGNMENTS 思考与练习

1. Describe the functions of indicator lights and warning lights.
2. Name out the main instrument gauges.
3. What's the function of warning lights?

4.3 Accessories for Comfort and Safety

4.3.1 Electrical Accessories

Electrical movement of windscreen wiper and washers, window, seats, mirrors and the sunroof are included in one section as the operation of each system is quite similar, which using one or several permanent magnet motors, together with a supply reversing circuit.

1. Windscreen Wipers and Washers

A **windscreen** wiper is a device used to remove rain, snow, ice and debris from a windscreen or windshield. A windscreen washer system is also used to **sprays** water or an **antifreeze** window washer fluid at the windshield using several **nozzles**.

The Wiper Assembly

A wiper generally consists of a metal arm, **pivoting** at one end and with a long rubber blade attached to the other. The arm is powered by a **permanent** magnetic motor, often an electric motor, although **pneumatic** power is also used in some vehicles. The **blade** is swung back and forth over the glass, pushing water or other **precipitation** from its surface. Figure 4-20 shows a windscreen wiper system.

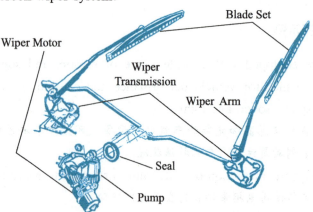

Figure 4-20　A Windscreen Wiper System

The speed is normally adjustable, with several continuous speeds and often one or more "intermittent" settings. Most automobiles use two synchronized radial type arms.

A self-parking switch in the wiper motor ensures that when the wiper switch is turned off, current will continue to flow to the motor. This will keep the motor rotating until the revolving switch breaks the wiper circuit and the wiper arms would have reached the parked position.

Windscreen Washers

A typical windscreen washer system consists of a reservoir, pump, hoses, connections and washer nozzles. The reservoir is normally located in the engine compartment.

When the windshield washer switch is activated, the wiper motor and pump turn on. The pump supplies a mixture of water, alcohol, and detergent from the reservoir to the windscreen. The fluid is dispensed through small nozzles mounted on the hood.

2. Power Windows

Power windows or electric windows can be raised and lowered by pressing a button or switch, as opposed to using a hand-turned crank handle.

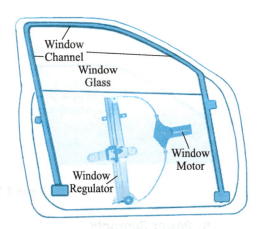

Figure 4-21 Electric Window Systems

The window lift on most cars uses a really neat linkage to lift the window glass while keeping it level. A small electric motor is attached to a worm gear and several other spur gears to create a large gear reduction, giving it enough torque to lift the window. Figure 4-21 shows an electric window system.

3. Power Door Locks

Power door locks, also known as central locking, allow the driver or front passenger to simultaneously lock or unlock all the doors of an automobile or truck, by pressing a button or flipping a switch.

The central locking in a car operates using a manual system, a remote keyless system or a combination of both (As a safety precaution against being locked in a car due to an electrical failure, power locks can be manually operated).

4. Power Seats

A power seat is a front seat which can be adjusted by using a switch or joystick and a set of small electric motors. Most cars with this feature have controls for the driver's seat only, though almost all luxury cars also have power controls for the front passenger seat.

Adjustment of a power seat (Figure 4-22) is achieved by using a number of motors to allow positioning of different parts of the seat. Some cars also have memory adjustments, which can recall (usually) two different adjustments of the seat by pressing a button.

5. Power Mirrors

A power mirror is a side-view mirror equipped with electrical means for **vertical** and **horizontal** adjustment from the inside of the automobile. The glass may also be electrically heated to prevent fogging or icing. Usually, a mirror is selected by a switch or a knob to control both left and right side mirrors. The mirror selector usually has a neutral position with none mirrors selected, to prevent accidental changes of the view. Power side mirrors (Figure 4-23) are convex mirrors.

Figure 4-22　Adjustment of a Power Seat

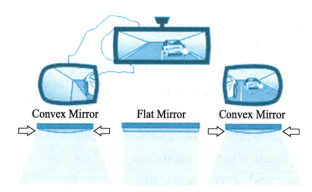

Figure 4-23　Power Side Mirrors

6. Power Sunroofs

An automotive sunroof is a movable (typically glass) panel that is operable to uncover an opening in an automobile roof, which allows light and fresh air to enter the passenger compartment. A **latching relay** locks into position each time it is energized, so that the roof can slide, tilt and stop in the closed position. A power sunroof is shown in Figure 4-24.

Figure 4-24　Power Sunroofs

▶ KEY TERMS 关键词

windscreen ['wɪndskriːn] n. 汽车挡风玻璃
spray [spreɪ] vt. 喷射
antifreeze ['æntɪfriːz] n. 防冻剂

nozzle ['nɒzl] n. 喷嘴
pivot ['pɪvət] vt. 以……为中心旋转
permanent ['pɜːmənənt] adj. 永久的，永恒的

pneumatic [njuːˈmætɪk] *adj*. 气动的
blade [bleɪd] *n*. 叶片
precipitation [prɪˌsɪpɪˈteɪʃn] *n*. 沉淀物
intermittent [ˌɪntəˈmɪtənt] *adj*. 间歇的
synchronized [ˈsɪŋkrənaɪzd] *adj*. 同步的
reservoir [ˈrezəvwɑː(r)] *n*. 储液器
flip [flɪp] *vt*. 轻按；拨动

remote [rɪˈməʊt] *n*. 远程
combination [ˌkɒmbɪˈneɪʃn] *n*. 结合；组合
adjustment [əˈdʒʌstmənt] *n*. 调整，调节
vertical [ˈvɜːtɪkl] *adj*. 垂直的
horizontal [ˌhɒrɪˈzɒntl] *adj*. 水平的
latching relay 闭锁继电器；自锁继电器

SENTENCES 翻译示例

❶ A windscreen wiper is a device used to remove rain, snow, ice and debris from a windscreen or windshield.
风窗玻璃刮水器是一种清除风窗玻璃上的雨水、雪、冰和碎屑的装置。

❷ A typical windshield washer system consists of a reservoir, pump, hoses, connections and washer nozzles.
典型的风窗玻璃清洗系统由储液罐、喷水泵、软管、连接件和清洗喷嘴组成。

❸ Power windows or electric windows are automobile windows which can be raised and lowered by pressing a button or switch, as opposed to using a hand-turned crank handle.
电动车窗可以通过按下按钮或开关自动升降窗户，而不是通过手摇曲柄。

ASIGNMENTS 思考与练习

1. Make a clearly labeled sketch to show a typical wiper motor linkage.
2. Describe the structure of a typical windshield washer system.
3. Describe how to achieve adjustment of the electrical seat and the ways of movement.

4.3.2 Heating and Air Conditioning Systems

The heating, ventilation, and air conditioning (HVAC) system is designed to help keep the interior of your vehicle nice and cool on hot summer days and toasty warm in the winter.

1. Air Conditioning (AC)

Automotive air conditioners cool the interior of the passenger's compartment by moving heat from inside the car to outside. There are five main components to the whole system, namely the compressor, condenser, receiver-dryer, expansion valve, and the evaporator.

There are slight variations between some systems, but Figure 4-25 is a good overall view of a generic AC system.

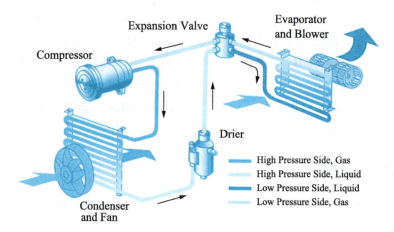

Figure 4-25   AC Systems

Refrigerant

Refrigerant is the generic name for the chemical blend that cycles through an air conditioner to cool the air, and features evaporating at a low temperature, then condensing again at a higher pressure. Freon R-12 refrigerant has been used for many years. But R-12 was harmful to the earth's ozone layer, it's been replaced with harmless R-134a refrigerant (Figure 4-26).

Compressors

The belt-driven compressor uses engine power to compress and circulate the refrigerant gas throughout the system. The compressor (Figure 4-27) pumps refrigerant vapors under high pressure coming from the evaporator to the condenser.

Figure 4-26   R134a Refrigerant   Figure 4-27   Compressors

Condensers

The condenser (Figure 4-28), is a device used to change the high-pressure refrigerant vapor to a liquid, is mounted in front of the engine's radiator. A great deal of heat is generated during condensing, and is removed from the condenser by outside air flowing.

Receiver Dryers or Accumulators

The dryer, also known as the receiver-dryer, is a small reservoir vessel for the liquid refrigerant, and removes any moisture that may leak into the refrigerant and causes **havoc**. If the system uses an orifice tube, there will be an **accumulator**. Their functions are same.

Thermal Expansion Valves (TXV) or Orifice Tubes

The thermal expansion valve (Figure 4-29) removes pressure from the liquid refrigerant so that it can expand and become refrigerant vapor in the evaporator. Here, the system changes from the high-pressure side to the low-pressure side.

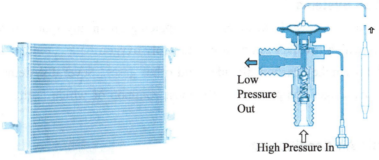

Figure 4-28 Condensers   Figure 4-29 Thermal Expansion Valves

The **orifice** tube (Figure 4-30) serves the same purpose as TXV. The orifice tube is simple and low cost, but the flow of refrigerant is fixed.

Figure 4-30 An Orifice Tube

Evaporators

The evaporator is another little radiator with its coil of tubes and fins that serves exactly the opposite task as the condenser, its job is to absorb heat rather than **dissipate** it.

2. Heating Systems

The automotive heating system (Figure 4-31) has been designed to work hand in hand with the cooling system to maintain proper temperatures inside the car. The primary components are the heater core, the heater control valve, the blower motor and the fan.

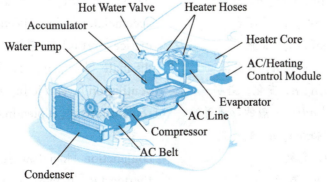

Figure 4-31 Heating Systems

Hot engine coolant is circulated through a small radiator, often called a heater core. A fan is positioned in front of the heater core to blow cold outside air over the fins. As this air travels over the heater core, it heats up and becomes the hot air which blows out your heater vents and into the passenger compartment. After giving up its heat, the coolant is then pumped out through the heater core outlet, where it is returned to the engine to be recirculated by the water pump.

The main component is the heater core; it is located behind the dashboard. Most have an aluminum core with plastic tanks.

3. Ventilation Systems

Ventilation is the process of exchanging or replacing air in any space to provide high indoor air quality which involves temperature control, oxygen **replenishment**, and removal of moisture, odors, smoke, carbon dioxide, and other gases. Several systems are used to vent air into the passenger compartment, the most common of which is the flow-through system.

4. Automatic Air Conditioning

When the "Auto" mode (Figure 4-32) is selected, the automatic air conditioner controls the air temperature and air flow rate automatically.

An automatic air conditioner allows you to set a desired temperature. These units work in **conjunction** with a built-in **thermostat**, which detects and monitors the current temperature and signals the air conditioner system to keep pumping out cool air until the desired temperature setting is reached.

Figure 4-32　Auto Mode

▶ KEY TERMS 关键词

toasty ['təʊsti] *adj*. 暖和舒适的
compressor [kəm'presə(r)] *n*. 压缩机
condenser [kən'densə] *n*. 冷凝器
expansion [ɪk'spænʃn] *n*. 膨胀
evaporator [ɪ'væpəˌreɪtə] *n*. 蒸发器
variation [ˌveərɪ'eɪʃn] *n*. 变化；差别
generic [dʒɪ'nerɪk] *adj*. 一般的，通用的
refrigerant [rɪ'frɪdʒərənt] *n*. 制冷剂
ozone ['əʊzəʊn] *n*. 臭氧
vapor ['veɪpə(r)] *n*. 蒸汽

radiator ['reɪdɪeɪtə(r)] *n*. 散热器
havoc ['hævək] *n*. 大破坏
accumulator [ə'kju:mjəleɪtə(r)] *n*. 贮液器
orifice ['ɒrɪfɪs] *n*. 孔口；孔
dissipate ['dɪsɪpeɪt] *vt*. 使……消散
ventilation [ˌventɪ'leɪʃn] *n*. 通风
replenishment [rɪ'plenɪʃmənt] *n*. 补充，补给
conjunction [kən'dʒʌŋkʃn] *n*. 连同
thermostat ['θɜːməstæt] *n*. 节温器

SENTENCES 翻译示例

① Refrigerant is the generic name for the chemical blend that cycles through an air conditioner to cool the air, and features evaporating at a low temperature, then condensing again at a higher pressure.

制冷剂是通过空调循环冷却空气的化学混合物的通用名称,其特征是低温蒸发,高压下会冷凝。

② The belt-driven compressor uses engine power to compress and circulate the refrigerant gas throughout the system.

发动机传动带驱动压缩机压缩制冷剂,并使制冷剂在整个系统内循环运行。

③ The evaporator is another little radiator with its coil of tubes and fins that serves exactly the opposite task as the condenser, its job is to absorb heat rather than dissipate it.

蒸发器是另一个由排管和散热片组成的小型散热器,但作用与冷凝器完全相反,是吸热而不是散热。

ASIGNMENTS 思考与练习

1. Name out the main components of an air conditioning system.
2. Describe the operation of the air conditioning system.
3. Describe the working process of the heating system.

4.3.3 Automotive Electronics

1. Immobilizers

An immobilizer is an electronic security device fitted to an automobile that prevents the engine from running unless the correct key (or other token) is present. Figure 4-33 shows immobilizer sign.

The microcircuit inside the key is activated by a small electromagnetic field which induces current to flow inside the key body, which in turn broadcasts a unique binary code

Figure 4-33　Immobilizer Sign

which is read by the automobile's electronic control unit (ECU). When the ECU determines that the coded key is both current and valid, the ECU activates the fuel-injection sequence.

2. Seatbelt Pretensioners

A seat belt is a vehicle safety device to secure the occupant against harmful movement during a collision or a sudden stop.

A pretensioner is to tighten up any slack in the belt webbing in the event of a crash. Like airbags, pretensioners are triggered by sensors in the car's body, and many pretensioners have used explosively expanding gas to drive a piston that retracts the belt.

Electric pretensioners (Figure 4-34) are often incorporated on vehicles equipped with precrash systems. It can operate on a repeated or sustained basis; provide better protection in the multiple collision accident.

Figure 4-34　Electric Pretensioners

3. Supplemental Restraint Systems (SRS)

An airbag (Figure 4-35) is an occupant restraint system for safety. The airbag module can inflate extremely rapidly to absorb energy then quickly deflate during a collision, impact with a surface or a rapid sudden deceleration. It consists of the airbag cushion, a flexible fabric bag, inflation module and impact sensor.

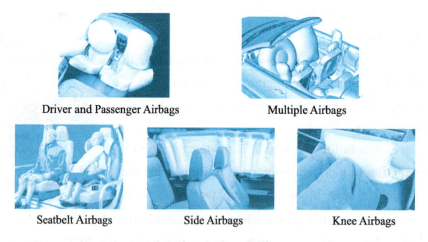

Figure 4-35　Airbags

During a crash event, the sensors provide crucial information to ECU, including collision type, angle and severity of impact. The airbag ECU determines if the crash event meets the criteria for deployment and triggers various firing circuits to deploy one or more airbag modules.

4. Child Safety Locks

Child safety locks tend to be built into the rear doors of most cars and are used to prevent rear seat passengers, particularly little ones, from opening the doors both during transit and while the vehicle is stationary.

The lock is typically engaged via a small switch on the edge of the door. When the child lock is engaged, the interior handle is rendered useless. The door can only be opened by lifting the outside handle. In some newer models, the child lock can be activated electronically from the driver position via a door control unit. Figure 4-36 shows some electrical child safety locks.

Figure 4-36　Electrical Child Safety Locks

5. Reversing Radar

This system, sometimes called obstacle avoidance radar, is an aid to reversing, which gives the driver some indication as to how much space is behind the car.

Reversing radar (Figure 4-37) is mainly composed of ultrasonic sensors, controllers, displays or buzzers, etc. This technique is, in effect, a range-finding system.

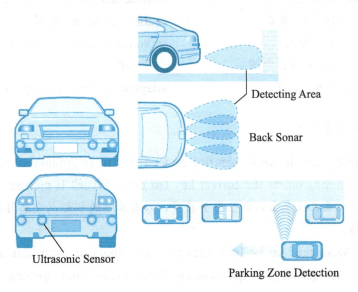

Figure 4-37　Reversing Radar

The output can be audio or visual, the latter being perhaps most appropriate, as the driver is likely to be looking backwards. The audible signal sounds "pip pip", the repetition frequency of which increases as the car comes nearer to the obstruction, and becomes almost continuous as impact is imminent.

6. Cruise Control Systems

Cruise control system is a system that automatically controls the speed of a motor vehicle. The system is a servomechanism that takes over the throttle of the car to maintain a steady speed as set by the driver.

Cruise control system is operated by ECU. It consists of several common components which include vehicle speed sensor, operator controls, control module and throttle actuator.

Some modern vehicles have systems for adaptive cruise control (ACC), which is a general term meaning improved cruise control. These improvements can be automatic braking or dynamic set-speed type controls.

KEY TERMS 关键词

immobilizer [iˈməubəlaɪzə(r)] n. 防盗控制系统
security [sɪˈkjʊərəti] n. 安全
microcircuit [ˈmaɪkrəˌsɜːkɪt] n. 微电路
binary [ˈbaɪnəri] adj. 二进制的；二元的
collision [kəˈlɪʒn] n. 碰撞
pretension [prɪˈtenʃn] n. 预紧
trigger [ˈtrɪɡə(r)] vt. 触发
retract [rɪˈtrækt] vt. 缩回；收缩
restraint [rɪˈstreɪnt] n. 约束

inflate [ɪnˈfleɪt] vi. 膨胀；充气
deflate [dɪˈfleɪt] vi. 放气；缩小
deceleration [ˌdiːseləˈreɪʃn] n. 减速
severity [sɪˈverəti] n. 严重；猛烈
avoidance [əˈvɔɪdəns] n. 避开；避免
obstruction [əbˈstrʌkʃn] n. 障碍；阻碍物
cruise [kruːz] n. 巡航
servomechanism [ˈsɜːvəʊˌmɪkəˌnɪzəm] n. 伺服机构
adaptive [əˈdæptɪv] adj. 适应的

SENTENCES 翻译示例

❶ An immobilizer is an electronic security device fitted to an automobile that prevents the engine from running unless the correct key (or other token) is present.
防盗器是一种安装在汽车上的电子安全装置，只有正确的钥匙（或采用其他方式）才会使发动机运转。

❷ Child safety locks tend to be built into the rear doors of most cars and are used to prevent rear seat passengers, particularly little ones, from opening the doors both during transit and while the vehicle is stationary.

儿童安全锁一般内置于大多数汽车的后门，目的是防止后座乘客（特别是儿童）在汽车行驶途中和静止时打开车门。

ASIGNMENTS 思考与练习

1. Describe the purpose of a seatbelt pretensioner briefly.
2. What is SRS? List airbags equipped in modern cars.
3. State the purpose of obstacle avoidance radar.

4.4　Test Equipment

4.4.1　Common Test Equipment

1. Multimeters

A *multimeter* is an standard electronic measuring instrument that combines several measurement functions (voltage, current and *resistance*) in one unit. *Analog* multimeters use a *microammeter* with a moving pointer to display readings. Digital multimeters (Figure 4-38) have a *numeric* display, may also show a *graphical* bar representing the measured value.

Figure 4-38　Digital Multimeters

Digital multimeters are now far more common due to their cost and *precision*, but analog multimeters are still preferable in some cases, such as when monitoring a rapidly varying value.

A multimeter has three parts, display, selection *knob*, ports.

Some special car multimeters can measure more *parameters*, such as frequency for crankshaft or camshaft sensor, DC volts for oxygen sensor, temperature, resistance or duty cycle for injectors, charging voltage, current, and RPM.

2. Oscilloscopes

An *oscilloscope* is a type of electronic test instrument that allows *observation* of varying signal voltages, usually as a *two-dimensional* plot of one or more signals as a function of time. Other signals (such as sound or vibration) can be converted to voltages and displayed.

Two types of oscilloscope are available, these are either analogue or digital. A digital oscilloscope has much the same end result as the analogue type but the signal can be thought of as being plotted rather than drawn on the screen.

The basic oscilloscope (Figure 4-39) is typically divided into four sections: the display, vertical controls, horizontal controls and trigger controls.

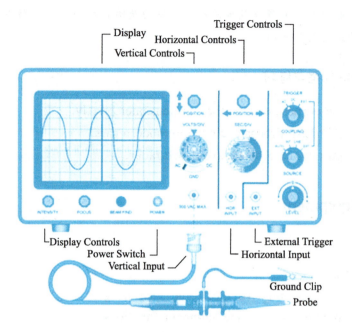

Figure 4-39　Oscilloscopes

A very useful piece of equipment becoming very popular is the "Scopemeter" (Figure 4-40). This is a hand-held digital oscilloscope that allows data to be stored and transferred to a PC for further investigation.

3. Engine Analyzers

Electronic engine analyzers were designed to diagnose the condition of a car's engine. Some form of engine analyzer has become an almost essential tool for fault-finding in modern vehicle engine systems. The latest machines are now generally based around a personal computer. This allows more facilities, which can be added to by simply changing the software.

The machine consists basically of three parts: multimeter, gas analyzer, oscilloscope.

Figure 4-40　Scopemeters

▶ KEY TERMS 关键词

multimeter [ˈmʌltɪmiːtə] n. 万用表
resistance [rɪˈzɪstəns] n. 电阻
analog [ˈænəlɔːg] adj. 模拟的；有长短针的
microammeter [maɪkrəʊˈæmɪtə(r)] n. [电] 微安计

numeric [njuːˈmerɪk] adj. 数值的；数字的
graphical [ˈɡræfɪkl] adj. 图形的；图像的
precision [prɪˈsɪʒn] n. 精度
knob [nɒb] n. 把手
parameter [pəˈræmɪtə(r)] n. 参数；系数

oscilloscope [əˈsɪləskəʊp] n. [电]示波器
observation [ˌɒbzəˈveɪʃn] n. 观察
two-dimensional [ˌtuːdɪˈmenʃənəl] adj. 二维的
investigation [ɪnˌvestɪˈgeɪʃn] n. 调查；调查研究
analyzer [ˈænəˌlaɪzə] n. [计]分析仪
diagnose [ˈdaɪəgnəʊz] v. 诊断
facility [fəˈsɪləti] n. 设备

SENTENCES 翻译示例

❶ A multimeter is a standard electronic measuring instrument that combines several measurement functions (voltage, current and resistance) in one unit.

万用表是一种标准的电子测量仪器，它将多个测量功能（电压、电流和电阻）组合在一个设备中。

❷ Digital multimeters are now far more common due to their cost and precision, but analog multimeters are still preferable in some cases, such as when monitoring a rapidly varying value.

数字万用表由于其成本低、精度高而被普遍使用，但在某些情况下，如监测快速变化的值时，模拟万用表仍然更可取。

❸ An oscilloscope is a type of electronic test instrument that allows observation of varying signal voltages, usually as a two-dimensional plot of one or more signals as a function of time.

示波器是一种电子测量仪器，允许观察变化的信号电压，通常显示为随时间变化的一个或多个信号的二维函数图。

ASIGNMENTS 思考与练习

1. State the types of multimeter and tell the reason why digital one is used widely.
2. What is an oscilloscope?
3. What is the function of the engine analyzer?

4.4.2 On-Board Diagnosis

On-board diagnosis (OBD) is an automotive term referring to a vehicle's self-diagnostic and reporting capability. OBD-II is the second-generation on-board diagnosis.

OBD technology benefits motorists, technicians and the environment by monitoring a vehicles performance every time it is driven, identifying performance and emissions problems immediately and providing technicians with information to help them quickly and accurately diagnose and repair malfunctions.

A basic OBD (Figure 4-41) consists of an ECU, which uses input information from various sensors to control the **actuators**, getting the desired performance. The "Check" light provides an early warning of malfunctions. A modern vehicle can support hundreds of parameters, such as vehicle and engine speed, steering angle, which can be accessed via the diagnostic link connector (DLC) using a scanner.

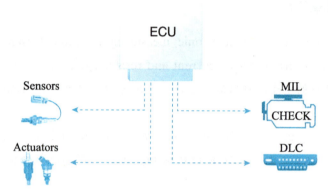

Figure 4-41　A Basic OBD

When a "Check Engine" light (Figure 4-42) on dashboard is illuminated, scanners connected to the OBD-II port record and display the trouble code that the vehicle is sending. Users can know what's wrong with the car. Once the problem has been fixed, clear the code from the vehicle's memory, **deactivate** the "Check Engine" light until the next issue arises.

Figure 4-42　Check Engine Lights

The scan tool (Figure 4-43) is one of the first and most widespread applications of the OBD-II scanner. But scan tools often just display the raw code, some sort of code reference are needed.

Data loggers are designed to be semi-permanently connected to the vehicle and monitor engine and vehicle under normal operation. A data logger (Figure 4-44) could be a good way to keep tabs on drivers' motoring habits.

Chapter 4 Electrical & Electronic Systems

Figure 4-43 Scan Tools   Figure 4-44 Date Loggers

Fuel economy meters are used to report vehicle fuel economy via the data supplied by the OBD-II port. The devices can extrapolate miles per gallon. Figure 4-45 shows a PLX Kiwi, which offer driving challenges to help train the user to be a more efficient driver.

A performance computer (Figure 4-46) is an OBD-II scanner with a focus on performance parameters and monitoring. Performance computers connected OBD-II can estimate horsepower, torque or provide a virtual tachometer for vehicles not equipped with an OEM tach.

Figure 4-45 A PLX Kiwi   Figure 4-46 A Performance Computer

The vehicle telematics (Figure 4-47) perform fleet tracking, monitor fuel efficiency, prevent unsafe driving, as well as for remote diagnostics and by pay-as-you-drive insurance.

Newer OBD-II scanners and readers are starting to integrate Wi-Fi technology to wirelessly connect to a nearby laptop or smartphone for easier monitoring of a vehicle in a garage or on the road. Figure 4-48 shows the future of the OBD-II apps monitor vehicle with global positioning system (GPS) on the iPhone.

Figure 4-47 Vehicle Telematic Boxs   Figure 4-48 IPhones as Scanners

KEY TERMS 关键词

diagnostic [ˌdaɪəɡˈnɒstɪk] *n.* 诊断
capability [ˌkeɪpəˈbɪləti] *n.* 能力
performance [pəˈfɔːməns] *n.* 性能
malfunction [mælˈfʌŋkʃn] *n.* 故障；失灵
actuator [ˈæktʃueɪtə] *n.* 执行器

deactivate [ˌdiːˈæktɪveɪt] *vt.* 关闭
extrapolate [ɪkˈstræpəleɪt] *vt.* 推断
tachometer [tæˈkɒmɪtə(r)] *n.* 转速表
telematic [teliˈmætɪk] *n.* 远程信息处理

SENTENCES 翻译示例

① On-board diagnosis (OBD) is an automotive term referring to a vehicle's self-diagnostic and reporting capability.
车载诊断系统是汽车术语，指的是车辆的自我诊断和报告功能。

② OBD technology benefits motorists, technicians and the environment by monitoring a vehicles performance every time it is driven, identifying performance and emissions problems immediately and providing technicians with information to help them quickly and accurately diagnose and repair malfunctions.
车载诊断技术对驾驶员、技术人员和环境都有好处，通过监测车辆在每次行驶时的性能，立即识别性能和排放问题，并向技术人员提供信息，帮助他们快速准确地诊断和修复故障。

③ Newer OBD-II scanners and readers are starting to integrate Wi-Fi technology to wirelessly connect to a nearby laptop or smartphone for easier monitoring of a vehicle in a garage or on the road.
新型的第二代车载诊断系统扫描读码器集成了无线保真技术，可以无线连接到附近的笔记本电脑或智能手机上，以便于在车库或道路上监控车辆。

ASIGNMENTS 思考与练习

1. What does OBD stand for?
2. Name out the main components of a basic OBD system.
3. List available applications of OBD-II scanner.

Case Study 实车案例

Waymo's Autonomous Cars Waymo 自动驾驶汽车

Waymo and Autonomous

Waymo is an autonomous car development company and subsidiary of Google's parent company, Alphabet Inc. On November 7, 2017, Waymo announced that it had begun testing driverless cars without a safety driver at the driver position. There is still an employee in the car.

An autonomous car (also known as a driverless car, self-driving car) is capable of sensing its environment and navigating without human input. So it is called an intelligent car.

Generations of Self-Driving Waymo Vehicles

Waymo's mission is to bring self-driving technology to the world, making it safe and easy for people and things to move around.

Waymo Vehicles Self-Driving

- Positioning and perceiving the environment around itself.

Rather than rely on GPS, Waymo's vehicles cross-reference their pre-built maps with realtime sensor data to precisely determine their location on the road. The detailed three-dimensional highlight information such as road profiles, curbs and sidewalks, lane markers, crosswalks, traffic lights, stop signs, and other road features.

- Detecting and Classifying objects

Processing information through the sensors and software to distinguish pedestrians, cyclists, vehicles, road work, obstructions, also estimate their speed, and acceleration over time, read traffic controls, from traffic light color and railroad crossing gates to temporary stop signs. Waymo vehicles can see up to 300 meters away (nearly three football fields) in every direction.

- Behavior prediction

Waymo vehicles can model, predict, and understand the intent of each object on the road. Because they have highly accurate models of how different road users are likely to behave, such as pedestrians, cyclists, and motorcyclists. The software predicts future movements of each object based on current speed and trajectory.

- Planner

The software considers all the information gathered above to find an appropriate route, and selects the exact trajectory, speed, lane, and steering maneuvers needed to progress along this route safely.

Waymo vehicles constantly monitoring the environment in 360 degrees around the vehicles, they are able to respond quickly and safely to any changes on the road.

The Software's Predictions   The Green Path is the Choice

Main Subsystems of Self-Driving

- The base vehicle, as certified by the OEM

Waymo's current generation self-driving vehicle is a modified version of the 2017 Chrysler Pacifica Hybrid Minivan, into which have been integrated the self-driving system. The car has been certified by the manufacturer.

- In-house hardware, including sensors and computers

To meet the complex demands of autonomous driving, Waymo has developed an array of sensors that allow our vehicle to see 360 degrees, both in daytime and at night, and up to nearly three football fields away.

This multi-layered sensor suite works together seamlessly to paint a detailed 3D picture of the world, showing dynamic and static objects including pedestrians, cyclists, other vehicles, traffic lights, construction cones, and other road features.

 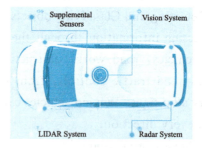

Chrysler Pacifica Hybrid Minivan   Sensors in a Car

These sensors mainly include LIDAR System, Vision (Camera) System, RADAR System, and Supplemental Sensors—including Audio Detection and GPS.

- The self-driving software that makes all the driving decisions

The self-driving software is the "brain" of a Waymo vehicle. It makes sense of the information from the sensors, and makes the best driving decisions for each situation.

Each of these subsystems is then combined to form a fully integrated self-driving vehicle, which is then further tested and validated.

Real-World Experience

Over the last eight years, Waymo has tested their vehicles in four U. S. states and self-driven in more than 20 cities, accumulating more than 3.5 million autonomous miles in the process.

汽车专业英语句法特点和翻译

长句与短句

汽车专业英语中大量使用结构复杂的长句,以准确、规范地传达意图。在翻译时应该理清句子成分,按照汉语的习惯,分成若干相对较短的句子,以便清晰而有条理地传达意愿。

1) Turn signals, formally called "direction indicators", are blinking lamps mounted near the left and right front and rear corners of a vehicle, and sometimes on the sides or on the side mirrors of a vehicle, activated by the driver on one side of the vehicle at a time to advertise intent to turn or change lanes towards that side.

   转向信号灯,也被称为"方向指示灯",安装在汽车左右两侧的前后角,有时也安装在汽车侧面或后视镜上,在汽车转向或并道时,由司机开启转向灯,并且一直闪烁。

2) An automotive sunroof is a movable (typically glass) panel that is operable to uncover an opening in an automobile roof, which allows light and fresh air to enter the passenger compartment.

   汽车天窗是一种可移动的(通常为玻璃)面板,按下开关按钮,天窗就会自动打开,让光和新鲜空气进入车内。

Chapter 5
Electric Vehicles

━━━▪ 基本要求 ▪━━━

1. 掌握纯电动汽车基本构造的英文表达。
2. 翻译纯电动汽车工作过程的英文表达。

━━━▪ 重点和难点 ▪━━━

1. 翻译纯电动汽车的驱动系统的英文描述。
2. 翻译纯电动汽车的电源系统的英文描述。
3. 翻译纯电动汽车的辅助系统的英文描述。
4. 翻译混合动力汽车的英文描述。
5. 翻译插电式混合动力汽车的英文描述。
6. 翻译燃料电池汽车的英文描述。
7. 翻译自动驾驶汽车的英文描述。

━━━▪ 导入新课 ▪━━━

With the rapid growing number of automobiles, new energy vehicle is becoming one of approaches to mitigate the dependence of the auto industry on petroleum so as to reduce pollutant emissions. Did you know? The environmental benefits of plug-in hybrids and electric vehicles increase if they are powered by electricity from "green" sources such as solar, wind or small-scale hydroelectricity. Find out more about green power.

5.1 Introduction

5.1.1 Differences between Electric and Traditional Vehicles

Electric vehicles share many of the same basic components found in traditional automobiles, but they have unique components that separate them from conventional vehicles, such as the lithium-ion battery and electric motor.

Batteries (Figure 5-1)

Most conventional gasoline-powered vehicles use lead-acid batteries. Electric vehicles, however, require large lithium-ion batteries or other batteries that use new technologies that provide more power and weigh less than older batteries of a similar size. Batteries in electric vehicles must also supply a much greater amount of electricity and recharge faster than those in conventional vehicles. Thus, electric vehicle batteries are much larger than conventional vehicle batteries; they usually weigh several hundred pounds, need to be replaced after several years, and can cost thousands of dollars. Scientists and engineers continue to develop new technologies to create smaller, lighter batteries that last longer and provide more power.

Electric Motors

Electric motors have been used for over a century; in fact, they were used in some of the earliest cars. Electric motors are powered by an electric current that creates a magnetic charge and turns a driveshaft. Electric motors waste less energy in the form of heat than internal combustion engines do, so they are more efficient. Torque (a measure of the turning force on an object) and revolutions per minute (RPM, or the speed that the motor turns) can be controlled by the electric motor as it adjusts the electrical current fed through the motor, even making a transmission unnecessary in some vehicles. See inner working of an electric motor (Figure 5-2) below.

Figure 5-1 Batteries

Figure 5-2 Inner Workings of an Electric Motor

Internal Combustion Engines (ICEs)

Most hybrid vehicles contain an internal combustion engine as the primary source of power, with a battery and electric motor acting as secondary power sources. Because power is also available from the battery and electric motor, these engines are typically smaller than those found in regular automobiles. Internal combustion engines in hybrid vehicles can also be used to recharge the battery. Plug-in hybrids get most of their power from the electric system and use the internal combustion engine to recharge the battery or to power the vehicle after the battery runs out.

5.1.2 Types of Electric Vehicles (Figure 5-3)

Electric vehicles can be classified as hybrids, plug-in hybrids, and all-electric vehicles. Each type of vehicle works in a different way and has its own advantages and disadvantages.

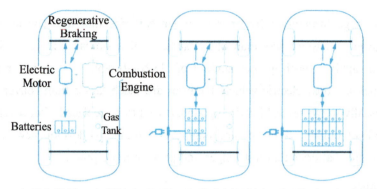

A. Hybrid Electric Vehicle   B. Plug-In Hybrid Vehicle   C. All-Electric Vehicle

Figure 5-3   Types of Electric Vehicles

Hybrid Electric Vehicles (HEVs)

Hybrid electric vehicles, commonly called hybrids, are powered by a combination of an internal combustion engine and an electric motor. There are several types of hybrid vehicles, and they vary depending on whether the engine or the motor is the primary source of power. Some are powered primarily by an internal combustion engine with additional power supplied by an electric motor. Others are powered by the electric motor with a gasoline engine as backup.

The electric motor is powered by a battery and generator. The generator, which receives power from the internal combustion engine, charges the battery and the battery powers the electric motor. In all cases, having an electric motor allows for a much smaller gas engine, which saves fuel and lowers tailpipe emissions. These vehicles may also employ regenerative braking; in which energy captured from the brakes is used to recharge the battery. This allows the vehicle to get better gas mileage when driving in the city and in stop-and-go traffic. These are currently the most popular type of electric vehicles in use today. Models are available from many manufacturers, including the Toyota Prius, Honda Civic Hybrid, and the Ford Escape Hybrid.

Plug-in Hybrid Vehicles (PHVs)

Plug-in hybrids have an electric motor and a gasoline engine like other hybrids, but they have a larger battery and can be charged from a secondary power source when they are in a resting state. Plug-in hybrids can drive anywhere from 10 to 40 miles (1 mile = 1 609.344 m) using just electricity before the battery runs out and the internal combustion engine turns on to power the vehicle. The Chevrolet Volt is an example of this type of vehicle.

All-electric Vehicles (EVs)

All-electric vehicles, also called battery electric vehicles, are powered by only a battery and an electric motor, and they do not contain a gasoline engine at all. When their power runs low, all-electric vehicles must be plugged in to an external source of electricity, such as a charging station, to recharge their batteries. Because their batteries are larger than batteries in other electric vehicles, all-electric vehicles can drive for about 100 miles before they must be recharged. However, they have no gasoline engine to take over when the battery runs low, so these vehicles have a lower overall mileage range than other types of electric vehicles. The major benefit of all-electric cars is that they consume no gasoline and have zero tailpipe emissions. The Nissan Leaf is an example of this type of vehicle.

▶ KEY TERMS 关键词

lithium [ˈlɪθiəm] n. 锂（符号 Li）
ion [ˈaɪən] n. ［化学］离子
lead [liːd] n. 铅
acid [ˈæsɪd] n. 酸
recharge [ˌriːˈtʃɑːdʒ] vt. 再充电
magnetic charge ［电磁］磁荷
torque [tɔːk] n. 转矩
hybrid vehicle 混合动力汽车

plug-in hybrids 插电式混合动力
all-electric vehicle 纯电动车
backup [ˈbækʌp] n. 备份
generator [ˈdʒenəreɪtə(r)] n. 发电机
regenerative [rɪˈdʒenərətɪv] adj. 再生的
capture [ˈkæptʃə(r)] vt. 捕获
mileage [ˈmaɪlɪdʒ] n. 英里数
stop-and-go [sˈtɒpˈændɡəʊ] adj. 走走停停的

▶ SENTENCES 翻译示例

❶ Electric vehicles share many of the same basic components found in traditional automobiles, but they have unique components that separate them from conventional vehicles, such as the lithium-ion battery and electric motor.
电动汽车与传统汽车有许多相同的基本部件，但它们有区别于传统汽车的独特部件，如锂离子电池和电动机。

❷ Most conventional gasoline-powered vehicles use lead-acid batteries. Electric vehicles, however, require large lithium-ion batteries or other batteries that use new technologies that provide more power and weigh less than older batteries of a similar size.
大多数传统的汽油动力汽车使用铅酸蓄电池。然而，电动汽车需要大型锂离子电池或其他使用新技术的电池，这些新技术能提供更多的电力，同样大小的电池重量比传统电池轻。

❸ Electric motors have been used for over a century; in fact, they were used in some of the earliest cars. Electric motors are powered by an electric current that creates a magnetic charge and turns a driveshaft.
电动机已经使用了一个多世纪，事实上，它们被用于一些最早的汽车。电动机由电流驱动，产生磁荷并转动传动轴。

❹ Some are powered primarily by an internal combustion engine with additional power supplied by an electric motor. Others are powered by the electric motor with a gasoline engine as backup.

有些混合动力汽车主要由内燃机提供动力,并由电动机提供额外动力。其他的混合动力汽车由电动机驱动,汽油发动机作为备用动力。

❺ Plug-in hybrids can drive anywhere from 10 to 40 miles using just electricity before the battery runs out and the internal combustion engine turns on to power the vehicle.

插电式混合动力汽车可以在电池电量耗尽前仅依靠电力行驶10到40英里的距离,电池电量耗尽后,由内燃机驱动车辆。

ASIGNMENTS 思考与练习

1. What are the differences between electric and traditional vehicles?
2. Name out three types of electrical vehicles.
3. What's the major benefit of all-electric cars?

5.2 All-Electric Vehicles

All-electric vehicles (EVs) run on electricity only. They are propelled by one or more electric motors powered by rechargeable battery packs. They are also called battery electric vehicles (BEVs), battery-only electric vehicles (BOEVs), and full electric vehicles (FEVs). They use electric motors and motor controllers instead of internal combustion engines (ICEs) for propulsion. See all-electric vehicle sketch (Figure 5-4) below.

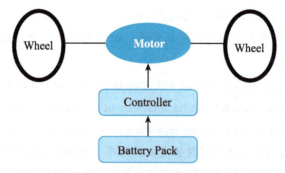

Figure 5-4　All-Electric Vehicle Sketch

All-electric vehicle (Figure 5-5) uses a large traction battery pack to power the electric motor and must be plugged in to a charging station or wall outlet to charge. Because it runs on electricity, the vehicle emits no exhaust from a tailpipe and does not contain the typical liquid fuel components, such as a fuel pump, fuel line, or fuel tank.

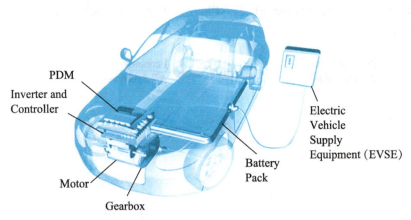

Figure 5-5 All-Electric Vehicles

5.2.1 Drive Systems (Figure 5-6)

Power Delivery Module

The Power Delivery Module (PDM) is an onboard charger for the battery pack, and converts alternating current (AC) power from the electric vehicle supply equipment (EVSE) to direct current (DC) to charge the battery pack.

Inverters & Controllers

The inverter modifies power coming from the batteries to be compatible with the motor.

The controller uses a Pulse Width Modulation (PWM) system that pulses on and off very quickly; the more the current is "on", the more power is delivered to the motor and the faster it will spin.

Electric Motors

BEVs generally use a variation of an AC motor. Due to possible heat issues, the electric motors are artificially limited to max out from 10~20k RPMs (revolutions per minute).

AC induction motors (Figure 5-7) use coils on the rotor, which produces "slip" (the rotor in the motor is slightly behind the magnetic field created by the stator). Because of this, they can produce max torque (twisting force) through high RPMs.

AC synchronous motors (Figure 5-8) use permanent magnets on the rotor, which keeps the motor in sync and reduces slip. They can be more efficient at lower

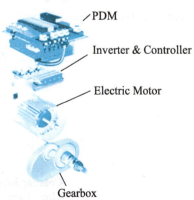

Figure 5-6 Drive Systems

RPMs, and produce max torque at 0 RPMs, which can make them well suited for "commuter" vehicles.

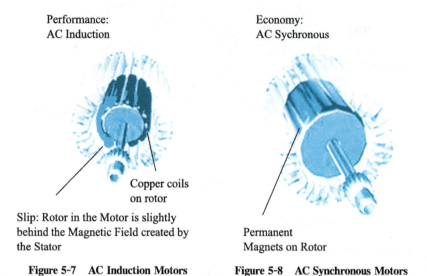

Figure 5-7　AC Induction Motors　　Figure 5-8　AC Synchronous Motors

Gearbox

Because of the electric motor's torque and high RPM abilities, most BEVs use a single speed, 9.7:1 ratio gearbox (the motor spins 9.7x for every 1 tire revolution), so the vehicles never "shift gears", but can still have top speeds between 70~160 mph (1 mph = 0.447 04 m/s).

Regenerative Braking

Some BEVs are designed to collect energy when coasting. When the "gas pedal" is released, the wheel/axle assembly pushes the gearbox; this turns the motor which generates electricity for the battery.

Aside from charging the battery, resistance in the motor can also significantly slow the vehicle. See regenerative braking (Figure 5-9) below.

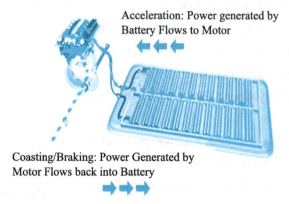

Figure 5-9　Regenerative Braking

5.2.2 Batteries

Li-Ions Batteries

The majority of BEVs use Lithium-ions (Li-ions) batteries for the battery pack. Lithium ion can store more energy while being smaller and lighter than lead-acid batteries (the type of battery in a regular car), and are more readily available than Nickle-Metal Hydride (NiMH) batteries.

Cold Temperature Performance

One drawback to Li-ion batteries is that at temperatures below freezing, they can be damaged if charged too quickly. Because of this, the batteries may charge slowly until they have "self-warmed" enough to charge at a higher rate.

Weight & Placement

At 400~1 200 lbs. (≈ 180~550 kilos), the location of the battery pack can greatly affect the vehicle's center of gravity (the average location of an object's weight). For most BEVs, the pack is under the cabin, which creates a low center of gravity and can improve handling.

Common Battery Designs (Figure 5-10)

Pouches:

A common battery pack design uses DC prismatic cells or "pouches" where each pouch is about as thick as a piece of cardboard. The pouches are usually stacked within modules, and the modules within the pack.

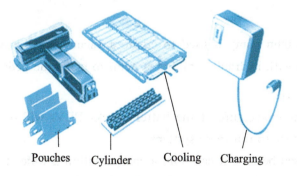

Pouches   Cylinder   Cooling   Charging

Figure 5-10   Common Battery Designs

Cylinders:

Other styles of battery use a cylindrical design for each battery. The cylinders are usually placed side-by-side within modules, and modules within the pack. This design allows for small gaps between individual batteries and may improve cooling.

Cooling:

Though battery packs can be air-cooled, water cooling is usually able to keep the batteries at a more consistent temperature. Batteries getting too hot can cause them to drain much more quickly, significantly decreasing the driving range of the car.

Charging:

Though regular home outlets can be used for charging, electric vehicle supply equipment (EVSE) stations safely supply higher voltages, which allow the onboard charger to recharge the battery pack more quickly.

5.2.3 Additional Systems (Figure 5-11)

The heating, cooling, steering and braking systems are completely electric.

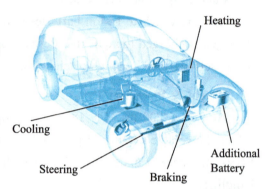

Figure 5-11 Additional Systems

Heating

Most BEVs use a positive temperature coefficient heater. This style of electric heater increases resistance as the temperature rises, preventing it from getting too hot.

Cooling

An electric compressor, similar to what's used in a refrigerator, is used to cool air for the A/C unit.

Steering

Generally, BEVs use rack and pinion steering assisted by an attached electrical motor.

Braking

An electric vacuum pump is used to create a vacuum on the back side of the brake pedal. This is used with hydraulic braking systems to make the pedal easier to push.

Additional batteries

To preserve the charge life of the battery pack, BEVs will often have an additional 12V, lead-acid battery to run these systems.

Lead acid is used because it can hold a charge within a wider temperature range than lithium ion and isn't usually damaged when charging below freezing temperatures.

▶ KEY TERMS 关键词

onboard charger 车载充电器
battery pack [电] 电池组
alternating current [电] 交流电

direct current [电] 直流电
inverter [ɪnˈvɜːtə] n. 逆变器
compatible [kəmˈpætəbl] adj. 兼容的

controller [kənˈtrəʊlə(r)] n. 控制器
Pulse Width Modulation 脉宽调制
artificially [ˌɑːtɪˈfɪʃəli] adv. 人工地
rotor [ˈrəʊtə(r)] n. [电][机][动力] 转子
stator [ˈsteɪtə] n. 定子
resistance [rɪˈzɪstəns] n. 电阻
Nickle-Metal Hydride 镍氢电池
prismatic [prɪzˈmætɪk] adj. 棱柱的
pouch [paʊtʃ] n. 袋

cardboard [ˈkɑːdbɔːd] n. 硬纸板
module [ˈmɒdjuːl] n. 模块
outlet [ˈaʊtlet] n. [电] 电源插座
coefficient [ˌkəʊɪˈfɪʃnt] n. 系数
rack [ræk] n. [机] 齿条
pinion [ˈpɪnjən] n. [机] 小齿轮
AC induction motors 交流异步电动机
AC synchronous motors 交流同步电机
regenerative braking 再生制动

SENTENCES 翻译示例

❶ The PDM is an onboard charger for the battery pack, and converts alternating current (AC) power from the electric vehicle supply equipment (EVSE) to direct current (DC) to charge the battery pack.
电源模块是车载电池组充电器,将来自于电动汽车供电设备的交流电转换为直流电,给电池组充电。

❷ The inverter modifies power coming from the batteries to be compatible with the motor. The controller uses a Pulse Width Modulation (PWM) system that pulses on and off very quickly; the more the current is "on", the more power is delivered to the motor and the faster it will spin.
逆变器改变电池的电能使之与电动机兼容。控制器使用脉宽调制系统,快速脉冲;电流越大,功率越高,电动机转速就越快

❸ Some BEVs are designed to collect energy when coasting. When the "gas pedal" is released, the wheel/axle assembly pushes the gearbox; this turns the motor which generates electricity for the battery. Aside from charging the battery, resistance in the motor can also significantly slow the vehicle.
一些纯电动汽车的设计是在滑行时收集能量。当松开"油门踏板"时,轮轴总成推动变速器;这就转动了为蓄电池供电的电动机。除了给蓄电池充电外,电动机的电阻也可以显著地减慢汽车的速度。

❹ A common battery pack design uses DC prismatic cells or "pouches" where each pouch is about as thick as a piece of cardboard. The pouches are usually stacked within modules, and the modules within the pack.
普通的电池组设计使用直流棱柱电池或称作"袋装电池(软包电池)",每个小袋的厚度相当于一块纸板。这些袋子通常都是在模块内堆叠起来的,模块在电池组内。

❺ Other styles of battery use a cylindrical design for each battery. The cylinders are usually placed side-by-side within modules, and modules within the pack. This design allows for small gaps between individual batteries and may improve cooling.

其他类型的电池为每个电池使用圆柱形设计。圆柱形电池通常在模块内并排放置，模块在电池组内。这种设计可以在单个电池之间产生小间隙，可以改善冷却情况。

ASIGNMENTS 思考与练习

1. How do all-electric cars work?
2. Name out the key components of an all-electric car.
3. What is regenerative braking?

5.3 Hybrid Electric Vehicles

Hybrid electric vehicles（HEVs）（Figure 5-12）combine the benefits of gasoline engines and electric motors. They can be designed to meet different goals, such as better fuel economy or more power. The main systems include batteries, electrical motors, a generator, and a second source of torque with its fuel source. The second source of torque is often an internal combustion engine, running on gasoline. In other cases, it may be an ICE powered by hydrogen, a diesel engine, a small gas turbine/generator, or a **Stirling engine** (the last two HEVs are still largely **theoretical**).

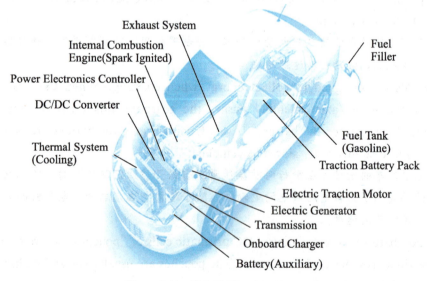

Figure 5-12　Hybrid Electric Vehicles

5.3.1　Structure

Torque sources：Internal combustion engine, relatively low power, about 20 **hp**. One, or more likely, several electric motors.

Energy storage: Battery (for electric motor) — usually a common car battery, but varies from car to car. Other energy storers like flywheels and "ultracapacitors" have not been as fully researched as batteries, but may be seen in the future.

Fuel cell: Gasoline or diesel for the average commercial car, other research is being done on hydrogen and other potential fuel sources.

Energy converter/ "Collector": Generator — the generator both converts electrical power from the battery to mechanical rotational and converts rotation back into energy in order to charge the battery. The torque source can be either the ICE or the wheel shaft in regenerative breaking.

Control: Transmission, various computerized and mechanical control systems. Control systems vary greatly from vehicle to vehicle. Like the one described below, they are all able to switch their drive mode from electrical to ICE, to a mode in which the two are working at once.

On the highway, when internal combustion engines are at their most efficient, and where the battery would be depleted very quickly in an electric car, the ICE is used. For shorter, city driving trips, the electric motor is either used exclusively, or in such a manner that the ICE also runs, at its peak efficiency.

5.3.2 Two Basic Configurations

There are two basic geometries to HEV systems: parallel and series (Figure 5-13).

Parallel

In parallel HEVs, both the internal combustion engine and electric motors drive the wheels; usually the electric motor and internal combustion engine drive the same transaxle. The Toyota Prius is the familiar example.

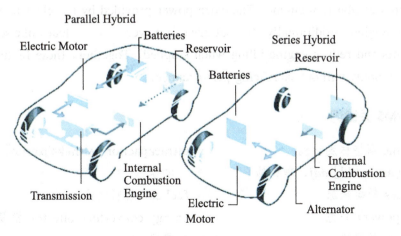

Figure 5-13 Parallel Hybrid and Series Hybrid

Series

In series HEVs, the internal combustion engine only drives a generator, which supplies power to batteries. The wheel drive motors are supplied only from the batteries or other onboard storage. The GM Volt will be a series Plug-in Hybrid Electric Vehicle (PHEV).

5.3.3 Three Advanced Technologies

Most hybrids use several advanced technologies.

Regenerative Braking

Regenerative braking recaptures energy normally lost during coasting or braking. It uses the forward motion of the wheels to turn the motor. This generates electricity and helps slow the vehicle.

Electric Motor Drive/Assist

The electric motor provides power to assist the engine in accelerating, passing, or hill climbing. This allows a smaller, more-efficient engine to be used. In some HEVs, the electric motor alone propels the vehicle at low speeds, where gasoline engines are least efficient.

Automatic Start/Stop

Automatically shuts off the engine when the vehicle comes to a stop and restarts it when the accelerator is pressed. This reduces wasted energy from idling.

Hybrid electric vehicles are powered by an internal combustion engine and an electric motor, which uses energy stored in batteries. A hybrid electric vehicle cannot be plugged in to charge the battery. Instead, the battery is charged through regenerative braking and by the internal combustion engine. The extra power provided by the electric motor allows for a smaller engine. Additionally, the battery can power auxiliary loads like sound systems and headlights and reduce engine idling when stopped. Together, these features result in better fuel economy without sacrificing performance.

▶ KEY TERMS 关键词

Stirling engine 斯特林发动机
theoretical [ˌθɪəˈretɪkl] *adj.* 理论的
torque sources 转矩来源
hp (horse power) 马力
energy storage 储能器

ultracapacitor [ˌʌltrækəˈpæsɪtə] *n.* 超级电容
fuel cell 燃料电池
energy converter/collector 能量转换器/收集器

computerized [kəmˈpjuːtəˌraɪzd] adj. 计算机化；电脑化

depleted [dɪˈplɪtɪd] adj. 耗尽的

exclusively [ɪkˈskluːsɪvli] adv. 唯一地；专有地

parallel [ˈpærəlel] n. 并行；并联

series [ˈsɪəriːz] n. [电] 串联

transaxle [ˈtrænsˌæksl] n. 变速驱动器

recapture [riːˈkæptʃə(r)] vt. 收回；重新利用

electric motor drive/assist 电动机驱动/辅助

accelerating [ækˈsæləreɪtɪŋ] n. 加速

automatic start/stop 自动启停

idling [aɪdlɪŋ] n. 怠速；空转

auxiliary [ɔːɡˈzɪliəri] adj. 辅助的

SENTENCES 翻译示例

1. Hybrid electric vehicles (HEVs) combine the benefits of gasoline engines and electric motors. They can be designed to meet different goals, such as better fuel economy or more power. The main systems include batteries, electrical motors, a generator, and a second source of torque with its fuel source. The second source of torque is often an internal combustion engine, running on gasoline. In other cases, it may be an ICE. powered by hydrogen, a diesel engine, a small gas turbine/generator, or a Stirling engine (the last two HEVs are still largely theoretical).

   混合动力汽车结合了汽油发动机和电动机的优点。它们可以被设计来满足不同的目标，比如更好的燃料经济性或更大的动力。主要系统包括蓄电池、电动机、发电机，以及带燃料源的第二个转矩源。第二个转矩源通常是靠汽油运行的内燃机。在其他情况下，可能是靠氢气驱动的内燃机、柴油发动机、小型燃气轮机/发电机、或斯特林发动机（最后两种混合动力汽车在很大程度上仍是理论性的）。

2. Torque sources：Internal combustion engine, relatively low power, about 20 hp. One, or more likely, several electric motors.

   转矩源：功率相对较低，约为 20 英马力的内燃机。一个或者多个电动机。

3. Energy storage：Battery (for electric motor) — usually a common car battery, but varies from car to car. Other energy storers like flywheels and "ultracapacitors" have not been as fully researched as batteries, but may be seen in the future.

   储能器：蓄电池（电动机）——通常是普通的汽车电池，但因车而异。其他像飞轮和"超级电容"这样的能量储存器还没有像电池那样得到充分研究，但未来可能会出现。

4. In parallel HEVs, both the internal combustion engine and electric motors drive the wheels; usually the electric motor and internal combustion engine drive the same transaxle. The Toyota Prius is the familiar example.

   在并联式混合动力汽车中，内燃机和电动机都驱动车轮；通常电动机和内燃机驱动相同的变速驱动桥。丰田普锐斯就是一个常见的例子。

5. Automatically shuts off the engine when the vehicle comes to a stop and restarts it when

the accelerator is pressed. This reduces wasted energy from idling.

当车辆停止时自动关闭发动机，并在踩下加速踏板时重新起动发动机，这就减少了怠速消耗的能量。

> **ASIGNMENTS 思考与练习**

1. Name out the key components of a hybrid electric car.
2. What is Automatic Start/Stop?
3. How do hybrid electric cars work?

5.4 Plug-In Hybrid Electric Vehicles

Plug-in hybrid electric vehicles (PHEVs) (Figure 5-14) use high-*capacity* batteries to power an electric motor and use another fuel, such as gasoline or diesel, to power an internal combustion engine. PHEV batteries can be charged using a wall outlet or charging station, by the internal combustion engine, or through regenerative braking. The vehicle runs on electric power until the battery is depleted, and then the vehicle automatically switches over to use the internal combustion engine.

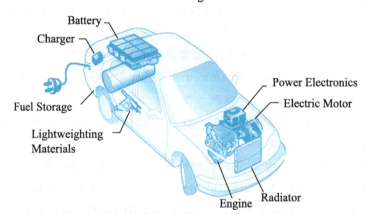

Figure 5-14 Plug-In Hybrid Electric Vehicle (PHEV) Diagram

Powered by Electric Motors and Engines

Plug-in hybrid electric vehicles have an internal combustion engine and an electric motor, which uses energy stored in batteries. PHEVs generally have larger battery packs than hybrid electric vehicles have. This makes it possible to drive *moderate* distances using just electricity (about 10 to 50-plus miles in current models), commonly referred to as the "all-electric range" of the vehicle.

During urban driving, most of a PHEV's power can come from stored electricity. For example, a light-duty PHEV driver might drive to and from work on all-electric power, plug in the vehicle to charge it at night, and be ready for another all-electric commute the next day. The internal combustion engine powers the vehicle when the battery is mostly depleted, during rapid acceleration, or when intensive heating or air conditioning is required. Some heavy-duty PHEVs work the opposite way, with the internal combustion engine used for driving to and from a job site and electricity used to power the vehicle's auxiliary equipment or control the cab's climate while at the job site.

Fueling and Driving Options

Plug-in hybrid electric vehicle batteries can be charged by an outside electric power source, by the internal combustion engine, or through regenerative braking. During braking, the electric motor acts as a generator, using the energy to charge the battery.

PHEV fuel consumption depends on the distance driven between battery charges. For example, if the vehicle is never plugged in to charge, fuel economy will be about the same as a similarly sized hybrid electric vehicle. If the vehicle is driven a shorter distance than its all-electric range and plugged in to charge between trips, it may be possible to use only electric power.

Fuel-Efficient System Design

Beyond battery storage and motor power, there are various ways to combine the power from the electric motor and the engine. The two main configurations are parallel and series. Some PHEVs use transmissions that allow them to operate in either parallel or series configurations, switching between the two based on the drive profile—this is called "blended mode" or "mixed mode."

▶ KEY TERMS 关键词

capacity [kəˈpæsəti] n. 容量
moderate [ˈmɒdərət] adj. 适度的，中等的
commute [kəˈmjuːt] n. 通勤
intensive [ɪnˈtensɪv] adj. 集中的
auxiliary [ɔːɡˈzɪliəri] adj. 辅助的
cab [kæb] n. 驾驶室

storage [ˈstɔːrɪdʒ] n. 存储
configuration [kənˌfɪɡəˈreɪʃn] n. 结构
profile [ˈprəʊfaɪl] n. 配置
blended [ˈblendɪd] adj. 混合的
power electronics 电力电子设备
lightweighting materials 轻量化材料

▶ SENTENCES 翻译示例

❶ Plug-in hybrid electric vehicles have an internal combustion engine and an electric motor, which uses energy stored in batteries. PHEVs generally have larger battcry packs than hybrid electric vehicles have. This makes it possible to drive moderate distances using just electricity (about 10 to 50-plus miles in current models), commonly referred to as the "all-electric range" of the vehicle.

插电式混合动力汽车装备有一个内燃机和一个电动机，它使用储存在电池中的能量。其电池组通常比混合动力汽车更大。这使得仅用电力就可以行驶适度的距离（目前的车型大约10到50多英里），这通常被称为车辆的"全电动范围"。

❷ During urban driving, most of a PHEV's power can come from stored electricity. For example, a light-duty PHEV driver might drive to and from work on all-electric power, plug in the vehicle to charge it at night, and be ready for another all-electric commute the next day. The internal combustion engine powers the vehicle when the battery is mostly depleted, during rapid acceleration, or when intensive heating or air conditioning is required.

在城市驾驶中，大部分的动力来自于储存的电能。例如，一名轻型的插电式混合动力汽车司机可能会用纯电力模式开车上下班，在夜间充电，准备第二天再进行纯电力通勤。当电池内的电量用尽时，急加速时，或在需要集中供暖或开空调时，内燃机为车辆提供动力。

❸ Plug-in hybrid electric vehicle batteries can be charged by an outside electric power source, by the internal combustion engine, or through regenerative braking. During braking, the electric motor acts as a generator, using the energy to charge the battery.

插电式混合动力汽车的电池可由外部电源充电，由内燃机充电，或通过再生制动充电。在制动过程中，电动机充当发电机，利用能量来给电池充电。

❹ PHEV fuel consumption depends on the distance driven between battery charges. For example, if the vehicle is never plugged in to charge, fuel economy will be about the same as a similarly sized hybrid electric vehicle.

插电式混合动力汽车燃料消耗取决于两次电池充电间隔期间汽车所行驶的距离。例如，如果汽车不充电，燃油经济性将与同样大小的混合动力电动汽车差不多。

▶ ASIGNMENTS 思考与练习

1. How do plug-in hybrid electric cars work?
2. What are the differences between hybrids and plug-in hybrids?
3. How can PHEV be charged?

5.5 Fuel Cell Electric Vehicles

Fuel Cell Electric Vehicle (FCEV) (Figure 5-15) also known as Fuel Cell Vehicle (FCV) or Zero Emission Vehicle (ZEV) is a type of electric vehicle that employs "fuel cell technology" to generate electricity required to run the vehicle. In these vehicles, chemical energy of fuel is converted directly into electric energy. The working principle of a "fuel cell" electric vehicle is different compared to that of a "plug in" electric vehicle in the sense that the electricity required to run this vehicle is generated on the vehicle itself.

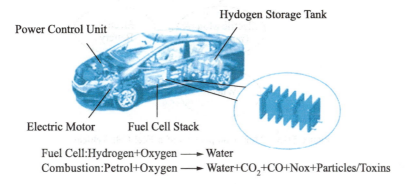

Figure 5-15 Fuel Cell Vehicles

Fuel Cell

Fuel cell is a device in which electrochemical reaction takes place between Hydrogen and Oxygen. The main components of a fuel cell include an anode, a cathode and an electrolyte. In presence of an electrolyte, the fuel ions i. e. Hydrogen ions react with the Oxygen ions to produce electricity, water vapor and heat. This reaction takes place at a temperature of $80^0 C$ only and thus it is also known as "cold combustion". The electricity so generated is utilized to drive an electric motor which in turn rotates the wheels of the vehicle.

The thickness of an individual fuel cell is about two millimeters and it can generate a potential difference of 1 volt only. Thus, an array of hundreds of fuel cells called "fuel cell stack" is used in a Fuel Cell Electric Vehicle.

Main Components of a Fuel Cell Electric Vehicle (FCEV) (Figure 5-16)

1. Hydrogen Storage Tank/ Fuel Tank

The gaseous Hydrogen is used a fuel in fuel cell electric vehicles. These storage tanks store Hydrogen under very high pressure of the order of 700 bars (1 bar = 10^5 Pa).

2. Fuel Cell Stack

This is the powerhouse of these vehicles where Hydrogen from the storage tank and

Oxygen from the ambient air react to form electricity.

3. Electric Motors

The electricity generated by the fuel cell stack is supplied to the electric motor which in turn rotates the wheels of the vehicle.

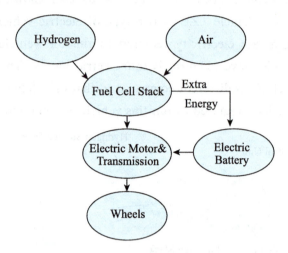

Figure 5-16 Main Components of a Fuel Cell Vehicle

4. Electric Batteries

The function of an electric battery is to store the extra electric energy generated by the fuel cell stack and to supply the same when more energy is needed by the vehicle to run.

5. Control Module

The control unit monitors the overall energy demand of the vehicle and thus regulates the functions of fuel cell stack, motor and battery to achieve optimum performance.

Advantages of Fuel Cell Electric Vehicle (FCEV)

Fuel cell vehicles are more efficient compared to any other conventional internal combustion engine.

The tail pipe emissions of these vehicles contain only the water vapor and hence are non-polluting vehicles.

Limitations of Fuel Cell Electric Vehicle (FCEV)

Storing Hydrogen under high pressure is a risky affair and may prove fatal in case of collisions.

The excess heat generated by the fuel cell is difficult to handle and also hampers the performance over the long run.

Fuel refilling stations equipped with the sophisticated handling capability are required to be commissioned.

▶ KEY TERMS 关键词

cell [sel] *n*. 电池
electrochemical [ɪˌlektrəʊˈkemɪkəl] *adj*.
　[化学]电化学的
hydrogen [ˈhaɪdrədʒən] *n*. [化学]氢
oxygen [ˈɒksɪdʒən] *n*. [化学]氧
anode [ˈænəʊd] *n*. 阳极
cathode [ˈkæθəʊd] *n*. 阴极
electrolyte [ɪˈlektrəlaɪt] *n*. 电解质

utilize [ˈjuːtəlaɪz] *vt*. 利用
array [əˈreɪ] *n*. 排列
fuel cell stack 燃料电池组
gaseous [ˈɡæsiəs] *adj*. 气态的，气体的
ambient [ˈæmbiənt] *adj*. 周围的；外界的
fatal [ˈfeɪtl] *adj*. 致命的
collision [kəˈlɪʒn] *n*. 碰撞
hamper [ˈhæmpə(r)] *vt*. 妨碍

▶ SENTENCES 翻译示例

❶ In these vehicles, chemical energy of fuel is converted directly into electric energy. The working principle of a "fuel cell" electric vehicle is different compared to that of a "plug in" electric vehicle in the sense that the electricity required to run this vehicle is generated on the vehicle itself.

在这些车辆中，燃料的化学能直接转化为电能。"燃料电池"电动汽车的工作原理与"插电式"电动汽车的工作原理不同，即运行该车辆所需的电力是车辆自身产生的。

❷ Fuel cell is a device in which electrochemical reaction takes place between Hydrogen and Oxygen. The main components of a fuel cell include an anode, a cathode and an electrolyte.

燃料电池是一种在氢气和氧气之间发生电化学反应的装置。燃料电池的主要组件包括阳极、阴极和电解质。

❸ The thickness of an individual fuel cell is about two millimeters and it can generate a potential difference of 1 volt only. Thus, an array of hundreds of fuel cells called "fuel cell stack" is used in a Fuel Cell Electric Vehicle.

单个燃料电池的厚度约为2毫米，仅可产生1伏特的电位差。因此，一组数百个燃料电池被称为"燃料电池堆"，应用于燃料电池电动车。

❹ The electricity generated by the fuel cell stack is supplied to the electric motor which in turn rotates the wheels of the vehicle.

由燃料电池组产生的电力被供应给电动机，电动机旋转车轮，驱动汽车。

❺ Storing Hydrogen under high pressure is a risky affair and may prove fatal in case of collisions. The excess heat generated by the fuel cell is difficult to handle and also hampers the performance over the long run.

在高压下储存氢气是一件危险的事情，在发生碰撞时可能会致命。燃料电池产生的多余热量很难处理，也妨碍了长期性能。

ASIGNMENTS 思考与练习

1. How do fuel cell vehicle work?
2. What is a fuel cell?
3. Name out the main components of a fuel cell electric vehicle.

5.6 Autonomous Vehicles

Autonomous Vehicles (AVs) use technology to partially or entirely replace the human driver in navigating a vehicle from an origin to a destination while avoiding road hazards and responding to traffic conditions. See primer on autonomous vehicles (Figure 5-17) below.

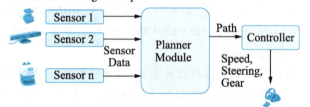

Figure 5-17　Primer on an Autonomous Vehicle

Autonomous Vehicle Technologies

AVs use combinations of technologies and sensors to sense the roadway, other vehicles, and objects on and along the roadway. The key technologies (Figure 5-18) and sensors are described below.

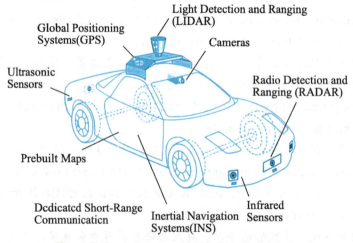

Figure 5-18　Autonomous Vehicle Key Technologies

Light Detection and Ranging (LIDAR): A 360-degree sensor that uses light beams to determine the distance between obstacles and the sensor.

Cameras: Frequently used inexpensive technology, however, complex algorithms are necessary to interpret the image data collected.

Radio Detection and Ranging (RADAR): A sensor that uses radio waves to determine the distance between obstacles and the sensor.

Infrared Sensors: Allow for the detection of lane marking, pedestrians, and bicycles that are hard for other sensors to detect in low lighting and certain environmental conditions.

Inertial Navigation Systems (INS): Typically used in combination with GPS to improve accuracy. INS uses gyroscopes and accelerometers to determine vehicle position, orientation and velocity.

Dedicated Short-Range Communication (DSRC): Used in Vehicle to Vehicle (V2V) (Figure 5-19) and Vehicle to Infrastructure (V2I) systems to send and receive critical data such as road conditions, congestion, crashes and possible rerouting. DSRC enables platooning, a train of vehicles that collectively travels together.

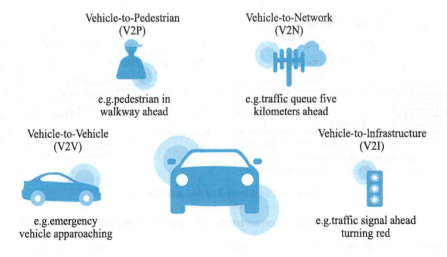

Figure 5-19 V2V, V2I, V2N and V2P

Prebuilt Maps: Sometimes utilized to correct inaccurate positioning due to errors that can occur when using GPS and INS. Given the constraints of mapping every road and drivable surface, relying on maps limits the routes an AV can take.

Ultrasonic sensors: Provide short distance data that are typically used in parking assistance systems and backup warning systems.

Global Positioning Systems (GPS): Locate the vehicle by using satellites to triangulate its position.

Technology Enablers

For both the self-driving cars and the smart roadway systems, endpoint telemetry, smart software, and cloud are essential enablers. The onboard cameras and sensors on an autonomous vehicle collect vast amounts of data, which must be processed in real time to keep the vehicle in the right lane and operating safely as it heads to its destination. There's a lot of local data processing that has to occur in real time, including the computations necessary to keep the car in its lane. At the same time, there are processing tasks that can happen remotely in the cloud, such as software updates and upgrading learning models. A scalable, highly-resilient cloud-based infrastructure is critical for handling this type of large-scale data processing, while cloud-based data management systems and intelligent agents take charge of aggregating and analyzing the real-time telemetric data—for example, vehicle speed and surrounding car proximity—to initiate actions like braking or switching lanes. See cloud-assisted architecture (Figure 5-20) below.

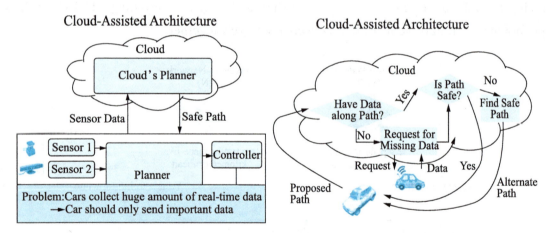

Figure 5-20　Cloud-Assisted Architecture

Cloud-based networking and connectivity is another important part of the mix. Autonomous vehicles will be outfitted with onboard systems that support machine-to-machine communications, allowing them to learn from other vehicles on the road to make adjustments that account for weather changes and shifting road conditions such as detours and in-path debris. Advanced algorithms, AI, and deep learning systems are central to ensuring that self-driving cars can quickly and automatically adapt to changing scenarios.

Beyond the specific components, scalability of cloud computing infrastructure along with intelligent data management and transmission capabilities are indispensable for ensuring all of the right information is processed properly and securely. This is especially true for destination and address data, which could be considered personally identifiable information. For example, built-in intelligence could determine if data storage and analysis happens in the cloud or onboard the vehicle in the event that the travel path crosses regions with sub-par network connectivity.

▶ KEY TERMS 关键词

autonomous [ɔːˈtɒnəməs] *adj*. 自主的
navigate [ˈnævɪɡeɪt] *vt*. 驾驶
hazard [ˈhæzəd] *n*. 危险
sensor [ˈsensə(r)] *n*. 传感器
obstacle [ˈɒbstəkl] *n*. 障碍物
algorithm [ˈælɡərɪðəm] *n*. [计][数] 算法
accuracy [ˈækjərəsi] *n*. 精确度，准确性
gyroscop [ˈdʒaɪrəskəʊp] *n*. 陀螺仪
GPS (global position system) *abbr*. 全球定位系统
accelerometer [əkˌseləˈrɒmɪtə(r)] *n*. [物] 加速计
orientation [ˌɔːriənˈteɪʃn] *n*. 方向
velocity [vəˈlɒsəti] *n*. [物] 速度
infrastructure [ˈɪnfrəstrʌktʃə(r)] *n*. 基础设施
congestion [kənˈdʒestʃən] *n*. 拥挤
constraint [kənˈstreɪnt] *n*. 约束，限制
triangulate [traɪˈæŋɡjuleɪt] *vt*. 对……作三角测量

endpoint [ˈendpɔɪt] *n*. 端点；末端
telemetry [tɪˈlemətri] *n*. 遥测技术
remotely [rɪˈməʊtli] *adv*. 远程地
scalable [ˈskeɪləbl] *adj*. 可伸缩的
resilient [rɪˈzɪliənt] *adj*. 有弹性的
agent [ˈeɪdʒənt] *n*. 代理
aggregate [ˈæɡrɪɡət] *vt*. 集合
telemetric [ˌteliˈmɪtrɪk] *adj*. 遥感勘测的
proximity [prɒkˈsɪməti] *n*. 接近
initiate [ɪˈnɪʃieɪt] *vt*. 发起
cloud-based 基于云计算的
outfit [ˈaʊtfɪt] *vi*. 配备
onboard system 车载系统
detour [ˈdiːtʊə(r)] *n*. 绕道
debris [ˈdebriː] *n*. 碎片，杂物
AI (artificial intelligence) *abbr*. 人工智能
scenario [səˈnɑːriəʊ] *n*. 场景
scalability [ˌskeɪləˈbɪlɪti] *n*. 可扩展性；可伸缩性
sub-par [ˈsʌbˈpɑː] *adj*. 低于标准的

▶ SENTENCES 翻译示例

❶ Autonomous vehicles (AVs) use technology to partially or entirely replace the human driver in navigating a vehicle from an origin to a destination while avoiding road hazards and responding to traffic conditions.
自动驾驶汽车使用技术来部分或完全取代驾驶员从起点到目的地对于车辆的驾驶，同时避免道路危险并对交通状况做出反应。

❷ Inertial Navigation Systems: Typically used in combination with GPS to improve accuracy. INS uses gyroscopes and accelerometers to determine vehicle position, orientation and velocity.

惯性导航系统：通常与全球定位系统相结合以提高精度。INS使用陀螺仪和加速计来确定车辆的位置、方向和速度。

❸ Prebuilt Maps：Sometimes utilized to correct inaccurate positioning due to errors that can occur when using GPS and INS. Given the constraints of mapping every road and drivable surface, relying on maps limits the routes an AV can take.

预建地图：有时用于纠正错误的定位，因为在使用全球定位系统和惯性导航系统时可能出现错误。考虑到绘制每条道路和可行驶路面的限制，依靠预先构建的地图可以限制自动驾驶汽车的路线。

❹ For both the self-driving cars and the smart roadway systems, endpoint telemetry, smart software, and cloud are essential enablers. The onboard cameras and sensors on an autonomous vehicle collect vast amounts of data, which must be processed in real time to keep the vehicle in the right lane and operating safely as it heads to its destination.

对于自动驾驶汽车和智能道路系统而言，终端遥测、智能软件和云都是必不可少的推动因素。自动驾驶汽车的车载摄像头和传感器收集大量的数据，这些数据必须实时处理，以保证汽车在正确的车道上行驶，并安全行驶到达目的地。

❺ Cloud-based networking and connectivity is another important part of the mix. Autonomous vehicles will be outfitted with onboard systems that support machine-to-machine communications, allowing them to learn from other vehicles on the road to make adjustments that account for weather changes and shifting road conditions such as detours and in-path debris. Advanced algorithms, AI, and deep learning systems are central to ensuring that self-driving cars can quickly and automatically adapt to changing scenarios.

云计算网络和连接是另一个重要组成部分。自动驾驶汽车将配备车载系统，支持机器对机器的通信，允许他们在路上学习其他汽车，进行调整，以适应天气变化和道路状况的变化，如绕开路面上的杂物。高级算法、人工智能和深度学习系统是确保自动驾驶汽车能够快速、自动地适应变化的场景的核心。

▶ ASIGNMENTS 思考与练习

1. What does autonomous car mean?
2. How driverless cars will work?
3. What are the essential enablers of self-driving cars?

Case study 实车案例

Toyota Prius Hybrid Electric Vehicle 丰田普锐斯混合动力汽车

The Toyota Prius is a hybrid electric vehicle developed and manufactured by the Toyota Motor Corporation. The Prius first went on sale in Japan in 1997, making it the first mass-produced hybrid vehicle. It was subsequently introduced worldwide in 2001. According to the United States Environmental Protection Agency, the 2008 Prius is the most fuel efficient car sold in the U.S., achieving 46 mpg. According to the UK Department for Transport, the Prius is tied with the diesel Mini Cooper D as the second least CO_2-emitting vehicle behind the Volkswagen Polo 1.4 TDI.

At the centre of Toyota's hybrid technology is the Hybrid Synergy Drive. This system makes intelligent use of a vehicle's electric motors and gas/petrol engine to take advantage of the key attributes of the two power sources to ensure that the car operates at optimum fuel efficiency.

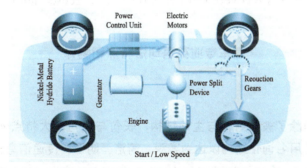

1. At start-off/low-speeds, Hybrid Synergy Drive runs the car on the electric motors only, since the gas/petrol engine does not perform efficiently. A gas/petrol engine cannot produce high torque in the low rpm range, whereas electric motors can—delivering a very responsive and smooth start.

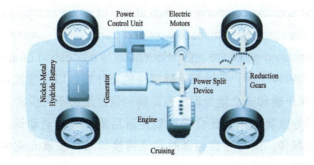

2. However, the gas/petrol engine is quite energy efficient for cruising. Power produced by the gas/petrol engine is used to drive the wheels and also the generator to

provide power to the electric motors or to charge the battery. By making use of the engine/motor dual powertrain, the energy produced by the gas/petrol engine is transferred to the road surface with minimal loss.

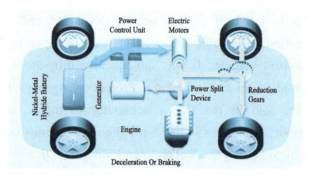

3. Under deceleration or braking, Hybrid Synergy Drive uses the car's kinetic energy to let the wheels turn the electric motors and recover regenerative energy to recharge the battery. Energy that is normally lost as friction heat under deceleration is converted into electrical energy, which is recovered in the battery to be reused later.

汽车专业英语句法特点和翻译

名词化结构

汽车专业英语除了被动结构与主动结构，长句与短句两大特点外，还有一些其他显著特点。如，使用名词化结构以达到客观、简洁、明了、传递信息量大的目的。

1) The thickness of an individual fuel cell is about two millimeters and it can generate a potential difference of 1 volt only.
   单个燃料电池的厚度约为2毫米，它只能产生1伏特的电位差。

2) Cloud-based networking and connectivity is another important part of the mix.
   云计算网络和连接是另一个重要组成部分。

3) Beyond the specific components, scalability of cloud computing infrastructure along with intelligent data management and transmission capabilities are indispensable for ensuring all of the right information is processed properly and securely.
   除了特定的组件之外，云计算基础架构的可伸缩性以及智能数据管理和传输能力对于确保正确和安全地处理所有正确的信息是必不可少的。

此外，在汽车专业英语中，还会接触到定语后置、非谓语动词、倒装结构等，可以酌情做出得体的翻译。同时注意翻译时灵活转换句法，积累专业知识使译文更客观严谨，提高翻译质量。

参考译文
Translation for Reference

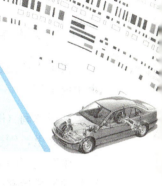

第一章 汽车概述

1.1 汽车构造

汽车，别名"auto"，也称作"motorcar"或者"car"，通常是四轮车辆，主要用于客运，通常使用挥发性燃料，由内燃机驱动。现代汽车是一个复杂的技术系统，采用具有特定设计功能的子系统。汽车的主要结构（图1-1）是发动机、底盘、车身和电气系统。这将在各种形式的机动车中找到。

发动机

发动机是汽车的"心脏"，靠内部燃烧运转，意思是提供动力的燃料在发动机内部燃烧。四冲程发动机是最常见的汽车发动机类型。发动机由活塞、气缸、输送燃料至气缸的管道和其他部件组成。每个系统都是汽车运行、减少噪声和污染所必需的。

底盘

底盘是汽车各部分安装的框架。底盘必须足够坚固，以承受汽车的重量，但为了承受转弯和路况所带来的冲击和张力，也得有一定的灵活性。底盘由传动系统、行驶系统、转向系统和制动系统四个部分组成。

车身

汽车的车身通常由钢或铝制成，也使用玻璃纤维和塑料。车身在形成客舱、提供储存空间、容纳汽车各系统的同时也有其他重要的功能。在大多数情况下，其坚固结构可以保护乘客免受事故的伤害。汽车的其他部分，比如车前部和发动机罩，被设计为容易起皱变形，从而承受撞车的大部分冲击。

电气系统

电力用于汽车的许多地方，从车头灯到收音机都用电，但其主要功能是提供点燃气缸内燃料所需的电火花。电气系统由蓄电池、起动机、交流发电机、分电器、点火线圈和点火开关组成。

181

1.2 汽车生产

汽车生产是逐步创造一辆新车的复杂过程。在离开装配线之前，一辆汽车将通过以下五个主要工序。

冲压车间（图1-2）

在这里，钢被塑造成型，形成即将成为车身外壳的面板。

生产过程的第一步是准备用来制造汽车的粗钢。钢板在被切割和制成单个部件之前是以钢卷的形式运来的，这些部件将被焊接在一起，制成一辆辆汽车。

在钢成形之前，必须先做好准备。将每个钢卷送到一个机器上，展开并使之平滑，这样钢卷就完全平整了。然后将金属切成板料并冲压成组成汽车基本结构的各个面板。成品面板被收集到机架中，然后依次送到焊接车间。

焊接车间（图1-3）

在焊接车间，冲压后的钢板被焊接在一起，形成一个车身外壳。每个车身外壳都有一个身份标签，并被保留在生产过程中。该标签由生产系统创建，用于确定汽车的颜色、发动机规格、内饰等。

焊接车间最简单的形式可以分为两部分，由熟练工人组成的焊接站，以及由机器驱动的焊接站。两个工作站将数千个独立的钢制部件结合在一起，形成新的车身外壳。

零件被组装成子装配体，这些子装配体组成汽车。在车身外壳生产线末端手工安装发动机罩和行李箱。这里的团队还做了最终的视觉检查，以确保车身完美连接，并且面板光滑没有凹痕、磨料或其他变形，它们在涂装时可能导致表面光洁问题。车身从这里被提升到一个传送带上，传送带将其送入涂装车间。

涂装车间（图1-4）

涂装车间要求绝对清洁。保持一尘不染的洁净环境对于每辆车涂装的质量和一致性至关重要。现在，为了达到下线的质量标准，喷漆包括四层：电泳、密封和聚氯乙烯喷涂、中涂（底漆）、面漆（光泽和颜色）。

表面预处理：离开焊接车间后，将清洗车身表面，以增加电泳涂装步骤时的防锈性和附着力。

电泳涂装：在表面预处理后，车身会被嵌入到电泳涂料槽中（电泳涂装过程—电泳涂层）。这个过程也被称为电沉积，以使表面更好喷漆。在从电泳涂料槽中取出后，车身将在烘箱中高温烘干，使涂料干燥并产生涂层的硬度。

密封和聚氯乙烯喷涂：这一步有助于密封钢材的边缘，防止在驾驶过程中的外部影响（防水和防噪声）。

底漆：提高面漆的附着力以及光泽度和颜色丰满度。在底漆层之后，车身将在高温下进行干燥过程。

面漆：这是一种为车辆创造美感的涂层，展示了车辆的真实颜色。因此，它的要求包括三个词"光泽度、耐久性和真实性"。通过静电喷涂工艺,将颜料喷到底漆层上。在此之后,车身将在烘箱中高温烘干。

完成后,在移动到装配车间之前,将对整个车身进行光洁的检查。

装配车间(图 1-5)

当车身外壳到达装配车间后,车门就会被拆卸,并被送到另一条线上,以便安装其饰板、玻璃、扬声器和车镜。与此同时,车身重要位置已经被包装保护,以保护漆面和部件免受潜在损害。

因为装配非常复杂,所以整个任务分为几个部分:内饰线、传动系线和终装线。

检查(图 1-6)

在交付给经销商之前,这是生产过程的最后一步。为了保证最高质量的产品,所有的车辆都必须经过最后检查,检查发动机、车灯、喇叭、轮胎平衡和充电系统。在这个阶段发现任何缺陷都要求将汽车送到中央维修区域,中央维修区域通常位于装配线末端附近。当车辆通过最后审核时,它会得到一份证书,然后被开到一个暂存区,等待被装运到目的地。

在几小时内,它就从金属板材变成了一辆高质量的汽车。

第二章 发动机

2.1 汽车发动机概述

汽油车发动机的目的是把汽油转化为运动,使汽车能够移动。目前,把汽油转化为运动的最简单方法是在发动机内燃烧汽油。因此,汽车发动机(图 2-1)是一种燃烧发生在内部的内燃机。

2.1.1 发动机的分类

汽车发动机在设计上有所不同,但某些部件在所有发动机中都是通用的,并被用于发动机分类。以下是分类的方法。

1. 燃烧的燃料

燃料燃烧提供了广泛的发动机分类。一般使用两种燃料:汽油和柴油。汽油发动机为点燃式,而柴油发动机为压燃式(无火花)。诸如液化石油气、乙醇汽油(90%汽油、10%酒精)和纯酒精之类的替代燃料在非常有限的情况下使用。

2. 缸体结构

实际上,在汽车中有三种不同的发动机结构:

直列式(图 2-2)——气缸按直线排成一排。

V 型(图 2-3)——气缸按一定的角度排成两排。

水平对置式（图2-4）——气缸在发动机的相对两侧排成两排。

3. 气缸数

气缸的数量经常与发动机缸体结构结合使用。气缸的数量是汽车发动机运行平稳的一个标志。一个八缸发动机比四缸发动机运行更平稳，因为做功行程发生的频率更高。气缸的数量也有助于输出功率；更多的气缸，更多的动力。然而，这并不总是一个很好的动力输出指标。一个涡轮增压的四缸发动机比自然吸气六缸发动机产生更大的动力。

4. 点火类型

点燃燃料有两种方法：火花点火和压燃点火。汽油车发动机使用火花点火，而柴油发动机使用压燃点火。该方法是压缩空气使其温度上升至柴油的燃点，添加柴油时即刻点火。

2.1.2 四冲程循环

目前，几乎所有的汽车都使用四冲程循环，将汽油转化为运动。四冲程循环也被称为奥托循环，以纪念尼古拉斯·奥托，他在1867年发明了四冲程发动机。四冲程（图2-5）是：进气行程、压缩行程、做功行程和排气行程。

以下是四冲程发动机的工作原理：

1. 活塞从上止点开始运动，进气门打开，活塞向下移动，空气汽油混合气被吸入气缸内。这是进气行程。只需要很少汽油混合到空气中即能工作。

2. 然后活塞向上移动，压缩这个燃料/空气混合气。压缩使爆发力更加强大。

3. 当活塞到达压缩行程的上止点时，火花塞产生电火花点燃汽油。气缸内的汽油燃烧，推动活塞向下运动。

4. 活塞到达下止点，排气门打开，废气通过排气管排出气缸。

现在发动机已经准备好下一个循环了，所以它吸入另外的空气燃油混合气。

在发动机中，活塞的往复运动被曲轴转化为旋转运动（图2-6）。旋转运动非常好，因为我们计划转动（旋转）汽车的车轮。

2.2 发动机缸体

如今，大多数汽车、货车、公共汽车、拖拉机等的发动机都采用了高度一体化的设计。因此，"发动机缸体""气缸体"或简单的"缸体"这些术语可能会在汽车修理厂或街上听到。

发动机缸体（图2-7）是内燃机车辆的关键部件，为车辆提供动力室。它被称为"缸体"，因为它通常是一个坚固的铸造汽车部件，在冷却和润滑的曲轴箱内安置气缸和相关的部件。缸体的设计是非常坚固的。

发动机缸体通常由适当等级的铁或铝合金铸造而成。铝制缸体的重量轻得多，并且能将热量更好地转移给冷却液，但是铁制缸体保留了一些优势，并继续被一些制造商使用。由于使用气缸套和轴瓦，铝的相对柔软性并不重要。

缸体内部有许多通道，包括冷却水套，这样的设计是用来将水从散热器输送到发动机的所有热区，防止过热。当水在发动机中循环后，它返回到散热器，由风扇冷却后再返回发动机。

发动机缸体的核心是气缸，顶部是气缸盖。气缸盖（图2-8）安装在缸体的顶部，就像房子的屋顶一样。底部到活塞顶部形成燃烧室。气缸的数量决定了气缸的大小和位置，大多数汽车的气缸在四到八个之间。这些气缸容纳活塞，通过控制气缸内的一系列爆炸，推动活塞转动曲轴来为车辆提供动力。

缸体底部附有油底壳，它密封发动机中的润滑油。油底壳通常由压制钢制成。油底壳和气缸体的下部一起被称为曲轴箱（图2-9）。

2.3 两大机构

2.3.1 曲柄连杆机构

曲柄连杆机构（图2-10）位于往复式活塞发动机的中心，其目的是将活塞的直线运动转化为旋转运动，以提取有用的功。曲柄连杆机构通常由活塞、连杆、曲轴和飞轮或动力输出装置组成。

活塞

活塞（图2-11）是一个圆柱形的金属，在气缸内上下移动。由于燃烧而产生的力推动活塞沿着气缸壁前进。沿着气缸的这种滑动将力传递给连杆。

为了有效地传递力，采用铝制活塞与空心结构相结合的方式，使活塞的惯性保持最小。活塞上装有两套活塞环，用来填补活塞和气缸之间的间隙。上部气环是为了防止燃烧的气体泄漏到下部而提供气密性密封。下部油环提供有效的密封，以防止发动机气缸中的油泄漏。

连杆

连杆（图2-12）连接活塞和曲轴。它可以在两端旋转，使它的角度可以随着活塞移动和曲轴旋转而改变。此外，在做功行程时它将活塞的滑动运动转换为曲轴的旋转运动。连杆小头通过活塞销连接到活塞上，连杆大头通过曲柄销连接到曲柄上。连杆是由特种钢或铝合金制成的。连杆的设计和制造必须特别小心，随着弯曲应力的变化，它容易受到不同拉伸和压缩应力的影响。

曲轴

曲轴（图2-13）把活塞的上下运动转变为旋转运动。轴上包含一些偏心部分，称为"曲柄"。连杆大头用曲柄销连接到曲柄上。曲柄销是曲轴的关键部分，因为通过活塞传递的力直接作用于它。

飞轮

飞轮（图2-14）是一个大而重的金属圆盘，安装在发动机曲轴的后部。它的目的是为了消除气缸内因燃烧而引起的震动。飞轮还提供了离合器从动盘安装面，轮缘上有齿圈与起动机啮合。

2.3.2 配气机构

配气机构（图2-15）包括气门、摇臂、推杆、挺柱和凸轮轴。配气机构的唯一工作是"交通警察"。它可以在正确的时间让空气和燃料进出发动机。时间由凸轮轴控制，凸轮轴通过链条或传动带与曲轴同步。

凸轮轴

凸轮轴上有精确加工的凸角来控制气门的开启。

凸轮的凸角

凸轮的凸角被精确地加工成形，它决定了气门开启时与活塞位置的关系，气门的位移距离，以及气门保持开启的时长。

推杆

发动机的凸轮轴位于发动机缸体上，使用推杆作用于摇臂，打开气门。推杆安装在挺柱上，靠凸轮轴凸角顶起。

液力挺柱

通常使用液力挺柱，因为它们可以通过保持零气门间隙（气门驱动机构的组件之间没有间隙）来减少配气机构的噪音。还有机械挺柱和滚轮挺柱。

气门

每个气缸至少有一个进气门和一个排气门。有些发动机每个气缸设计有两组气门。进气门的直径大于排气门直径，从而最大限度地增加气缸内的空气流量。排气门必须承受比进气门更高的温度，因为空气流过进气门，使进气门保持在较低的温度。

顶置气门

顶置气门发动机（图2-16）是一种气门被置于气缸盖内的发动机。在顶置气门发动机中，只有一个凸轮，位于相对的气缸组的"V"结构之间。顶置气门发动机几乎都是每个气缸只有两个气门，但也并非总是如此。

顶置凸轮轴

在顶置凸轮轴（图2-17）发动机中，无论是V形结构还是直列结构，驱动气门的凸轮都直接位于气门的顶部。凸轮旋转，凸角沿气门杆向下推动，使气门打开，然后当凸角旋转后气门关闭。气门弹簧当然提供了回弹力。传动链或同步带用于将顶置凸轮连接到主轴上，而且每个气缸通常有多个进气门和排气门。

2.4 五大系统

2.4.1 燃油供给系统

汽油在进入气缸之前必须与空气充分混合。汽油和空气的结合造成更大的爆炸。燃油泵从安装在汽车后部的油箱中抽取汽油。有些汽车上的汽油被吸入化油器，而其他汽车采用燃油喷射的方式。这两种装置都将汽油与空气混合（空气和汽油的比例约为14：1），并将该混合物以雾状喷入气缸中。燃油供给系统的其他部分（图2-18）包括空气滤清器（一个过滤器以确保混入空气中的燃料无杂质）和进气歧管（将可燃混合物分配到各个气缸）。

油箱

油箱基本上就是燃料的储存罐。当你在加油站加满油时，气体沿着加油管进入油箱。在油箱里有一个发送装置，它告诉油量表油箱里有多少汽油。近年来，油箱变得略为复杂，因为它现在通常安装燃油泵，并且具有更多的排放控制，以防止气体泄漏到空气中。

燃油泵

新式汽车上，燃油泵（图2-19）通常安装在燃油箱内。老式汽车将燃油泵连接到发动机或油箱与发动机之间的车架导轨上。如果燃油泵在油箱内或车架导轨上，那么它就是电动的，由汽车蓄电池驱动。安装在发动机上的燃油泵是利用发动机的运动来泵出燃油，通常由凸轮轴驱动，但有时也会由曲轴驱动。

燃油滤清器

清洁燃料对发动机的寿命和性能至关重要。喷油器和化油器有微小的孔，很容易堵塞，所以过滤燃油是必要的。燃油滤清器（图2-20）可以在燃油泵的前或后使用，有时前后都使用。燃油滤清器通常是由纸制滤芯制成，但也可以是不锈钢或合成材料，并被设计成在大多数情况下是可一次性使用的。一些高性能燃油滤清器将具有可清洗的滤网，无需更换。

喷油器

1986年以后的大多数国产车和早期来自工厂的外国车都使用燃油喷射。计算机对喷油器何时打开以使燃油进入发动机进行控制，取代了使用化油器来混合燃油和空气的方式。这降低了排放且具有更好的燃油经济性。喷油器基本上是一个微小的电磁阀，利用电信号控制其开启和关闭。在图2-21中，你可以看到喷油器朝向进气口的外部。在靠近气缸盖的位置喷射燃料，燃料雾化（以微小颗粒的形式），因此当被火花塞点燃时，燃料会更好地燃烧。

化油器

化油器在没有电脑干预的情况下将燃油与空气混合。虽然操作简单，但他们往往需要频繁调整和重建。这就是新车已经取消了化油器而采用燃油喷射的原因。

电控燃油喷射系统

电控燃油喷射是向发动机供应燃料的一种技术和机械结构。这些系统在汽车和货车中最常见。电子控制装置使用一系列电路和压力表来精确且高速地打开和关闭燃料阀。

系统中包含多个传感器，主要用于确保将正确的燃油量输送到喷油器，然后再输送到进气门。这些传感器包括发动机转速传感器、电压传感器、冷却液温度传感器、节气门位置传感器、氧传感器和空气流量传感器。另外，进气歧管绝对压力传感器监测进气歧管中的空气压力，以决定产生的功率。

在顺序燃油喷射系统中，喷油器与每个气缸的开启相配合，一次打开一个。其他一些喷射系统可能会同时打开所有喷油器。顺序喷射的方式是有利的，因为当驾驶员操作突变时，它可以更快地响应。

整个喷射系统由一个电子控制单元控制，该单元用作所有各种传感器输入信息的中央交换机。电子控制单元使用这些信息来确定脉冲长度、点火提前角和其他元素。

2.4.2 润滑系统

润滑系统（图 2-22）的目的是在发动机内循环机油。发动机必须有良好的润滑系统。没有它，运动部件接触时的摩擦热就会磨损部件并造成功率损耗。机油以油膜形式隔开两个运动部件，防止零件互相摩擦，并缓冲部件，使发动机运转更加安静平稳。

机油起着至关重要的作用。因为机油每分钟循环数千次，所以它能润滑、清洁和冷却发动机的许多运动部件。它减少了发动机部件的磨损，并确保在受控温度下一切工作有效。保持新鲜的润滑油通过润滑系统，减少维修次数，延长发动机使用寿命。

发动机有几十个运动部件，它们都需要良好润滑，以提供平稳、一致的性能。当机油流经发动机时，它会在以下各部件之间流动。

机油泵

机油泵对机油进行加压，使其通过发动机并保持组件持续润滑。多叶转子泵是最常见的油泵类型。外部安装的油泵（图 2-23）通常在泵体上安装滤清器。

油底壳

油底壳通常位于发动机的底部，作为储油室，也被称为 sump。是发动机关闭时收集机油的地方。大多数车辆在油底壳内容纳 4 至 8 夸特的机油。

油底壳的类型

油底壳分两种。第一种是大多数汽车都使用的湿式油底壳（图 2-24）。此种油底壳位于发动机的底部。这种设计对于大多数车辆来说都是实用的，因为油底壳靠近机油泵的出油位置，而且制造和修理相对便宜。

第二种是干式油底壳（图 2-25），常见于高性能的车辆上。这种油底壳位于发动机的其它地方，特别不在底部。这种设计允许汽车更靠近地面，降低重心并改善操控性。它还有助于防止机油在高转弯负载下从油管中滑落而引起的断油。

吸油管

当发动机起动时，这个油管在油泵的驱动下从油底壳里吸油，把机油送到机油滤清器之后送给整个发动机。

限压阀

调节油压，使其在负载和发动机转速变化时保持一致的流量。

机油滤清器

机油滤清器（图 2-26）过滤掉可能会磨损发动机或损坏发动机部件的杂质、污垢、金属颗粒和其他污染物。

喷射孔和油道
钻入或铸入气缸体及其部件的通道和孔，确保机油均匀地分布于各部件。

油位指示器
油位指示器也被称为机油尺，指示油底壳的油位，有时还包含制造商推荐的机油类型等信息。有些车辆在油底壳装有电子传感器，以指示低油位。

2.4.3 冷却系统

冷却系统（图2-27）的主要工作是通过将热量传递给空气来防止发动机过热。冷却系统的另一个重要工作是让发动机尽可能快地升温，然后让发动机保持恒定的温度。

在汽车上有两种类型的冷却系统：水冷和风冷。

水冷
水冷汽车的冷却系统通过发动机中的管道和通道循环冷却液。当冷却液流经高温发动机时会吸收热量，从而降低发动机的温度。冷却液流过发动机后，转而流向热交换器（或散热器），通过热交换器将热量散发到空气中。

风冷
一些老式汽车和少数现代汽车采用风冷式冷却系统。这种冷却方法不是在发动机中进行液体循环，而是通过发动机缸体覆盖的铝制散热片对气缸进行散热。一个功率强大的风扇向这些散热片吹风，将热量传递给空气来冷却发动机。

冷却液
水是保持热量最有效的液体之一，但水的凝固点太高，不适用于汽车发动机。大多数汽车使用的液体是水和乙二烯乙二醇（$C_2H_6O_2$）的混合液，也称为防冻液。通过将乙二烯乙二醇添加到水中，可以显著提高沸点、降低凝固点。

水泵
水泵是一个简单的离心泵（图2-28），由连接到发动机曲轴的传动带驱动。当发动机运转时，水泵使冷却液循环流动。

散热器
散热器（图2-29）是一种换热装置。它的设计目的是将热量从流经它的热冷却液传递到风扇吹过的空气中。大多数现代汽车都使用铝制散热器。

压力水箱盖
散热器盖（图2-30）实际上是将冷却液的沸点提高约45华氏度（25摄氏度），它实际上是一个压力释放阀，在汽车上通常设置为15磅力每平方英寸。当水处于压力之下时，水的沸点会升高。

节温器

节温器（图2-31）的主要工作是让发动机快速升温，然后使发动机保持在恒定的温度。它通过调节流经散热器的水量来实现这一点。在低温下，散热器的出口被完全堵塞——所有的冷却液都通过发动机重新循环。

风扇

和节温器一样，必须控制冷却风扇，以使发动机保持恒温。

循环

由于大多数汽车都是水冷的，所以我们将着重对水冷系统进行说明。水泵将冷却液输送到发动机缸体，冷却液便开始在气缸周围的发动机通道里流动。然后冷却液通过发动机的气缸盖返回。节温器位于冷却液离开发动机的位置。若节温器关闭，其周围的管道将冷却液直接送回水泵。若节温器打开，冷却液先通过散热器，然后再流回水泵。

2.4.4 点火系统

点火系统（图2-33）执行两个任务。首先，它必须创造一个足够高的电压（20 000伏特以上），以击穿火花塞间隙，从而产生足够强的火花来点燃空气/燃料混合气。第二，它必须控制点火时间，使它在准确的时间发生，并将其发送到正确的气缸。

点火线圈

点火线圈（图2-34）是将相对较弱的电池能量转化成足以点燃可燃混合气的电火花的装置。在传统的点火线圈内部是两个导线线圈，这些线圈称为绕组（图2-35）。一个绕组称为初级绕组，另一个绕组称为次级绕组。初级绕组获得电流点火，次级绕组将其送出给分电器。

分电器、分电器盖和转子

分电器（图2-36）基本上是一个非常精确的旋转器。当它旋转时，它会在正确的时间将火花分配到单个的火花塞上。它通过使用来自线圈电线的强大火花来分配火花，并通过旋转的电接触器（转子）发送。转子之所以旋转，是因为它连在分电器的轴上。当转子旋转时，它会与许多点（4、6、8或12，这取决于你的发动机有多少个气缸）接触，并通过该点将火花发送到另一端的插头线上。现代的分电器有电子辅助，可以改变点火时间。

火花塞和电线

火花通过火花塞电线到达火花塞。火花塞（图2-37）被拧入气缸盖，这意味着火花塞的顶端位于气缸顶部，在这个位置上点火。当进气门打开，适量可燃混合气进入气缸时，火花塞在分电器提供的精确时间产生精密的蓝色炽热火花，点燃混合气并产生燃烧。

点火模块

在过去，分电器依靠许多"机械直觉"来保持点火时间的完美。它是通过一个称为积分－电容系统的装置来实现的。点火点设置为一个特定的间隙，在电容器调节时产生最佳火花。现如今这都是由电脑处理的。直接调节点火系统的计算机称为点火模块,即点火控制模块。

2.4.5 起动系统

起动发动机可能是汽车电气系统最重要的功能。起动系统(图2-38)通过将蓄电池的电能转化为起动机的机械能来实现这个功能。然后,起动机将机械能通过齿轮传递到发动机曲轴的飞轮上。在起动过程中,飞轮旋转,可燃混合气被吸入气缸,压缩并点火以起动发动机。起动系统由点火开关控制,并通过熔断线路保护。

起动机

起动机是一台电动机,它可以转动曲轴从而起动发动机。起动机由蓄电池供电。起动机有一个电磁开关,能移动一个旋转齿轮(驱动齿轮),与发动机飞轮上的环形齿轮相啮合或断开。减速起动机包含图2-39所显示的组件。它有一个紧凑高速的电动机和一套减速器。尽管电动机比传统的起动机更小更轻,但它的运行速度更快。减速起动机替代了大多数传统的起动机。

起动机电磁线圈

起动机电磁线圈用作强大的继电器。当被激活时,它会关闭电路并将电流发送给起动机。同时,起动机电磁线圈向前推动起动机齿轮,使其与发动机飞轮齿圈啮合。

蓄电池电缆

由于起动机需要大电流来起动发动机,所以用粗(大规格)电缆(图2-41)将它与蓄电池连接。负极(接地)电缆连接电池"-"端和发动机气缸体,靠近起动机。正极电缆连接电池"+"端和起动机电磁线圈。

空挡安全开关

出于安全原因,起动机只能在自动变速器处于停车或空挡位置时进行操作;或者,如果汽车有手动变速器,当离合器踏板处于踩下状态时进行操作。为了做到这一点,在自动变速器换挡装置或手动变速器离合器踏板上安装了一个空挡安全开关。

起动继电器

继电器是一种允许少量电流控制大量电流的装置。起动继电器(图2-42)串联在蓄电池与起动机之间。一些汽车使用起动机电磁线圈来实现同样的目的,允许来自于点火开关的少量电流控制从蓄电池流向起动机的大电流。

点火开关

点火开关一般有四个挡位:锁止挡、附件通电挡、接通挡和起动挡。一些汽车有关闭和锁止两个锁车挡位,一个是车熄火,另一个是允许拔出钥匙。

蓄电池

蓄电池的作用是为起动机提供电流,在起动时为点火系统提供电流,当发电机过载时,可以协助发电机向用电设备供电，它还可以作为一个储电器。

2.5 排放控制系统

在汽车中，排放控制系统（图2-43）是用来限制从内燃机和其他部件排放有害气体的。这些气体有三个主要来源：发动机废气、曲轴箱、油箱和化油器。排气管排放出燃烧的和未燃烧的碳氢化合物、一氧化碳、氮和硫的氧化物，以及各种酸、醇和酚。曲轴箱是未燃烧的碳氢化合物和少量一氧化碳的第二个来源。在油箱和（早期汽车的）化油器中，从汽油中不断蒸发的碳氢化合物也构成了污染因素。各种系统已被开发出来控制这些排放。

曲轴箱强制通风（图2-44）

在曲轴箱中，气缸下部放置曲轴的发动机缸体部分泄漏的燃烧气体与通风空气相结合，回到进气歧管，在燃烧室中重新燃烧。执行此功能的装置称为曲轴箱强制通风阀或PCV阀。

废气再循环

为了控制占发动机总污染物三分之二的废气排放，使用了两种类型的系统：空气喷射系统和废气再循环系统。在废气再循环系统中（图2-45），一定比例的废气被引导回气缸盖，它们与可燃混合气一起进入燃烧室。再循环的废气有助于降低燃烧的温度，这有利于抑制氮氧化物产生（尽管发动机效率降低）。在典型的空气喷射系统中，发动机驱动的空气泵将空气注入排气歧管，空气与未燃烧的碳氢化合物和一氧化碳在高温下结合继续燃烧过程。这样，大量的通过排气系统排出的污染物就被燃烧掉。

催化转化器

另一个额外燃烧的地方是催化转化器（图2-46），由包含陶瓷颗粒的绝热室或涂有金属如铂和钯的薄层的陶瓷蜂窝结构组成。当废气通过填充颗粒或蜂窝时，金属充当催化剂以引起废气中的碳氢化合物、一氧化碳和氮氧化物转化为水蒸气、二氧化碳和氮气。这些系统并不完全有效：在预热过程中，温度很低，不能催化排放物。预热催化转化器是解决这个问题的可行方案。例如，混合动力汽车中的高压电池可以提供足够的电力来迅速地加热转换器。

活性炭罐

过去，从油箱和化油器蒸发出来的燃油蒸汽直接排放到大气中。今天，由于密封油箱盖和燃油蒸发排放控制系统（图2-47）的使用，这些排放物已经大大减少了。燃油蒸发排放控制系统的核心部件是一个活性炭罐，能吸附高达其自重35%的燃料蒸汽。在操作中，油箱内溢出的汽油蒸汽流向蒸汽分离阀，它将原燃料返回到油箱，燃料蒸汽通过清洗阀输送到活性炭罐中。活性炭罐充当了贮存装置：当发动机运转时，吸附在活性炭罐内的燃油蒸汽经真空软管吸出，经过过滤器，进入燃烧室内燃烧。

计算机控制整个燃烧过程。提高了燃烧效率。这种控制确保了上述系统最有效的操作。此外，计算机控制的燃油喷射系统确保了更精确的可燃混合气，从而提高燃烧效率和降低污染物的产生。

第二代车载诊断

早在 1994 年,一些美国车辆就配备了新的政府授权的第二代车载诊断(OBD II)系统。1996 年款起,所有新车和轻型卡车都需要配备第二代车载诊断系统,用于检测排放问题。当检测到一个问题时,检查发动机警告灯亮起来,诊断故障代码存储在动力总成控制模块中。之后,可以使用扫描工具读取代码,确定问题的性质。

2.6 涡轮增压器

涡轮增压器(图 2-48)是一种排气驱动装置,可以提高发动机的输出功率。通常,活塞的向下运动将空气吸入发动机,空气和燃料混合在一起,燃烧产生动力。踩加速踏板会增加可吸入的空气量。(所以你不是真的踩着油门,你踩着空气!)

涡轮增压器使用一对安装在共用轴上的扇形铸件。一台(称为涡轮机)通过管道连接至排气口,另一台(压缩机)通过管道连接至进气口。排气流旋转涡轮机,导致压缩机转动。压缩机将空气以更快的速度吹入发动机中。更大量的空气可以与更大量的燃料混合,从而增加功率输出。涡轮增压器结构图如图 2-49 所示。

涡轮增压器用螺栓固定在发动机的排气歧管上。来自气缸的废气旋转涡轮机,就像燃气涡轮发动机一样工作。涡轮机通过轴连接到位于空气滤清器和进气歧管之间的压缩机。压缩机对进入活塞的空气加压。来自气缸的废气通过涡轮叶片,导致涡轮旋转。通过叶片的排气越多,它们旋转得越快。请参见下面的涡轮增压器工作原理图(图 2-50)。

在涡轮机所连接的轴的另一端,压缩机将空气泵入气缸中。压缩机是一种离心泵,它将空气吸进其叶片的中心,并在旋转时向外甩出。

为了使涡轮增压器工作,需要有足够的排气压力来旋转("加速")涡轮机。直到发动机的速度达到每分钟 2 000~3 000 转时才可能发生这种情况,这叫做涡轮迟滞。请注意,一旦涡轮加速,结果通常是一股强劲的力量,有时伴有喷气发动机般的哨声。

3.1 传动系统

3.1.1 离合器

离合器位于发动机后部和变速器前部之间。其目的是为操作者提供接合和分离发动机飞轮与变速器的能力。

离合器(图 3-1)由离合器盖、压盘和一个带有摩擦衬面的离合器从动盘组成。离合器盖用螺栓固定在发动机飞轮上。因此,它一直随着发动机一起旋转。压盘在离合器盖内,它也随着离合器盖和飞轮旋转。夹在压盘和飞轮之间的是离合器从动盘。该盘通过花键连接到变速器输入轴。

1. 结构

离合器的基本部件如图 3-2 所示。

飞轮

飞轮（图 3-3）用螺栓固定在发动机的曲轴上，是一个钢制或铝制的大"圆盘"。作为发动机的平衡器，飞轮有许多作用，减轻每个气缸燃烧引起的发动机振动，并提供一个光滑加工的"摩擦"表面用以和离合器接触。但其主要功能是将发动机转矩从发动机传递到变速器。飞轮圆周压有齿圈，当起动发动机时可与起动机的驱动齿轮啮合。

压盘

压盘（图 3-4）是一个弹簧加载装置，可以使离合器从动盘和飞轮接合或分离。离合器从动盘安装在飞轮和压盘之间。大多数压盘使用膜片式弹簧，少数使用多个螺旋弹簧。

离合器从动盘

离合器从动盘（图 3-5）基本上是一块钢板，覆盖有摩擦材料，位于飞轮和压盘之间。盘中心是花键毂，其设计用于安装在变速器输入轴的花键上。当离合器接合时，离合器从动盘在飞轮和压盘之间被"挤压"，发动机的动力通过盘毂传送到变速器的输入轴上。

膜片弹簧

膜片弹簧（图 3-6）由弹簧钢制成。它是用铆接或用螺栓联接到离合器盖。在膜片弹簧的每一侧都有一个支撑坏，当膜片弹簧工作时，它起着一个支点的作用。

离合器分离机构

离合器分离机构允许驾驶员操作离合器。通常，它由离合器踏板总成、机械联动装置、拉索或液压回路、分离轴承和离合器拨叉组成。

手动拉索式：离合器拉索机构（图 3-7）使用柔性外壳内的钢缆将踏板运动传递到离合器拨叉。拉索通常固定在离合器踏板的上端，拉索的另一端连接到离合器拨叉。拉索壳安装在固定位置。这样，只要离合器踏板移动，拉索就能在壳内滑动。离合器拉索壳体的一端具有用于离合器调节的螺纹。

液压式：液压式离合器分离机构（图 3-8）使用一个简单的液压回路将离合器踏板动作传递给离合器拨叉。它有三个基本部分——主缸、液压管路和工作缸。离合器踏板的运动会在主缸中产生液压，从而启动工作缸。然后工作缸移动离合器拨叉。

主缸是开发液压压力的控制缸。工作缸是操作缸，由主缸的压力驱动。

分离轴承

分离轴承（图 3-9）也称为 throw-out bearing，是一种滚珠轴承。它位于离合器拨叉和压盘膜片之间。轴承仅在离合器分离时才起作用。它减少了压盘分离杠杆和分离叉之间的摩擦。分离轴承是带有润滑剂的密封单元组件。它在从手动变速器前部伸出的轮毂套上滑动，并通过液压或手动压力进行移动。

离合器拨叉

离合器拨叉（图3-10）也称为 clutch arm 或 release arm，将运动从分离机构传递到分离轴承和压盘。当离合器拨叉被分离机构移动时，它会撬开分离轴承以释放离合器。

离合器踏板

离合器踏板通过压下踏板而产生来自主缸的液压。该液压被施加到工作缸，离合器最终接合和分离。

2. 原理

分离

当驾驶员希望分离离合器时，他/她通过踩下离合器踏板来实现。通过一系列机械连杆机构或液压系统，此动作可使离合器拨叉相对于分离轴承移动。该轴承允许轴向力从离合器拨叉传递到膜片弹簧。此动作导致膜片弹簧将压盘从摩擦盘上拉开。此时，转矩不能传递到传动轴，离合器分离。

接合

当驾驶员松开离合器踏板时，压盘内的弹簧压力向前推动离合器从动盘。该动作将飞轮、离合器从动盘和压盘锁定在一起。发动机再次转动变速器输入轴。原理如图3-11所示。

车辆离合器有许多不同的类型和设计，但作用相同。这有助于将汽车发动机产生的旋转运动转换为车轮的旋转运动。大多数设计都是基于一个或两个摩擦片紧紧地压在一起或靠着飞轮的结构。离合器可以使用离合器踏板接合和分离，离合器踏板始终位于制动踏板的左侧。

3.1.2 手动变速器

手动变速器（图3-12）有两个作用。变速器的一个作用是为驾驶员提供操纵车辆前后行驶的选择。这是所有汽车的基本要求。几乎所有车辆都有多个前进传动比，但大多数情况下，只有一个传动比用于倒车。另一个作用是为驾驶员提供发动机和车轮之间的传动比选择，以便车辆能够在各种运行条件和负载下以最佳效率运行。

1. 结构

变速器壳体

变速器壳体为轴承和轴提供支撑，并为润滑油提供外壳。手动变速器壳体由铁或铝铸造而成。因为铝重量较轻，所以是首选。为维修而设置了放油塞和加注塞。放油塞位于壳体的底部。

变速器轴

手动变速器通常在变速器内安装三个钢轴，分别是输入轴、中间轴和主轴（输出轴）。

输入轴：输入轴也称为离合器轴，将离合器从动盘的旋转传递到中间轴齿轮。轴的外端是花键。内端有一个与中间轴啮合的机加工齿轮。变速器壳体中的轴承支撑壳体中的输入轴。当离合器从动盘转动时，输入轴齿轮和中间轴齿轮转动。

中间轴：中间轴也称为集束齿轮轴，为中间轴齿轮与变速器内的输入轴齿轮和其他齿轮啮合提供支撑。它位于离合器轴一侧的稍下方。

输出轴：输出轴固定输出齿轮和同步器。轴的后部延伸至壳体后部，在那里它连接到驱动轴以转动车辆的车轮。轴上的齿轮可以自由旋转，但同步器锁定在轴上。同步器只有在轴转动时才会转动。

同步器

同步器（图 3-13）是一个通过拨叉在主轴上来回滑动的套筒。一般来说，它的每侧都有一个青铜锥体与齿轮上的锥形配合锥啮合。同步器有两个功能。

- 将输出轴齿轮锁定到输出轴上。
- 在换挡期间防止齿轮碰撞或磨削。

当同步器沿着主轴移动时，锥体起到离合器的作用。在接触到要接合的挡位时，输出轴加速或减速直到输出轴和挡位的速度同步。当同步器滑到一个挡位时，齿轮锁定在同步器和输出轴上。接下来，动力就从变速器传送到车轮上。

换挡拨叉

换挡拨叉安装在同步器套筒周围，以将运动从换挡连杆传递到套筒上。换挡拨叉位于同步器套筒的槽中。连杆或换挡滑轨将换挡拨叉连接到驾驶员的换挡杆上。

2. 动力流

现在已经了解了手动变速器的基本部件和结构，我们将通过四挡手动变速器来介绍动力流的情况。动力流如图 3-14 所示。

3.1.3 自动变速器

与手动变速器一样，自动变速器的主要工作是允许发动机在其狭窄的速度范围内运行，同时提供较宽的输出速度范围。自动变速器和手动变速器作用完全相同，但是工作方式完全不同。自动变速器和手动变速器有两大区别。

- 自动变速器车中没有离合器踏板。
- 一旦将变速器推至前进挡，其他一切都是自动完成的。

手动变速器与自动变速器的主要区别在于，手动变速器可锁定和解锁输出轴上的不同齿轮组以达到各种齿轮比，而在自动变速器中，同一组齿轮可产生所有不同的齿轮比。行星齿轮组是使自动变速器成为可能的装置。

1. 结构

组成自动变速器的主要部件包括：

行星齿轮组

基本的行星齿轮组齿轮（图 3-15）由三个主要部分组成：一个位于中心位置的太阳

轮、安装有多个行星齿轮的行星架和一个带内齿的环形齿轮，所有这些齿轮都保持恒定的啮合关系。当行星齿轮围绕太阳轮旋转时，行星齿轮和行星架是一个单一的单元。齿轮组的任何部件都可以固定，也可以旋转。要传递转矩，必须固定其中一个元件。如果所有的部件都允许转动，则没有转矩可以传递，齿轮组处在空挡位置。

液力变矩器

在自动变速器上，液力变矩器取代了配用标准变速装置车上的离合器。液力变矩器安装在发动机和变速器之间。当车辆停驶时，仍然能够维持发动机继续运转。如图 3-16 所示，液力变矩器的原理就好比是将风扇插入墙壁电源通电，向另外一个没有通电的风扇吹风。如果抓住未通电风扇上的叶片，它将停转，一旦松手，风扇就会开始加速，直到接近那台通电的风扇的速度。与之不同的是，液力变矩器不是使用空气，更准确地说，而是使用油或传动液。

液力变矩器（图 3-17）由三个内部元件组成，它们一起工作以将动力传递给变速器。这三个元件分别是泵轮、涡轮和导轮。泵轮直接安装在变矩器壳体上，而变矩器壳体又直接用螺栓固定在发动机的曲轴上，并以发动机转速转动。涡轮在壳体内并直接连接到变速器的输入轴，以提供动力驱动汽车。导轮安装在一个单向离合器上，因此它可以在一个方向上自由旋转，但不能在另一个方向上旋转。三个元件均安装叶片，以精确引导油流经变矩器。

2. 原理

随着发动机运转，传动液进入泵内并被离心力甩向外侧，到达涡轮，使其开始转动。传动液以循环运动的方式继续冲向涡轮的中心，进入导轮。如果涡轮的运动速度比泵轮慢得多，那么传动液将与导轮叶片的前部接触，将导轮推入单向离合器并防止其转动。导轮停止时，传动液由导轮叶片引导以"帮助"的角度重新进入泵轮，增加转矩。当涡轮和泵轮速度同步时，传动液开始撞击背面的导轮叶片，导致导轮与泵轮和涡轮相同的方向转动。随着速度的增加，三个元件开始以相同的速度转动。

3.1.4 无级变速器

与传统的自动变速器不同，无级变速器没有带有一套齿轮的变速器，这意味着它们没有联锁的齿轮。最常见类型的无级变速器可以在设计精巧的带轮系统上操作，该带轮系统可以在最高挡位和最低挡位之间提供无限的可变性，而没有不连续的步骤或换挡。

带式无级变速器

大多数无级变速器只有三个基本组件：大扭矩的金属带或橡胶带、可变半径的输入主动轮和输出从动轮。

无级变速器还有各种微处理器和传感器，但上述三个组件是使技术得以运用的关键要素。

可变直径带轮（图 3-18）是无级变速器的核心。每个带轮由两个彼此相对锥面组成。传动带在两个锥面之间的凹槽中传动。之所以选用 V 形传动带，是由于横截面部分成 V 形，增加传动带接触面的摩擦力。

钢带

新材料的引入使无级变速器更加可靠和高效。其中，最重要的进步之一是与带轮相连接的金属带的设计和发展。这些柔韧的传动带由几片薄钢带组成，这些薄钢带将高强度的蝴蝶结形金属片连接在一起。钢带如图3-19所示。

金属带不易滑动，并且高度耐用，使无级变速器可以传递更大的发动机转矩。运行时，比橡胶带式的无级变速器噪声小。

工作过程

当一个带轮半径增大时，另一个半径减小以保持传动带紧固。随着两个带轮改变它们相互的半径，会实现无数个传动比——从低到高的所有值连续不断。例如，当主动带轮上的节圆半径较小而从动带轮上的节圆半径较大时，从动带轮的转速降低，实现低速挡。当主动带轮上节圆半径较大而从动带轮上的节圆半径较小时，则从动带轮的转速增加，实现高速挡。因此，理论上，无级变速器有无数个挡位，它可以随时在任何发动机或车速下运行。无级变速器可以使用液压、离心力或弹簧张力来产生调节带轮所需的力。工作过程如图3-20所示。

可变直径带轮必须是成对出现。其中一个被称为主动带轮的带轮连接到发动机的曲轴上。主动带轮也称为输入带轮，因为它是发动机的能量进入变速器的地方。第二个带轮称为从动带轮，因为主动带轮使它转动。从动带轮作为输出带轮，将能量传递给传动轴。

无级变速器的简单性和无级性使其成为各种机器和设备的理想传动装置，而不仅仅在汽车上应用。无级变速器已经在电动工具和钻床上使用了多年。它也被用于各种车辆，包括拖拉机和雪地摩托车。无级变速器在所有这些应用中，都依赖于易滑动、易拉伸的高密度橡胶带，所以会降低传动效率。

3.1.5　万向传动装置

在传统的纵向安装的发动机前置后轮驱动车辆中，传动轴用于将来自发动机的转矩通过变速器输出轴传递至差速器，差速器继而将转矩传递至车轮。传动系统如图3-21所示。

传动轴

传动轴（图3-22）可以用钢或铝制成，可以是实心的，也可以是空心的。传动轴可随路面条件升降，并用花键吸收长度变化。

大多数车辆使用单个一体式传动轴。但许多卡车都使用一个分体式传动轴。这将减少每个轴的长度以避免行驶振动。由于传动轴在高速时以全发动机转速旋转，所以它必须是笔直的，并且是完全平衡的。如果不平衡，传动轴会剧烈振动。为了防止这种振动，传动轴上焊有平衡块。小块金属配重焊接在轻的一侧以抵消重的一侧的重量达到顺利运行的目的。

万向节

万向节（图3-23）也称为万向接头。万向节的作用是吸收由差速器相对于变速器的相对位置变化所引起的角度变化，以这种方式平稳地将动力从变速器传递到差速器。胡克（十字轴）式万向节因其结构简单和功能准确而被普遍使用。一个简单的万向节由一个十字轴和两个万向节叉三个基本部件组成。

中间支承轴承

中间支承轴承（图 3-24）用螺栓安装在车架横梁或车身底架上。它支撑两段轴汇合处的传动轴的中心位置。密封的滚珠轴承可以使传动轴自由旋转。滚珠轴承的外部由一个厚橡胶支撑。橡胶底座可防止震动和噪音传入驾驶室。

3.1.6 驱动桥总成

驱动桥总成（图 3-25）由驱动桥壳及其内部的主减速器、差速器和半轴组成。驱动桥总成的作用是降低来自万向节的速度并且增加转矩，然后将动力分配给驱动轮。

1. 主减速器

主减速器是动力传动系统的一部分，位于传动轴和差速器之间。其功能是将传动轴传递的动力的方向改变 90 度，再传给传动轴。同时，它提供了一个固定的减速的值，该值介于在传动轴的速度和驱动轮轴速度之间。主减速器减速比或传动比取决于环形齿轮齿数和小齿轮齿数。客车的传动比在 3∶1 到 5∶1 之间，货车是在 5∶1 到 11∶1 之间。

主减速器的主要部件包括连接到传动轴的小齿轮，以及用螺栓联接或铆接在差速器壳体上的锥齿轮或环形齿轮。

小齿轮

传动轴旋转时，小齿轮（图 3-26）转动环形齿轮。小齿轮的外端用花键连接到万向节叉上。小齿轮的内端与环形齿轮的齿啮合。

环形齿轮

小齿轮驱动环形齿轮（图 3-27）。环形齿轮可靠地固定在差速器壳体上，齿数比小齿轮更多。环形齿轮通过 90 度的角度变化来传递旋转动力。

2. 差速器

传动系中的另一个重要部件是差速器（图 3-28），它由主减速器驱动。差速器位于两根半轴之间，允许两轴以不同的速度转动。当车辆转弯或在不平坦的路面上行驶时，半轴速度的变化是必要的。同时，差速器将发动机转矩传输至驱动桥。

差速器总成利用传动轴的旋转将动力传递至半轴。差速器这个术语可以通过两个单词"different"和"axle"来记忆。差速器必须能够为两根半轴提供转矩，即使它们以不同的速度转弯。差速器总成由差速器壳体和差速器齿轮构成。

差速器壳体

差速器壳体内装有环形齿轮，行星齿轮和半轴的内端。

差速器齿轮

差速器齿轮是一组小的锥齿轮，包括两个半轴齿轮（差速器侧齿轮）和两个小齿轮（差速器空转齿轮）。差速器齿轮安装在差速器壳内。小齿轮轴穿过两个半轴齿轮和壳体。两个半轴齿轮与车轴的内端啮合。

限滑差速器

当两个车轮具有相同的牵引力时，传统差速器向每个后轮提供相同量的转矩。当一个车轮比另一个车轮牵引力小时，例如，当一个车轮在冰上滑动时，另一个车轮不能传递转矩。所有转向的结果都体现在滑动车轮上。为了提供良好的均匀牵引力，即使只有一个车轮滑动，许多车辆使用限滑差速器。它与标准差速器非常相似，但有一些防止车轮旋转和牵引力丧失的手段。标准差速器以最小的牵引力向车轮提供最大转矩。限滑差速器以最大牵引力向车轮提供最大转矩。

3.2 行驶系统

3.2.1 车架

车架是底盘的主要部分，底盘的其他部分安装在车架上。车架必须具有足够的强度和刚度，以承受车辆在道路上行驶时受到的冲击、扭转、应力和振动。它也被称为底盘大梁架。车架支撑在车轮和轮胎组件上。车架前部较窄，可为前轮提供较短的转弯半径。车架后侧加宽以提供更大的乘坐空间。

1. 车架类型

多年来一直有一些不同的框架设计。两种基本的框架结构是非承载式车身和承载式车身。

非承载式车身

非承载式车身由薄板和隔离框架通过在其间插入橡胶软垫制成。车辆结构的独立框架和车身类型是生产大部分全尺寸货车时最常用的技术。在此类型结构中，车架和车身是分开制造的，而且每一个都是一个完整的单元。车架的设计是为了支撑车身的重量和吸收所有的负荷。车身仅仅容纳并且在某些情况下保护货物。

车身通常用螺栓固定在车架上的几个点上，以允许车架弯曲并将载荷分配到预期的载重构件上。这种类型的车架由侧构件、横构件和角撑板组成。典型的车架设计如图3-29所示。

侧构件或导轨是车架中最重的部分。侧构件的形状适应车身并支撑重量。它们在车辆的前部变窄，以便为车轮提供更短的转弯半径，然后在车身固定到车架的主体部分下方加宽。横构件被固定到侧构件以防止车架的扭曲。横梁的数量、尺寸和布置取决于车架的设计类型。通常，前横梁支撑散热器和发动机前部；后横梁支撑乘用车上的油箱和后行李箱。非承载式车身如图3-30所示。

承载式车身

词语"unibody"（图3-31）或"unit body"是"unitized body"的缩写。在这种结构类型中，没有车架。这个单体和框架单元由许多不同的冲压金属薄板焊接在一起组成。底部由地板、通道和箱体部分焊接成一个单元。这种设计通常比具有单独的主体和框架的车辆更轻且更坚固。该组件取代了车架。与传统的独立框架和车身结构相比减少了整体重量。传统的非承载式车身框架结构已经转向了现在大多数汽车上使用的较轻的车身结构。

2. 副车架

降低噪声、振动和声振粗糙度（NVH）是现代汽车的一个非常重要的问题。传统的悬架直接安装在底盘上（尽管通过橡胶衬套），因此 NVH 可以轻松传输到客舱。其中一种常用的解决方案是将悬架安装到一个由铝合金制成的副车架上（图 3-32）（仍然通过衬套），以减轻重量。副车架本身可以吸收一些 NVH。它又通过更多的套管安装到车身上，从而进一步降低 NVH。

3.2.2 悬架

用于将车轮连接到底盘的导向机构、弹簧、减振器被称为悬架系统。它通常有两个作用，分别是控制车辆的操纵和制动安全，并保持乘客的舒适性，避免颠簸、振动等。这也有助于保持正确的车辆高度。汽车的前后悬架设计可能不同。典型的后轮驱动汽车上的悬架系统如图 3-33 所示。

1. 结构

弹簧

弹簧是一种机械装置，通常用于储存能量并随后释放，用以吸收冲击或保持接触面之间的力。当今的弹簧系统是基于四种基本设计之一。

钢板弹簧：钢板弹簧（图 3-34）是最古老和最简单的悬架中的弹簧。几个长而薄的钢片通过夹子捆在一起。钢板弹簧通过 U 型螺栓夹住钢板固定在车轴上。弹簧一端通过弹簧销与车架相连，另一端采用铰链连接。结合钢板弹簧本身的弯曲，保障了悬架的运动，为行驶作缓冲。钢板弹簧如今仍在大多数卡车和重型车辆上使用。

螺旋弹簧：螺旋弹簧（图 3-35）也被称为 helical spring。它由弹簧材料盘绕成螺旋形制成。螺旋弹簧压缩、膨胀以吸收车轮的运动。

扭杆弹簧：扭杆弹簧（图 3-36）利用钢杆的扭曲特性来提供螺旋弹簧般的性能。扭杆弹簧的作用是扭转而不是压缩。由于预压处理，他们具有定向的性质。以下是其工作方式：扭杆弹簧的一端固定在车架上，另一端与悬架控制臂相连，控制臂的作用类似于垂直于扭杆移动的杠杆。当车轮碰撞时，垂直运动转移到控制臂，然后通过杠杆作用传递到扭杆，扭杆沿其轴线扭转以提供弹簧力。

空气弹簧：空气弹簧（图 3-37）由安装在车轮和车架之间的圆柱形空气室组成，利用气体的可压缩性来吸收车轮的振动能量。空气弹簧这个概念实际上已经有一百多年的历史，在马车上早有应用，那时的空气弹簧是由充气的皮革隔膜制成的，非常像风箱。20 世纪 30 年代它们被模压橡胶空气弹簧取代。

减振器

减振器（图 3-38）（也称为"shocks"）是悬架部件，用来减缓车辆弹簧的上下弹跳运动，并通过一种称为减振的过程来抑制弹簧跳跃。如果没有减振器，弹簧将继续以固有频率跳动，直至将它们从路面所吸收能量释放完为止。毋庸置疑，这将会产生一种极为颠簸的乘坐感，由于地形路况不同，车辆还可能会很难控制。

从本质上讲，减振器通过将悬架行程的动能转化为热能来控制不需要的弹簧运动，该热能使用液压流体引导。与其压缩周期（变短）相比，大多数标准减振器在其延伸周期内会产生更大的阻力（变长）。减振器在每个车轮附近的车架和悬架构件之间用螺栓联接。安装点通常被描述为"吊耳"（螺栓穿过的圆形套管）。减振器内部是一根连接到活塞上的金属杆，活塞可在充满液压油的缸体内上下移动。大多数现代的减震器还含有氮气，以减少由于热积聚而产生的充气和起气泡时减振器性能的退化。

控制臂

控制臂（图 3-39）是汽车上最枯燥但最给人带来机械感的部件之一。用最简单的话来说，控制臂在保证转向节、转轴和车桥牢牢固定在车上的同时，保障悬臂的上下运动。近一个世纪以来，控制臂一直是悬架系统的组成部分，虽然形状、尺寸和材料多样，但功能都是相同的：把一切连接在一起。

现在，你在讨论控制臂时，不得不谈论球形接头和橡胶控制臂衬套，因为它们连接在一起共同发挥作用。绝大多数控制臂上都安装有一个橡胶衬套或球形接头，作用是允许控制臂上下旋转不受束缚。

老式控制臂通常由冲压钢制成，因为便宜、快速、简单。多年来，许多控制臂已经从简单的冲压钢结构发展为精密铝铸件，比以前更坚固更轻。

2. 悬架系统的分类

悬架可以通过位置（前方或后方）或类型（非独立或独立）来分类。轿车上已不再使用非独立车桥前悬架悬架，因此，在了解非独立车桥前悬架仅在车辆后部使用后，我们按照类型对悬架进行分类。有三种主要类型的悬架，它们是非独立悬架、独立悬架和半独立悬架系统。

（1）独立悬架系统

该系统意味着悬架装置的设置方式允许车辆左右侧车轮在不平坦路面行驶时垂直上下移动。作用在单个车轮上的力不会影响另一车轮，因为同一辆车的两个轮毂之间没有机械连接。在大多数车辆中，它被用于前轮。独立悬架如图 3-40 所示。

这种类型的悬架通常由于较少的簧下重量而提供更好的乘坐质量和操纵性。独立悬架的主要优点是它们需要较少的空间，更容易转向，重量更轻等。独立悬架的例子有：

麦弗逊式悬架

麦弗逊式悬架（图 3-41，图 3-42）是由福特公司的 Earl S. McPherson 于 20 世纪 40 年代发明。它在 1950 年的英国福特车上被推出，由于结构紧凑、成本低廉，已成为世界上主导的悬架系统之一。

麦弗逊式悬架将减振器和螺旋弹簧组合在一起，提供了可用于前轮驱动车辆的更紧凑和更轻的悬架系统。与其他悬架设计不同，在麦弗逊式悬架中，减振器也可用作控制车轮位置的连接，因此节省了控制臂。此外，由于支柱垂直放置，整个悬架非常紧凑。对于前轮驱动的汽车来说，它们的发动机和变速器都位于前部车厢内，它们需要占用车辆宽度很小的前部悬架。毫无疑问，麦弗逊式悬架是最合适的。

双叉臂式独立悬架

双叉臂（或"A臂"）式悬架（图3-43，图3-44）是最理想的悬架。它可以被应用在前轮和后轮上。请注意，控制臂的长度不等，上臂比下臂短。这种设计被称为短臂/长臂或平行臂设计。虽然有几种不同可能的配置，但这种设计通常使用两个叉形臂来定位车轮。每个叉臂有两个安装到车架上的位置，其中一个安装位置在车轮上，承载一个减振器和一个螺旋弹簧以吸收振动。双叉臂式独立悬架可以更好地控制车轮的外倾角。它比麦弗逊式和扭杆式更昂贵，因为它涉及更多的部件和更多的车身悬挂点。由于这些原因，很少有小型车采用它。

多连杆式独立悬架

由于它没有严格的定义，我们很难描述它的结构。理论上，任何具有三个或更多控制臂的独立悬架都是多连杆的。不同的设计具有不同的几何排列和特征。多连杆式独立悬架（图3-45）源自双叉臂，是一种通常用于独立悬架的车辆悬架设计，使用三个或更多横向臂和一个或多个纵向臂。这些横臂和纵臂长度不一定相等。

通常每个臂在每端都有一个球形接头或橡胶衬套。因此，他们沿着它们自己的长度，在拉伸和压缩中反应载荷。一些多连杆使用摆臂或叉骨。似乎多连杆在操作和空间效率之间能提供更好的折中方案。

（2）非独立悬架系统

同一轴的两侧车轮之间有一个刚性连接。作用在一个车轮上的力将影响相对的车轮。由道路不平引起的车轮的运动也影响相对的车轮。非独立悬架如图3-46所示。

坚固的车轴连同车轮安装在车梁两端。当需要高承载能力时，通常使用这种系统，因为它们非常坚固。非独立悬架系统的例子如下：

霍奇基斯悬架

称为霍奇基斯悬架的实心轴或横梁（图3-47，图3-48）是一种非独立型悬架。它主要应用于后轮，由两个板簧支撑。一个车轮的垂直运动会影响另一个车轮。霍奇基斯悬架制造简单且造价低。它们非常坚硬，在颠簸路面不会改变轮距和前束，这有助于减少轮胎的磨损。主要缺点是簧下质量大，舒适性差。

（3）半独立悬架

在半独立悬架中，车轮能够像独立悬架那样相对于彼此移动，但是当一个车轮跳动时，另外一个车轮也受到影响。这种效应是通过在负载下扭转或偏转悬挂部件来实现的。最常见的半独立悬架类型是扭力梁式半独立悬架。

扭力梁式半独立悬架

大多数现代微型汽车至中型车（例如大众高尔夫）采用扭力梁作为后悬架。为什么？与双叉臂和多连杆独立悬架相比，它宽度小，从而使后座空间更大。它主要用于汽车的后轮。由于其成本低和非常耐用，因此非常有利。它设计简单，重量轻。实际上，扭力梁式悬架（图3-49）只是半独立的，扭力梁将两个车轮连接在一起，这样在受力时允许有限的自由度。对于一些要求不高的小型车来说，这可以节省防侧倾杆。相反，它不能提供与双叉臂或多连杆悬架相同的行驶和操控水平。

3. 横向稳定杆

横向稳定杆（图3-50），也称为防侧倾稳定杆或平衡杆，必须用于独立前悬架。它减少了转弯时车辆的横向侧倾。通常情况下，它只是一根合金钢棒，每端连接到独立悬挂系统的下臂。它被支撑固定于车架的衬套内，与横梁平行。当两个车轮上下运动相同量时，横向稳定杆在衬套内自由转动，不起作用。

3.2.3 车轮和轮胎

1. 车轮

车轮必须具有足够的强度来承载车重，承受广泛的车速变化，适应不同的道路条件。车轮结构如图3-51所示。

深槽轮辋

深槽轮辋（图3-52）是一体的，由于其安装和拆卸轮胎更容易，所以通常用于乘用车。

2. 轮胎

轮胎安装在车轮的轮辋上。轮辋和轮胎之间是内胎。内胎内充满一定压力的空气。内胎内的空气压力使轮胎保持充气状态。轮胎承载车辆载荷并起到缓冲的作用。它吸收由于车辆在不平路面上行驶而产生的一些振动。它也抵消车辆在行驶或转弯时过度转向的倾向。汽车行驶时，轮胎必须产生最小的噪声，在任何情况下都应该提供良好的抓地能力。

（1）轮胎类型

车辆使用两种类型的轮胎。

斜交轮胎

斜交轮胎（图3-53）是一种老式结构的轮胎。其帘线的位置使胎体容易弯曲。这种设计优化了缓冲作用，使得汽车在崎岖不平的道路上平稳行驶。此种轮胎具有从一侧胎圈到另一侧胎圈以一定角度排列的帘布层。帘线角度也从一个帘布层翻转到另一帘布层，形成交叉图案。胎面直接粘合到顶层。斜交轮胎的一个主要缺点是帘布层和胎面薄弱性降低了高速行驶时的牵引力，增加了滚动阻力。

子午线轮胎

子午线轮胎（图3-54）胎侧柔软，胎面较硬。这种设计提供了非常稳定的接地面积（胎面接触路面的面积),从而提高了安全性,改善了转弯、制动和磨损情况。此种轮胎有从一侧胎圈到另一侧胎圈平行径向排列的帘线,带束层直接布置在胎面下方。带束层可以由钢、玻璃纤维或其他材料制成。此种轮胎的一个主要缺点是它在低速时会左右晃动。在粗糙的路面上行驶时坚硬的胎面不会产生弯曲。

(2) 轮胎结构

轮胎结构如图 3-55 所示。

胎体:胎体,也被称为"carcass"或"casing",是轮胎的核心。胎体是轮胎的框架,是指由轮胎帘线构成的所有层。它吸收轮胎的内部气压、重量和振动。

胎面:它由许多天然橡胶和合成橡胶以及其他成分制成。胎面由厚的橡胶层组成,与路面直接接触。

胎肩:位于胎面和胎侧之间,是轮胎中最厚的部分。因此胎肩的设计能够快速方便地驱散开车时积聚在轮胎内部的热量。

胎侧:位于胎肩和胎圈之间,保护内侧的胎体,并且由于其在驾驶期间的灵活性而提供舒适的乘坐体验。此外,轮胎的类型、尺寸、结构、胎面花纹、制造商、品牌名称和其他详细信息都标注于其上。

胎圈:胎圈缠绕在帘线末端并将轮胎固定到轮辋上。它是将轮胎夹紧在轮辋上的高强度带橡胶涂层的钢丝圈。一般情况下,轮辋稍微收紧,因此在行驶时气压突然降低的情况下,轮胎不会从轮辋上松开。

缓冲层(带束层):带束层是放置在轮胎胎面和胎体之间以保护胎体的帘线层。它吸收外部冲击并防止胎面直接与胎体接触,造成伤害。它是位于胎面和胎体之间的径向轮胎周围的强化增强层。

橡胶密封层:橡胶密封层替代轮胎内部的内胎,由低透气性的橡胶层构成。橡胶层通常由丁基橡胶和合成橡胶组成。其主要功能是将高压空气保持在内。

轮胎规格

我们必须知道一些重要的轮胎规格(图 3-56)。这些将在下图进行说明和描述。

胎侧标识

胎侧标识(图 3-57)包含我们需要知道的一些信息。

扁平率

我们应当了解轮胎的另一个结构,尽管严格来说,它只是一个计算出来的比率,而不是真实存在的结构。它被称为轮胎的扁平率(图 3-58)。扁平率是指在正确尺寸的轮辋上安装并充气时轮胎高度与宽度的比率关系。

为什么我们关心轮胎的扁平率?因为高度与宽度的关系决定了轮辋上轮胎的形状,更重要的是决定了轮胎的性能特征。若胎壁高度稍微降低,则胎壁刚度将大大增加。高扁平率的轮胎在负载状态下挠度更大,接触地面时更为柔和。低扁平率的轮胎提供更大的抓地面积、更好的回弹性能、更小的滑动角度、更低的弯曲率和更小的挠度。

3. 车轮定位

除了允许车辆转向之外，还必须设置转向系统，允许车辆在没有驾驶员的转向输入的情况下直线前进。因此，车轮定位是车辆的重要设计因素。车轮定位包括调整车轮的角度，使它们垂直于地面并相互平行。这些调整的目的是为了最大限度地延长轮胎寿命。设计人员设定了四个参数，并且必须定期检查这些参数，以确保它们符合原车规格。这里讨论的四个参数如下。

前轮前束

前束的定义（图3-59）是从上往下看时轮胎方向和车辆方向产生的角度。如果轮胎的前方向内，则称为前束；如果向外，称为后束。过多的后束通常会导致轮胎内胎表面的快速磨损。相反，太多的前束会使胎面外表面快速磨损。两种情况都会导致更差的乘坐舒适性和更低的燃油效率。

前轮外倾

外倾角的定义（图3-60）是从车前面或后面观察的转向轴线和地面垂线产生的角度，以度为单位测量。如果车轮的顶端向外倾斜，形成正的外倾角；如果车轮的顶端向内倾斜，形成负的外倾角。如果轮胎完全垂直于地面，则称为零外倾角。如果外倾没有调校好，则会导致轮胎胎面出现单边磨损。

随着悬架和车辆技术的发展，当今大多数车辆都具有负外倾角，这增加了外胎的接触面积并提供了稳定的转弯性能。在许多前轮驱动车辆上，外倾角不可调整。如果这些车辆出现外倾角，则表示有部件发生磨损或弯曲，这有可能是由事故造成的，必须进行维修或更换。

主销内倾角

主销内倾角（图3-61）是指从车辆前方看到的主销轴向车身内侧倾斜的度数。当车轮以主销为中心回转时，此角度会使车辆前部略微抬起。此动作利用车的自重使转向车轮回位。

主销后倾角

主销后倾角（图3-62）是指从侧面看转向主销与地面垂线产生的角度。如果转向轴向后倾斜，称为正的主销后倾角；如果向前倾斜，称为负的主销后倾角。通常情况下，正的主销后倾角会使车辆在高速下更加稳定。

校正不正确通常会导致轮胎磨损更快。因此，无论何时安装新轮胎或悬架组件，或出现不寻常的轮胎磨损时，都应检查校准。在车辆经过重大危险道路或路缘后，还应该检查校正。

3.3 转向系统

转向系统（图3-63）允许驾驶员沿着道路行驶，并根据需要左转或右转。转向器总成中的齿轮不仅可以转动前轮，同时还可以作为减速齿轮，通过增加输出转矩来减少转向盘的转向力度。起初大部分转向系都是手动的，后来动力转向开始流行起来，并安装在当今制造的大多数车辆中。

3.3.1 机械转向系统

转向盘

转向盘是驾驶员和汽车之间的关键联系装置。操纵转向。

转向柱

转向柱包括将转向盘的旋转传递至转向器的转向主轴，以及将转向主轴固定于车身的柱管。转向盘通过螺母安装在转向主轴的顶端。转向柱包含一个冲击力吸收机构，该机构吸收在碰撞时对驾驶员施加的推力。转向主轴的底端通常通过柔性接头或万向节连接到转向器，以使从转向器到转向盘的路面冲击传递最小化。

转向器

转向器的作用是把来自转向盘的转向力矩和转向角进行适当的变换，再输出给转向拉杆机构，从而使汽车转向。

转向器有多种类型，最常见的有：齿轮齿条式和循环球式。

（1）**齿轮齿条式**（图 3-64）

齿轮齿条式转向器是一对将旋转运动转换为直线运动的齿轮。机械齿条齿轮式转向器基本上由转向器轴、小齿轮、齿条、推力弹簧、轴承、密封件和转向器壳组成。在齿轮齿条式转向系统中，转向器轴的端部包含与长齿条啮合的小齿轮。齿条通过转向横拉杆连接到转向节臂，这些拉杆是可调节的，以保持适当的前束角度。当转向盘转动时，转向轴末端的小齿轮转动。小齿轮将齿条从一侧移动到另一侧。这个动作推动或拉动转向横拉杆。这将车轮转向一侧或另一侧，这样车辆就可以转向。

（2）**循环球式**

循环球式转向器如图 3-65 所示。在循环球式转向器中，转向器的输入轴与蜗轮相连，但是在循环球组件中的蜗轮是直的。球状螺母有内螺旋槽，可以与蜗轮的螺纹配合。螺母另一侧有外齿，与扇形齿轮相啮合。

在球状螺母与蜗轮槽中有小钢球。小钢球使蜗轮与螺母相啮合并以很小的摩擦进行运动。当转向盘转动时，输入轴使蜗轮旋转。小钢球将来自蜗轮的转动力传递给螺母，使球状螺母相对于蜗轮上下运动。导管与螺母的内螺旋槽两端相连。这样小钢球就可以在一个连续的环形通道中循环。

当球状螺母在蜗轮上上下运动时，它会带动扇形齿轮转动，依次带动转向摇臂前后运动。这种运动被传递到转向摇臂和转向节上来转动车轮。

转向连杆

转向连杆是转向杆和转向臂的组合，作用是将转向器的运动传递到左右前轮。转向连杆必须准确地将转向盘的运动传递给前轮。

3.3.2 动力转向系统

为了提高驾驶舒适性，大多数现代汽车都使用宽幅、低压轮胎，这增加了轮胎与路面的接触面积，因此需要更大的转向力。增加转向器的传动比可以减少转向力。但是，这会在车辆转弯时导致转向盘产生更大的旋转运动，从而不能急转弯。因此，要保持转向速度快，同时转向的力度小，需要使用某种转向辅助装置。换言之，主要用于大型车辆的动力转向系统现在也用于小型客车。动力转向也允许机械转向随时可用，即使发动机未运转或动力辅助系统发生故障。

常见的动力转向有液压助力转向、电控液压助力转向和电动助力转向。

（1）液压助力转向

液压助力转向系统（图3-66）采用液压泵，该泵靠发动机驱动，可使少量流体受到压力。当转动转向盘时，这个压力帮助转向机构引导轮胎。这种动力转向系统通常包括液压泵、动力转向液、压力软管组件、控制阀和回油管路。

液压泵

液压泵（图3-67）由发动机曲轴带轮和传动带驱动，并在压力下将液压油输送到齿轮箱。泵的排量与发动机转速成正比，但是输送到齿轮箱的液压油量由流量控制阀调节，多余的液压油返回吸入侧。

储油罐

储油罐供应动力转向液压油。它直接安装在泵体上或单独安装。如果未安装在泵体上，则通过两根软管连接到泵体上。通常情况下，储油罐盖有一个液位计，用于检查液压油位。

流量控制阀

流量控制阀控制从液压泵到齿轮箱的液压油流量，无论泵的转速如何，都能保持恒定的流量。

转阀

动力转向系统只在驾驶员转动转向盘时（例如开始转弯时）才起作用。当驾驶员没有施加力量时（例如直线行驶时），系统不会起任何作用。能感应到施加在转向盘上的作用力的装置称为转阀（图3-68）。

转阀的核心部件是扭力杆。扭力杆是一根很细的金属杆，当有力作用在上面时它就会扭曲。扭力杆的顶端与转向盘相连，底端与小齿轮或蜗轮（使轮子转动）相连，因此作用在扭力杆上的扭矩等于驾驶员转动转向盘的转矩。驾驶员作用在转向盘上的转矩越大，扭力杆扭曲得越严重。

随着扭力杆的弯曲，它带动滑阀的内部部件旋转。由于滑阀的内部部分也同时连接到转向轴（也就相当于连接到转向盘），所以滑阀的内部和外部之间的转数取决于驾驶员施加到转向盘的转矩。当转向盘没有转动时，两条液压管都向转向器供给相同的液压。但是，如果滑阀转向一侧或另一侧,则端口打开以向相应的油路提供高压油。

由于传统液压动力转向系统消耗的燃料中有 70% 以上是不必要的,并且是可以避免的,所以节能是新车开发中最重要的问题之一,尤其是动力转向系统。因此,应用更先进的动力转向系统(如电动助力转向系统和电控液压助力转向)可以节省大量能源。商用车辆特别需要新型动力转向系统。

(2) 电控液压助力转向

电控液压助力转向系统(图 3-69)与其他液压助力转向系统一样,主要的区别在于,在传统液压系统中,液压系统将从发动机提取功率,从而降低总功率输出,轻微减少汽车的燃料里程。在电控液压助力转向系统中,液压系统的动力由电动机直接驱动而不是直接由发动机驱动。这意味着发动机负载不会随着蓄电池和电动机的功率而变化。

(3) 电动助力转向系统

电动助力转向系统(图 3-70)全部是电子式的。它旨在使用电动机为车辆驾驶员提供方向控制。电动助力转向系统不需要发动机动力。因此,装备有电动助力转向系统的车辆可能比具有传统液压动力转向装置的相同车辆高出 3% 的燃料经济性。还有一个好处,发动机的更多动力传输到车轮。电动助力转向系统正在取代液压转向系统,并将很快成为汽车制造商中的主流。

电动助力转向系统由四个主要部分组成。
- 电动助力转向系统控制模块,从电动助力转向系统组件收集数据并发送所需信息;
- 电动助力转向系统电动机,其速度和方向由电动助力转向系统控制单元控制;
- 减速机构,将动力辅助输入到转向齿条组件;
- 转矩传感器监控驾驶员的输入和电动助力转向系统的机械输出。

3.4 制动系统

制动系统(图 3-71)有两种类型:驻车制动器和行车制动器。驻车制动器也称为"紧急制动器",是用于"稳定"车辆的制动器。行车制动器是用于减慢车辆速度或停车的系统。

每次踩下制动踏板时,行车制动器都会启动,并将液压制动力分配至前轮和后轮。

驻车制动器通常采用拉线操作,并将力施加至后制动盘内的专用制动蹄或通过活塞到制动钳中。它通常位于前排座椅之间,可以通过单独的踏板或手柄操作。

3.4.1 液压制动系统

制动系统的液压操作是 60 多年来的通用设计。油压或液压制动系统的完整部件由主缸、钢线、橡胶软管、助力器和每个车轮上的制动装置组成。

1. 结构

真空助力器

真空助力器(图 3-72)位于制动踏板联动装置和主缸之间。制动助力器是一种利用发动机真空与大气之间的压力差来增强制动推力的装置。当驾驶员踩下制动踏板时，制动助力器增加了主缸内活塞的压力，驾驶员不必增加制动踏板压力。当车辆由柴油机驱动时，由于进气歧管不真空，需要使用辅助真空泵。该泵可以由发动机或电动机驱动。

主缸

主缸（图3-73）位于助力器前面。主缸是一种将制动踏板施加的操作力转换为液压的装置。目前，主缸内有两个活塞，在双管路液压制动系统中产生液压，然后将液压施加到盘式制动器卡钳或鼓式制动器的轮缸上。

制动液和储液罐

储液罐用来吸收由制动液温度变化引起的体积变化。制动液是一种特殊的油，具有特定的性能。制动液和储液罐如图3-74所示。由于液体没有明显的可压缩性，所以制动液需要在压力下传递制动压力。制动会产生大量热量，制动液必须具有高沸点、低凝点才能保持有效。液位传感器检测储液罐中的液位，若低于最低液位，则制动系统警告灯亮起。制动液不能暴露在空气中，否则会吸收水分，降低沸点。

制动管路和软管

为了安全，液压制动系统的刚性管线或管道使用钢管制成。橡胶软管只在需要灵活性的地方使用，例如前轮，它们可以上下移动，也可以转向。系统的其余部分使用非腐蚀性无缝钢管，在所有连接点都配有特殊配件。制动管路和软管（图3-75）内有高压制动液，流体就像一根实心杆，将制动力传递到轮缸和卡钳活塞。

鼓式制动器

早期的汽车制动系统在四个车轮上都采用了鼓式设计。由于这些组件被放置在与车轮一起旋转的圆形鼓中，因此被称为鼓式制动器（图3-76）。鼓式制动器释放时（图3-77），在制动蹄和制动鼓之间留下空隙。鼓式制动器在工作时（图3-78）将迫使制动蹄压在制动鼓上，使车轮减速。制动液用于将制动踏板的运动转移到制动蹄的运动中，而制动蹄本身由类似于离合器从动盘上使用的耐热摩擦材料制成。

这种基本设计在大多数情况下都能发挥制动作用，但它有一个主要缺陷。当制动鼓被强制制动加热时，其直径会因材料的膨胀而增大，并且必须进一步踩下制动器以获得有效的制动作用。踏板运动的这种增加被称为制动衰减，并且可能导致在极端情况下的制动失效。通常这种制动失效是鼓内热量过多的结果，因此大多数现代汽车都不再使用鼓式制动器。但是，由于其重量和成本优势，有些汽车上仍然使用。

（1）制动底板

底板上安装着各种部件。底板安装在车轴的固定位置上，它是固定不动的，上面装有轮缸、制动蹄和各种硬件。它很少出问题。

（2）制动轮缸

轮缸是一个内部有两个活塞的缸，两端各有一个活塞。每个活塞都有一个橡胶密封件和一个连接活塞和制动蹄的轴。当施加制动压力时，活塞被推出顶向制动蹄与制动鼓接触。如果轮缸出现泄漏迹象，则必须维修或更换。

(3) 回位弹簧

压力从轮缸释放后，回位弹簧将制动蹄片拉回到其静止位置。如果弹簧较弱并且不能完全将制动蹄拉回，则会导致衬片过早磨损，因为衬片会与制动鼓保持接触。

(4) 制动鼓

制动鼓由铁制成，内侧有机加工表面和制动蹄接触。

(5) 制动蹄

制动蹄和制动块一样，由带摩擦材料的钢制蹄组成，摩擦衬片可以铆接或粘接在制动蹄上，也像制动块一样，衬片最终会磨损并且必须更换。

(6) 间隙自动调整装置

间隙自动调整装置的部件应该干净并且能够自由移动，以确保制动器在衬片寿命期间保持其调整功能。如果间隙自动调整装置停止工作，你会注意到，必须进一步踩下制动踏板才会感觉到制动器起作用。盘式制动器是自我调节的，不需要其他辅助机构。

盘式制动器

尽管盘式制动器（图3-79）依靠相同的基本原理来减缓车辆的速度，但其设计远远优于鼓式制动器。盘式制动器不是将主要部件装在金属鼓内，而是使用纤薄的制动盘和小卡钳来阻止车轮运动。制动钳内部有两个制动衬块，分别装在制动盘两侧。当踩下刹车踏板时，制动衬块夹紧。制动液用于将制动踏板的运动转移到制动衬块的运动中。

鼓式制动器在强制动时可使制动鼓内积聚热量，与此不同的是，用于盘式制动器的制动盘完全暴露在外部空气中。这种设计的作用是持续冷却制动盘，大大减少了过热或失效的趋势。

(1) 制动盘

制动盘的设计（图3-80）略有不同。许多镂空的叶片将制动盘的两个接触面连接在一起。这种"通风"的设计有助于散热。一些摩托车和跑车制动器上设计有许多小孔，也是此目的。另外，这些孔也有助于制动衬块从制动盘表面擦拭水。其他设计包括"槽"——加工在制动盘中的浅槽，有助于从制动衬块中去除用过的制动材料。这种开槽制动盘通常不用于普通汽车，因为会很快磨损制动衬块。但是，这种制动盘去除摩擦材料效果好，对赛车有利，它使制动衬块保持柔软。

(2) 制动钳

制动钳（图3-81）是安装制动衬块和活塞的组件。活塞通常由铝或镀铬铁制成。

(3) 制动衬块

每个制动钳安装两个制动衬块（图3-82）。制动盘两侧各有一个制动衬块安装在制动钳上。制动衬块不是永久使用，每次制动衬块与制动盘接触时，都会磨损一点，逐渐地变得越来越薄。

制动衬块必须定期更换，并且大多数汽车都有制动衬块报警。一些车型有软金属薄片会在制动衬块过薄时引起制动器尖叫声，而其它车型报警片则嵌入制动衬块材料中，在制动衬块变薄时关闭电路并点亮警告灯。更昂贵的汽车可能会使用电子传感器。

2. 制动钳的类型

制动钳有两种类型：浮动式和固定式。

（1）浮动式制动钳

单活塞浮动卡钳（图 3-83）是最流行的，也是制造和维修成本最低的。浮动卡钳"浮动"或在其支撑的轨道中移动，以使其可以在制动盘的中心位置。在施加制动压力时，液压油会将活塞压在内侧制动衬块上，而内侧制动衬块则会推向制动盘。它还将卡钳向相反的方向推靠在外侧制动衬块上，将其压向制动盘的另一侧。

（2）固定式制动钳

整个卡钳是固定安装的，并在制动盘两侧有一个或多个活塞。活塞将两个制动衬块推到制动盘的两侧。固定卡钳（图 3-84）使用多个活塞，分成两个、四个或六个活塞。固定卡钳可以施加更多的挤压动力，并在制动过程中更均匀地施加该动力。无论何时驾驶员使用制动器，固定卡钳还可以通过制动踏板提供更好的感觉，这对于豪华车和高性能车来说更可取。

这两种盘式制动器作为有效制动系统的一部分都是有效的。很明显，力量不够强大的浮动式比固定式制动钳应用的多。

浮动或滑动卡钳对于大多数车辆来说已经足够了，因为它更轻更便宜。只有当车辆以极大的速度行驶时，或者是具有合理速度的重型车辆时才需要固定卡钳，此时更强大的制动优先于低成本和重量的优势。

3. 原理

液压制动系统如图 3-85 所示。当踩下制动踏板时，制动踏板上的压力移动主缸内的活塞，迫使制动液压力升高，通过制动管路和柔性软管进入卡钳和轮缸。施加在制动踏板上的力在每个活塞上产生一定比例的作用力。制动钳和轮缸包含活塞，活塞连接到盘式制动衬块或制动蹄片上。每个轮缸活塞将附着的摩擦材料推靠在制动盘的表面或制动鼓壁上，从而减慢车轮的旋转。当释放踏板压力时，制动衬块和制动蹄恢复到释放位置。

3.4.2 驻车制动器和防抱死制动系统

1. 驻车制动器

驻车制动器（图 3-86）不依赖于液压系统，而是依靠钢丝拉线或电动伺服系统工作。拉起手柄、踩下驻车制动踏板或启动电子驻车系统将牵引钢丝拉线，机械地接合制动器。在装有后鼓式制动器的汽车上，钢丝拉线连接到制动蹄上。在装有后盘式制动器的汽车上，驻车制动器可以是一组制动蹄片，仅用于驻车制动系统。

有时，驻车制动系统被称为"紧急制动系统"，因为在液压油损失或其他制动问题的情况下，可以用驻车制动系统来减速。

2. 防抱死制动系统

防抱死制动系统是汽车安全领域的最大进步之一。在应用防抱死制动系统之前，惊慌失措的司机经常猛踩刹车将刹车锁定，导致滑行。这就是为什么驾驶学校会教导学生快速踩下制动踏板的原因。防抱死制动系统使用车载计算机、液压泵和电磁阀以及传感器来防止制动器锁死。因此，当驾驶员踩下制动踏板，防抱死制动系统本质上自动控制制动器制动力的大小并且比驾驶员操作更快。

（1）结构

该系统主要由电子控制单元、液压执行器和每个车轮上的车轮速度传感器组成。

防抱死制动系统计算机

防抱死制动系统计算机使用来自轮速传感器的信号来控制液压执行器的操作。如果检测到车轮抱死倾向，电脑将命令适当的轮缸电磁阀位置，调节部分或全部液压回路中的制动液压力，以防止车轮抱死并提供最佳制动。

液压执行器

位于发动机舱内的液压执行器（图3-87）包含电磁阀和液压泵电动机。电磁阀有三个位置。

- 在位置1，电磁阀打开；来自主缸的压力直接通过制动器。
- 在位置2，电磁阀关闭，将制动器与主缸隔离。这可以防止压力进一步上升。
- 在位置3，电磁阀释放制动器的部分压力。

由于电磁阀能够释放制动器的压力，所以必须有某种方法来恢复压力。这就是液压泵电动机的功能。当一个电磁阀降低管路中的压力时，液压泵就会恢复压力。

在大多数情况下，防抱死制动系统通过保持轮胎—路面处于最大摩擦系数缩短制动距离。然而，它的主要好处是通过抑制任何车轮的锁定来保持车辆控制。

车轮速度传感器

防抱死制动系统需要某种方式来检测车轮的运动状态。位于每个车轮上的防抱死制动系统轮速传感器（图3-88）提供了这一信息。

（2）原理

标准的防抱死制动系统包括一个中央电子控制单元，四个车轮转速传感器和制动液压系内的液压阀。防抱死制动工作系统如图3-89所示。电子控制单元持续监控每个车轮的转速。如果它检测到一个车轮转动明显慢于其他车轮，表示即将发生车轮锁定的情况，它会起动电磁阀以减少受影响车轮上的制动液压，降低该车轮上的制动力，车轮转动加快。相反，如果电子控制单元检测到车轮转向明显快于其他车轮，则车轮的制动液压会增加，重新施加制动力，此车轮减速。这个过程不断重复，并且可以由驾驶员通过制动踏板跳动来检测。

第四章 电气电子系统

4.1 电源系统

4.1.1 铅酸蓄电池

大多数汽车使用铅酸蓄电池。铅酸蓄电池是一种电化学装置，它储存和提供电能，并且大部分可以反复充电。

蓄电池为起动机和点火系统供电以起动发动机。当电力需求超过充电系统的输出电量时，它们还提供必要的电流。

结构

铅酸蓄电池（图4-1）由各种部件组成，主要部件为极板、电解液、蓄电池壳体等。

蓄电池壳体由玻璃、硬质橡胶或塑料制成。通常它被分成由单个电池组成的一些单独的隔间。标称12V铅酸蓄电池的基本结构由六个串联的电池组成，每个电池为2伏。

活性材料被放置在栅格中以形成正极板和负极板。图4-2显示了一个电池中极板的排列。第一块和最后一块板是负极板。

正极板由过氧化铅和铸造的金属栅架组成。

负极板由海绵状铅和铸造的金属栅架组成。

在每块正极板和负极板之间放置木制或纸制隔板以防止短路，并且必须能够允许电解液自由循环。

电解液是一种由35%的硫酸和65%的蒸馏水混合而成，通过内部化学反应形成电流的溶液。混合时，把酸倒入蒸馏水中。

充电与放电（图4-3）

蓄电池充电：在充电过程中，化学反应被逆转。极板上的硫酸盐将以硫酸的形式回到电解液中，极板材质也恢复为过氧化铅和海绵状铅。

蓄电池放电：在放电过程中，正极板和负极板均变为硫酸铅，并且电解液失去了大部分溶解的硫酸，主要变成水。

充电方法

正常充电（慢速充电）——所选择的充电电流约为电池容量的1/10，充电时间超过8至12小时。

快速充电（快速充电）——在短时间内充电且充电电流非常大。即使在紧急情况下，安全限值也不应超过电池的容量值。

跨接起动汽车

当跨接起动汽车时，将跨接电缆正极连接到无电蓄电池正极，将电缆负极连接到无法起动车辆的发动机接地端。图 4-4 显示了用于跨接起动汽车的连接。

4.1.2 充电系统

在起动过程中，蓄电池供应车辆需要的全部电力。但是，一旦发动机运转，充电系统（图 4-5）负责产生足够的电量以满足电气系统中所有负载的需求，同时为蓄电池充电。

充电系统由交流发电机、调节器和互连线路组成。充电系统的主要部件是交流发电机，它产生直流电给蓄电池充电，并为车辆电气负载供电。

发电机的运行

交流发电机（图 4-6）由四个主要部分组成：定子、转子、二极管整流器和稳压器。

交流发电机使用电磁原理产生电流。典型的交流发电机电路如图 4-7 所示。转子基本上是一块磁铁或一组磁铁，在一个称为定子的铜线套内高速旋转。

转子是一个围绕定子旋转的旋转磁铁，铁芯包裹在铜线中。这些转子、定子相对彼此旋转并产生交流电，该交流电由二极管组整流为直流电，用于为蓄电池充电并为车辆的其他电气部件供电。电压调节器控制并保持交流发电机发出的电量。

当汽车蓄电池电量耗尽时，允许电流从交流发电机回流，循环往复。

主要部件

转子（图 4-8）组件由传动轴、线圈和两个极靴组成。转子轴头安装带轮，允许转子由曲轴带轮的传动带驱动，高速旋转。转子有两个电磁铁互锁部分，像手指形状，两端有南北极，均匀地分布在转子的外部。

定子（图 4-9）安装在交流发电机的主体上并保持静止。中心刚好有足够的空间来安装转子，并且能够在没有任何接触的情况下旋转。它包含三组导线，在交流发电机内部，以 120 度间隔开。导线有三角形连接和 Y 形（星形）连接（图 4-10）两种形式的连接。

二极管是电流的单向止回阀，只允许电流单向流动。来自交流发电机的所有电压都对准一个方向，通过使用安装在整流器组件中的 6 个二极管将交流电转换为直流电。

电压调节器调节交流发电机产生的充电电压，使其保持在 13.5 伏和 14.5 伏之间，以保护整个车辆的电气元件。

电压调节器可以安装在交流发电机外壳的内部或外部。现代大多数电压调节器都是内置组件。

充电系统的故障检测

充电系统的检查步骤如下：

- 手眼检查——传动带张力是否正常，所有的连接需清洁和紧密。
- 检查电池——必须充电 70%。
- 测量交流发电机的电源电压——电池电压。
- 最大输出电流——电流表读数在额定最大输出的 10% 左右。
- 调节电压（电流表读数小于等于 10 A）——14.2 V±0.2 V。
- 电路电压降——最大值是 0.5 V。

4.2 照明、信号和仪表装置

4.2.1 照明系统

1. 介绍

汽车的照明系统具有多种用途和功能：

首先，为驾驶员在黑暗中安全驾驶提供照明。

其次，汽车灯光提高了汽车的可视性。

第三，车灯作为警示信号，展示汽车的存在、位置、大小、速度和方向的实际信息。

照明系统包括各种照明和信号装置或部件，固定安装在车辆的前部、侧部、后部和内部，如图4-11所示。

根据车灯的位置和功能，它们可被分为外部灯、内部灯、信号灯和仪表板上的指示灯等。

用于汽车外部照明的光源类型包括白炽灯泡、钨卤素灯泡、氙气灯子系统、霓虹灯光源、发光二极管光源等。

2. 外部灯

前照灯

前照灯装于汽车头部，用于夜间行车道路的照明。通常要求前照灯灯光为白光。现代前照灯是电动操作的，成对安装在汽车头部的一侧或两侧，每个灯泡功率约为40~60瓦。

侧转向灯

应在汽车的前部安装两个小于7瓦的灯。它们被封闭在一个塑料外壳中，可被包含在前照灯组件中。

尾灯

尾灯也称为"tail lamp"或者是"rear position lamps"，仅产生红光。两个尾灯功率不得小于5瓦。可以与车辆的刹车灯组合，也可以与其分开。

倒车灯

倒车灯不得超过两盏，每个最高瓦数为24瓦。灯光为白色。当变速器挂在倒挡时，倒车灯打开以照亮汽车后方区域并警告其他车辆和行人。

牌照灯

法律要求必须安装牌照灯，但没有规定照明要求。后牌照必须清晰可见，且不许遮挡。

刹车灯（制动灯）

通常有两个灯组合在一起，每个灯的功率分别为15瓦和36瓦。红色稳定的制动灯比尾灯更亮，当司机刹车时，激活刹车灯。

驻车灯

驻车灯或前位置灯可发出白色或琥珀色的光。它是汽车前灯外侧的附加调光灯,可提高停放汽车的可见度。

雾灯

雾灯提供宽阔的条形光束,用于大雾、下雨或下雪天气行车时,在极低速度下提高能见度。前雾灯光色为黄色,后雾灯光色为白色。

3. 前照灯的光束和光学系统

光束

前照灯系统需要产生近光束和远光束,可以通过单个单功能灯或单个多功能灯来实现。图 4-12 显示了道路的近光和远光照明。

近光前照灯提供的光线分布满足前向和侧向照明,并限制光线射向其他道路使用者的眼睛,控制眩光。

远光前照灯提供明亮的、重点分布于中央的光线,不能控制其照向其他道路使用者。

前照灯光学系统

前照灯(图 4-13)由三个基本部件组成:反射镜、灯丝和特殊的配光镜,它们在气密单元中紧密融合。

前灯反射镜将灯泡发出的光线聚合成强光束。其内表面镀银、铬或镀铝,然后被抛光处理。

配光镜在一定程度上将反射镜反射出的光束和杂散光线重新分布,由此获得更好的整体道路照明,同时获得最少的眩光。

灯丝对前照灯很重要。卤素灯泡、气体放电灯和发光二极管广泛用于前照灯,但光线模式不同。

4. 内部灯

内部灯包括车辆内部使用的不同类型的强光照明装置,如钥匙灯、发动机舱灯、储物箱灯、行李箱灯、行李箱盖灯、驾驶室灯、仪表显示灯等。

汽车钥匙指示灯一般安装在门锁上方或锁孔侧面,是一种明亮的微型闪光信号灯。

仪表显示灯包括双转速表、高度计、风速、升降速度速度表、电流表、发动机组合仪表等小型机械装置灯。

4.2.2 信号系统

转向信号

转向信号灯正式的称呼是"方向指示灯",安装在汽车左右两侧的前后角,有时安装在汽车侧面或后视镜上,在汽车转向或并道时,由司机开启转向灯,并且一直闪烁。

汽车转向信号灯开启后,会反复闪烁,闪烁频率稳定保持在每分钟 60~120 次(1~2Hz)。图 4-14 显示了转向信号的国际标准符号。打转向时需要音频指示或视觉指示灯来通知驾驶员。指示灯位于车辆组合仪表上，转向操作时产生循环的"滴答声"。

倒车信号设备

汽车后方的盲点是一个大问题。出于安全原因，一些报警装置配备倒车灯、蜂鸣器和语音报警，由安装在变速器中的换向开关自动控制。

倒车灯（图4-15）用于警告相邻车辆驾驶员和行人，车辆正在倒车，并向后方提供照明。

倒车蜂鸣器是一个原本用于警示途经汽车的行人"该车正在倒车"的装置。现在这种装置倒车时自动发出蜂鸣声，即使在没有行人经过的情况下也如此。

语音报警器使听者能够立即找到声音的来源和方向。

喇叭

喇叭是大多数国家对汽车的合法要求。喇叭的目的是警告或提醒接近的行人或驾驶员。喇叭可以是单个的，也可以是成对的。

常用的汽车喇叭有三种：高音喇叭、气动多音喇叭（高低音喇叭）、气喇叭。

与气喇叭不同，电喇叭通过电动振铃机构使金属膜片振动，从而发出声音。

汽车喇叭通常是电动的，由一个扁平的圆形钢制膜片驱动，该膜片上有电磁铁，并连接到一个反复中断该电磁铁电流的接触器上。现代电喇叭如图4-16所示。

4.2.3 仪表装置

仪表板（图4-17）也称为"instrument panel"，是位于车辆驾驶员前方的控制面板，用于显示车辆操作的仪表和控制的装置。

现代汽车配备了各种传感器和复杂的车载电子设备，可监控车辆性能，并通过显示屏、声音和指示灯警告驾驶员注意车辆的特殊状况。

1. 仪表

仪表为驾驶员提供了系统状态的缩放指示，例如油箱已满。基本上有两种类型的显示仪表：模拟显示仪表和数字显示仪表。

燃油表

磁式燃油表由两个平衡线圈和一个电枢组成。线圈磁力之间的差值使得电枢带动指针在表盘内转动。

发送单元中的可变电阻控制通过加热线圈的电流。加热线圈加热双金属臂，使其弯曲并使仪表指针偏转。

水温表

水温表分磁力式和热敏式仪表，与前面讨论过的燃油表类似。

机油压力表

可变电阻型传感器单元通常是一个变阻器（它是一个带弧刷臂的绕线线圈）。膜片的运动改变了电阻，导致电路电压改变。

车速表

在过去,车速表由连接在变速器齿轮上的传动电缆驱动。但是,几乎所有的新型车辆都使用电子车速表。

2. 仪表板灯和报警装置

指示灯是用来告知驾驶员某个系统被启用了,例如后窗除雾器开始工作时灯亮了。报警灯通知驾驶员系统中的某些部件无法正常工作,或者存在必须纠正的情况。常见报警灯如图4-18 所示。

3. 报警电路

指示灯和报警装置通常通过关闭开关来激活。各种类型的音频发生器,包括蜂鸣器、钟声和语音合成器被用于提醒驾驶员车辆状况。图 4-19 显示了一个电路,该电路会警告"低油位"或"发电机不充电",如果在发动机不运转的情况下灯仍然亮着,也会发出声音。

4.3 安全舒适附件

4.3.1 电气附件

玻璃清洗系统、车窗、座椅、后视镜和天窗的电动运动包括在电气附件内,因为每个系统的操作都非常相似,都是使用一个或多个永磁电机以及电源换向电路。

1. 玻璃清洗系统

风窗玻璃刮水器是一种用于清除风窗玻璃上的雨水、雪、冰和碎屑的装置。风窗玻璃清洗器系统也用于使用多个喷嘴将水或防冻玻璃清洗液喷射到挡风玻璃上。

刮水器组件

刮水器通常由金属臂组成,以一端为中心旋转,另一端是长橡胶刮片。刮水刷臂由永磁电机驱动,通常是电动机,但某些车辆也使用气动动力。刮片在玻璃上来回摆动,从玻璃表面刮掉水或其他沉淀物。图 4-20 显示了风窗玻璃刮水器系统。

它的速度通常可调,有几个连续挡位,还有一个或多个"间歇"挡位。大多数汽车使用两个同步径向型转动臂。

刮水器电动机中的自动复位开关确保当刮水器开关关闭时,电流将继续流向电动机。这将保持电动机旋转,直到旋转开关切断雨刷电路,雨刷臂复位。

玻璃清洗器

典型的风窗玻璃清洗器系统由储液罐、喷水泵、软管、连接件和清洗喷嘴组成。储液罐通常位于发动机舱内。

当风窗玻璃清洗器开关启动时,刮水器电机和喷水泵开始工作。喷水泵把储水罐中的水、酒精和洗涤剂的混合物通过安装在机罩上的小喷嘴喷向风窗玻璃。

2. 电动车窗

电动车窗可以通过按下按钮或开关来自动升降窗户,而不是通过手摇曲柄。

大多数车窗升降器使用非常精巧的联动装置来升降玻璃，同时保持玻璃的水平。一个小型电动机连接到一个蜗轮和几个其他直齿圆柱齿轮上，以产生较大的齿轮减速比，从而提供足够的转矩来升起玻璃。图 4-21 显示了电动车窗系统。

3. 电动门锁

电动门锁也称为中控锁，允许司机和乘客同时操作，通过按下按钮或扳动开关锁定或解锁全部车门。

汽车的中控锁采用手动系统、遥控无钥匙系统或两者结合（作为防止因电气故障被锁在汽车中的安全措施，可手动操作电动门锁）。

4. 电动座椅

电动座椅是前排座椅，可通过使用开关或操纵杆和一组小型电动机进行调节。大多数具有此功能的汽车只能控制驾驶员座位，但几乎所有的豪华汽车都有前排乘客座椅的电源控制。

调整电动座椅（图 4-22）是通过使用多个电机来实现座椅不同部位的定位。一些汽车也有记忆调整，通过按下按钮可以调用（通常）两种不同的座椅调节。

5. 电动后视镜

电动后视镜是一种侧视镜，配备有用于从汽车内部进行垂直和水平调节的电气装置。玻璃也可以被电加热以防止起雾或结冰。通常，通过开关或旋钮选择镜像来控制左侧和右侧后视镜。电动后视镜选择开关通常有一个空挡位置，在此位置开关不起作用，以免由于误操作造成的镜像改变。电动后视镜（图 4-23）是凸面镜。

6. 电动天窗

汽车天窗是一种可移动的（通常为玻璃）面板，按下开关按钮，天窗就会自动打开，让光和新鲜空气进入车内。每次通电时，锁定继电器都会锁定到位，以便天窗可以滑动、倾斜和关闭。图 4-24 为电动天窗。

4.3.2 暖风和空调系统

供热、通风和空气调节系统旨在帮助车辆内部在炎热的夏季保持凉爽，在冬季保持温暖。

1. 空调系统

汽车空调通过将车内的热量传递到车外来降低车内温度。整个系统有五个主要部件，即压缩机、冷凝器、储液干燥器、膨胀阀和蒸发器。

有些系统之间有些细微的差异，但是图 4-25 是一个通用的空调系统的完整视图。

制冷剂

制冷剂是通过空调循环冷却空气的化学混合物的通用名称，其特点是低温蒸发，高压下会冷凝。氟利昂 R-12 制冷剂已使用多年。但是 R-12 对地球的臭氧层有害，已经被无害的 R-134a 制冷剂取代（图 4-26）。

压缩机

发动机传动带驱动压缩机压缩制冷剂,并使制冷剂在整个系统内循环。压缩机(图 4-27)将来自蒸发器的高压制冷剂蒸气泵送到冷凝器。

冷凝器

冷凝器(图 4-28)是一种用于将高压制冷剂蒸气变为液体的装置,安装在发动机散热器的前方。冷凝过程中产生大量热量,并通过外部空气流动从冷凝器中排出。

储液干燥器

干燥器也称为储液干燥器,是一种用于液体制冷剂的小型储存容器,可去除可能泄漏到制冷剂中的造成严重破坏的任何水分。如果系统使用节流管,则会有储液器。它们的功能是相同的。

热力膨胀阀或节流管

热力膨胀阀(图 4-29)可消除液体制冷剂的压力,使其膨胀并在蒸发器中变成制冷剂蒸气。在这里,系统从高压侧变为低压侧。

节流管(图 4-30)的用途与膨胀阀相同。节流管的结构简单且成本低,但制冷剂的流量是固定的。

蒸发器

蒸发器是另一个由排管和散热片组成的小型散热器,但作用与冷凝器完全相反,是吸热而不是散热。

2. 暖风系统

汽车暖风系统(图 4-31)的设计目的是与冷却系统配合使用,以保持车内适当的温度。主要部件是加热器芯、加热器控制阀、鼓风机电机和风扇。

热的发动机冷却液通过一个小型散热器循环,此小型散热器称为加热器芯。风扇位于加热器芯体的前方,用于将冷空气吹到散热叶片上。当空气流经加热器芯时,它会温度升高变成热空气,从加热器通风口吹进车内。在停止加热后,冷却剂通过加热器芯的出口被泵出,返回到发动机以通过水泵再循环。

主要部件是加热器芯,它位于仪表板后面。大多数是带塑料壳的铝芯。

3. 通风系统

通风是指在任何空间交换或更换空气的过程,以提供高质量的室内空气,包括控制温度,补充氧气和去除水分、气味、烟雾、二氧化碳和其他气体。有几种用于将空气排入车内的系统,其中最常见的是自然通风系统。

4. 自动空调

当选择自动模式(图 4-32)时,自动空调会自动控制空气温度和空气流量。

自动空调可以设定所需的温度。这些装置与内置恒温器一起工作,该恒温器检测并监测当前温度，并发出信号通知空调系统继续泵出冷空气直到达到设定的所需温度。

4.3.3 汽车电子器件

1. 防盗器

防盗器是一种安装在汽车上的电子安全装置，只有正确的钥匙（或采用其他方式）才会使发动机运转。防盗标志如图 4-33 所示。

钥匙内部的微电路由一个小电磁场激活，该电磁场引发电流在钥匙体内流动，从而发出由汽车电子控制单元读取的唯一二进制代码。当电子控制单元确定编码钥匙有效时，激活燃油喷射。

2. 安全带预紧器

安全带是一种车辆安全装置，用于在碰撞或突然停车期间保护乘客免受冲撞伤害。

安全带预紧装置在发生碰撞时收紧安全带。与安全气囊一样，预紧器由车身传感器触发，许多预紧装置使用爆炸性膨胀气体驱动活塞，使活塞缩回传动带。

电动预紧器（图 4-34）通常安装在装有预碰撞系统的车辆上。它可以重复或持续运行，在多次碰撞事故中提供更好的保护。

3. 辅助约束系统

安全气囊（图 4-35）是保证安全的乘客约束系统。安全气囊组件能够迅速膨胀以吸收冲击能量，然后在碰撞、冲击物体表面或突然减速时快速放气。它由安全气囊垫、柔性织物袋、充气模块和碰撞传感器组成。

在碰撞事故中，传感器向电子控制单元提供关键信息，包括碰撞类型、角度和撞击的严重程度。安全气囊电子控制单元确定碰撞事件是否符合打开标准，并触发各种发射电路以打开一个或多个安全气囊组件。

4. 儿童安全锁

儿童安全锁一般内置于大多数汽车的后门，目的是防止后座乘客（特别是儿童）在汽车行驶途中和静止时打开车门。

锁通常通过门边缘的小开关锁止。当使用儿童锁时，内部把手变得毫无用处，只能通过拉动外部手柄才能打开门。在新车型中，儿童锁可以通过门控单元以电子方式从驾驶员位置启动。图 4-36 展示了一些电子儿童安全锁。

5. 倒车雷达

此系统有时称为避障雷达，是一种倒车辅助装置，为驾驶员提供指示，指出车后有多少空间。

倒车雷达（图 4-37）主要由超声波传感器、控制器、显示器或蜂鸣器等组成，这种技术实际上是一种测距系统。

输出可以是音频或视频，视频可能最合适，因为使用音频，驾驶员可能会向后看。声音听起来是"哔哔"声，其重复频率随着汽车接近障碍物而增加，并且随着碰撞即将发生而变得几乎连续。

6. 巡航控制系统

巡航控制系统是一种自动控制汽车速度的系统。该系统是一个伺服机构,接管汽车油门以保持驾驶员设定的稳定速度。

巡航控制系统由电子控制单元操作。它由几个常见部件组成,其中包括车速传感器、驾驶员控制装置、控制模块和油门执行器。

一些现代车辆具有自适应巡航控制系统,这是一个通用术语,意思是改进的巡航控制。这些改进可以是自动制动或动态设定速度型控制。

4.4 检测设备

4.4.1 常用检测设备

1. 万用表

万用表是一种标准的电子测量仪器,它将多个测量功能(电压、电流和电阻)组合在一个设备中。模拟万用表使用带移动指针的微安表来显示读数。数字万用表(图4-38)具有数字显示屏,也可以显示代表测量值的图形条。

数字万用表由于其成本低、精度高而被普遍使用。但在某些情况下,如监测快速变化的值时,模拟万用表仍然更可取。

万用表有显示器、选择旋钮和端口三部分。

一些特殊的汽车万用表可测量更多参数,如曲轴或凸轮轴传感器的频率、氧传感器的直流电压、喷油器的温度、电阻或占空比、充电电压、电流和转速。

2. 示波器

示波器是一种电子测量仪器,允许观察变化的信号电压,通常显示为随时间变化的一个或多个信号的二维函数图。其他信号(如声音或振动)可以转换为电压并显示。

示波器分两种,模拟示波器和数字示波器。数字示波器具有与模拟类型相同的最终结果,但信号可以被认为是重绘波形而不是描绘在屏幕上。

基本的示波器(图4-39)通常分为四个部分:显示器、垂直控制器、水平控制器和触发器控制器。

示波表(图4-40)是一个非常有用且流行的设备。这是一种手持式数字示波器,可以将数据存储并传输到个人计算机以供进一步研究。

3. 发动机分析仪

电子发动机分析仪被设计用于诊断汽车发动机的状况。某些形式的发动机分析仪在现代汽车发动机系统中已成为故障查找的基本工具。最新的机器现在通常基于个人计算机。这允许添加更多的设备,只需更改软件即可。

发动机分析仪基本上由三部分组成:万用表、气体分析仪、示波器。

4.4.2 车载诊断系统

车载诊断系统是汽车术语，指的是车辆的自我诊断和报告功能。OBD-II 是第二代车载诊断系统。

车载诊断技术对驾驶员、技术人员和环境都有好处，通过监测车辆在每次行驶时的性能，立即识别性能和排放问题，并向技术人员提供信息，帮助他们快速准确地诊断和修复故障。

基本的车载诊断系统（图 4-41）包含一个电子控制单元，它使用来自各种传感器的输入信息来控制执行器以获得所需的性能。"检查"指示灯提供故障的早期警告。现代车辆可以支持数百个参数，例如车辆和发动机转速、转向角度，可以通过诊断数据连接器使用扫描仪进行访问。

当仪表板上的检查发动机指示灯（图 4-42）亮起时，连接到第二代车载诊断系统端口的扫描仪会记录并显示车辆正在发送的故障码，用户可以知道汽车出了什么问题。一旦问题得到解决，清除车辆内存中的代码，检查发动机指示灯关闭，直到出现下一个问题才会亮起。

读码器（图 4-43）是第二代车载诊断系统应用最早和最广泛的数据扫描仪之一。但是读码器只能显示原始代码，需要专门的工具将代码进行翻译和解释。

数据记录器被设计成半永久性地连接到汽车上，在正常工况下监测发动机和车辆。数据记录器（图 4-44）可能是一个很好的记录驾驶员驾驶习惯的方法。

节油表通过第二代车载诊断系统端口提供的数据报告车辆的燃油经济性。这些设备可以推算每加仑英里数。图 4-45 显示了 PLX Kiwi 节油记录仪，它提供了驾驶挑战，帮助培训用户成为更高效的驾驶员。

性能解析仪是一种专注于性能参数及性能监控的第二代车载诊断系统读码器。与第二代车载诊断系统连接的性能解析仪可以估算输出功率、输出转矩，或者为未配备原厂转速计的汽车提供一个虚拟转速表。

车辆远程信息处理（图 4-47）执行车队跟踪、监控燃油效率、防止危险驾驶、以及远程诊断和按需付费驾驶保险。

新型的第二代车载诊断系统扫描读码器集成了无线保真技术，可以无线连接到附近的笔记本电脑或智能手机上，以便于在车库或道路上监控车辆。图 4-48 展示了第二代车载诊断系统通过带有全球定位系统的苹果手机应用软件，来监控汽车性能的未来愿景。

第五章 电动汽车

5.1 概述

5.1.1 电动汽车和传统汽车的区别

电动汽车与传统汽车有许多相同的基本部件，但它们有区别于传统汽车的独特部件，如锂离子电池和电动机。

电池(图 5-1)

大多数传统的汽油动力汽车都使用铅酸蓄电池。然而，电动汽车需要大型锂离子电池或其他使用新技术的电池，这些新技术提供更多的电力，同样大小的电池重量比传统电池轻。电动汽车中的电池也必须提供比常规车辆更大的电量和更快的充电速度。因此，电动汽车电池比传统的汽车电池大得多；通常重量达几百磅，几年之后需要更换，而且可能花费数千美元。科学家和工程师们继续开发新技术，制造更小、更轻的电池，使用寿命更长，功率更大。

电动机（图 5-2)

电动机已经使用了一个多世纪，事实上，它们被用于一些最早的汽车。电动机是由电流驱动，产生磁荷并转动传动轴。电动机比内燃机浪费更少的热能，所以更有效率。电动机调节通过的电流，可以控制转矩（使物体发生转动的力）和每分钟转数（转速，或电动机转动的速度），在某些车辆中甚至不需要变速器。电动机的内部运作如下所示（图 5-2)。

内燃机

大多数混合动力汽车都以内燃机为主要动力来源，电池和电动机充当辅助动力源。由于电池和电动机也可以提供动力，因此这些发动机通常比普通汽车的发动机小。混合动力汽车的内燃机也可以用来给电池充电。插电式混合动力汽车的大部分动力来自电力系统，并使用内燃机来给电池充电或在电池电量耗尽后给汽车提供动力。

5.1.2 电动汽车的类型（图 5-3）

电动汽车可以分为混合动力电动汽车、插电式混合动力汽车和纯电动汽车。每种类型都有不同的工作方式，各有优缺点。

混合动力电动汽车

混合动力电动汽车通常称为混合动力汽车，由内燃机和电动机共同驱动。有几种类型的混合动力汽车，它们根据发动机或电动机是否是主要动力来源而有所不同。有些混合动力汽车主要由内燃机提供动力，并由电动机提供额外动力。其他的混合动力汽车由电动机驱动，汽油发动机作为备用动力。

电动机由电池和发电机供电。从内燃机接收动力的发电机对电池充电，并且电池为电动机供电。在任何情况下，使用电动机都可以使用更小型的内燃机，从而节省燃油并减少尾气排放。这些车辆也可以采用再生制动，其中从制动器捕获的能量被用于对电池进行再充电。这使得车辆在城市中行驶时，以及在走走停停的交通状况中获得更好的燃油里程。这种车目前是当今最流行的电动车型。许多汽车制造商都有这种车型，包括丰田普锐斯、本田思域混合动力车和福特翼虎混合动力车。

插电式混合动力汽车

插电式混合动力汽车与其他混合动力汽车一样，有一个电动机和一个汽油发动机，但是它们有一个更大的电池，当它们处于静止状态时可以通过一个辅助电源进行充电。插电式混合动力汽车可以在电池电量耗尽之前仅依靠电力行驶 10 到 40 英里的距离，电池电量耗尽后，由内燃机驱动车辆。雪佛兰沃蓝达是这种车型。

纯电动汽车

纯电动汽车也称作"battery electric vehicles"，仅靠蓄电池和电动机驱动，没有汽油发动机。当蓄电池电量不足时，必须接入外部电源，例如充电桩，进行再次充电。因为它们的蓄电池比其它电动车的电池大，所以在再次充电前可以行使 100 英里。但是，当蓄电池电量不足时，因为没有汽油发动机，所以总里程比其它电动汽车少。纯电动汽车的主要好处是不消耗汽油、零排放。日产聆风就是此种车型。

5.2 纯电动汽车

纯电动汽车只靠电力行驶。由一个或多个电动机驱动，电动机由可充电电池供电。纯电动汽车也被称为"battery electric vehicles""battery-only electric vehicles""full electric vehicles"。它们使用电动机和电机控制器代替内燃机来推进。见下图（图 5-4）。

纯电动汽车（图 5-5）使用大型牵引电池组为电动机供电，并且必须插入充电站或墙上插座才能充电。因为它是依靠电力行驶，所以不会从排气管排放废气，也没有燃油泵、油管和油箱等液体燃料部件。

5.2.1 驱动系统（图 5-6）

电源分配模块

电源分配模块是车载电池组充电器，将来自于电动汽车供电设备的交流电转换为直流电，给电池组充电。

逆变器和控制器

逆变器改变电池的电能使之与电动机兼容。控制器使用脉宽调制系统，快速脉冲；电流越大，功率越高，电动机转速就越快。

电动机

纯电动汽车一般使用交流电动机的变体。由于可能产生的发热问题，电动机被人为限制最大转数约每分钟 10k～20k 转。

交流异步电动机（图 5-7）在转子上使用线圈，从而产生"滑动"（电动机中的转子略低于定子产生的磁场）。因此，它们可以通过高转速（每分钟转数）产生最大转矩（旋转力）。

交流同步电动机（图 5-8）在转子上使用永磁体，使电动机保持同步并减少滑动。它们可以在更低的转速下效率更高，并在 0 转速时产生最大转矩，这使其非常适合"通勤"车辆。

变速器

由于电动机的转矩和高转速能力，大多数纯电动汽车使用单速 9.7∶1 比例的变速器

（电动机每旋转 9.7x 就旋转 1 圈），因此车辆从不"换挡"，但仍能达到最高速度在每小时 70~160 英里之间。

再生制动

一些纯电动汽车的设计是在滑行时收集能量。当松开"油门踏板"时，轮轴总成推动变速器，这就转动了为蓄电池供电的电动机。

除了给蓄电池充电外，电动机的电阻也会显著减慢车辆的速度。参见下面的再生制动（图 5-9）。

5.2.2 电源系统

锂离子电池

大多数纯电动汽车使用锂离子电池作为电池组。锂离子可以存储更多的能量，同时比铅酸蓄电池（常规汽车中的电池类型）更小更轻，并且比镍氢电池更容易获得。

低温性能

锂离子电池的一个缺点是在温度低于零度时，如果充电速度过快，可能会损坏。因此，电池可能会缓慢充电，直到它们具有足够的"自热"，再以更高的速率充电。

重量和位置

由于重量在 400~1 200 磅（约为 180~550 千克）之间，电池组的位置会极大地影响车辆的重心（物体重量的平均位置）。对于大多数纯电动汽车来说，电池组位于驾驶室的下方，可以降低重心并改善操控状况。

常见的电池设计（图 5-10）

软包电池：

普通的电池组设计使用直流棱柱电池或袋装电池（软包电池），其中每个小袋的厚度相当于一块纸板。这些袋子通常都是在模块内堆叠起来的，模块在电池组内。

圆柱形电池：

其他类型的电池为每个电池使用圆柱形设计。圆柱形电池通常在模块内并排放置，模块在电池组内。这种设计可以在单个电池之间产生小间隙，改善冷却情况。

冷却：

虽然电池组可以采用风冷，但水冷却通常能够使电池保持更加稳定的温度。电池过热可能会加快损耗，从而显著降低汽车的行驶里程。

充电：

虽然普通的家用插座可用于充电，但电动汽车充电站可以安全地提供更高的电压，使车载充电器能够更快速地为电池组充电。

5.2.3 辅助系统（图 5-11）

加热、冷却、转向和制动系统是完全电动的。

加热

大多数纯电动汽车使用正温度系数加热器。随着温度升高,这种类型的电加热器会增加电阻,防止它变得太热。

冷却

电动压缩机与电冰箱中使用的相类似,用于冷却空调机组的空气。

转向

通常情况下,纯电动汽车使用由电动机辅助的齿轮齿条式转向器。

制动

电动真空泵用于在制动踏板的背面制造真空环境。这应用于液压制动系统,使踏板更容易被推动。

辅助蓄电池

为了保护电池组的充电寿命,纯电动汽车通常会附加一个12伏的铅酸蓄电池来运行辅助系统。

使用铅酸蓄电池是因为它可以比锂离子电池在更宽的温度范围内保持电荷,并且在低于冰点温度充电时不会损坏。

5.3 混合动力汽车

混合动力汽车(图5-12)结合了汽油发动机和电动机的优点。他们可以被设计来满足不同的目标,比如更好的燃油经济性或更大的动力。主要系统包括蓄电池、电动机、发电机和带燃料源的第二个转矩源。第二个转矩源通常是靠汽油运行的内燃机。在其他情况下,它可能是由氢气驱动的内燃机、柴油发动机、小型燃气轮机/发电机或斯特林发动机(最后两种混合动力汽车在很大程度上仍然是理论性的)。

5.3.1 构造

转矩源:功率相对较低,约20英马力的内燃机。一个或者多个电动机。

储能器:蓄电池(电动机)——通常是普通的汽车电池,但因车而异。其他如飞轮和"超级电容器"这样的储能器还没有像电池那样得到充分研究,但未来可能会出现。

燃料:普通商用车的汽油或柴油,其他燃料研究正在进行,包括氢和其他潜在燃料源。

能量转换器/"收集器":发电机——发电机既将电池的电力转换为机械转动,又将旋转转换回能量给电池充电。转矩源可以是内燃机或处于再生制动时的轮轴。

控制:变速器、各种计算机和机械控制系统。不同车辆的控制系统差别很大。像下面描述的那样,它们都能够将驱动模式从电动模式切换到内燃机驱动模式或两者同时工作的模式。

在高速公路上行驶时,内燃机处于最有效的状态,电动汽车的电池电量很快就会耗尽,因此在这种情况下使用内燃机驱动。对于较短的城市驾驶出行，电动机可以单独使用，或者内燃机也同时在最佳工况下工作。

5.3.2 两种基本结构

混合动力电动汽车有两种基本的几何形式：并联式和串联式（图 5-13）。

并联式

在并联式混合动力汽车中，内燃机和电动机都驱动车轮；通常电动机和内燃机驱动相同的变速驱动桥。丰田普锐斯就是一个常见的例子。

串联式

在串联式混合动力汽车中，内燃机仅驱动发电机，为蓄电池供电。车轮驱动电机仅由电池或其他车载存储器供电。通用沃蓝达是串联式的插电式混合动力电动汽车。

5.3.3 三项先进技术

大多数混合动力汽车使用多种先进技术。

再生制动

再生制动能够重新捕获滑行或制动期间损失的能量。它利用车轮的前进运动来转动电动机。这会产生电力并有助于减慢车辆速度。

电动机驱动/辅助

电动机提供动力以协助发动机加速、行驶或爬坡。这样就可以使用更小、更高效的发动机。在一些混合动力汽车中，电动机在汽车低速行驶时独自驱动汽车，此时汽油发动机效率最低。

自动起动/停止

当车辆停止时自动关闭发动机，并在踩下加速踏板时重新起动发动机。这就减少了怠速消耗的能量。

混合动力汽车由内燃机和电动机驱动，该电动机使用储存在蓄电池中的能量。混合动力汽车不能插电给蓄电池充电。相反，蓄电池通过再生制动和内燃机充电。电动机提供的额外动力允许汽车使用较小的发动机。此外，蓄电池可为辅助负载（如音响系统和前照灯）供电，并在停止时减少发动机空转。这些特性结合在一起，就能在不影响性能的前提下提高燃油经济性。

5.4 插电式混合动力汽车

插电式混合动力汽车（图 5-14）使用大容量电池为电动机供电，并使用其他燃料（如汽油或柴油）来驱动内燃机。插电式混合动力汽车的电池可以使用壁式插座或充电桩、内燃机或再生制动进行充电。车辆依靠电力行驶，电量耗尽后车辆自动切换，使用内燃机驱动。

电动机和发动机驱动

插电式混合动力汽车装备有一个内燃机和一个电动机，它使用储存在电池中的能量。其电池组通常比混合动力汽车更大。这使得仅用电力就可以行驶适度的距离（目前的车型大约10 到 50 多英里），这通常被称为车辆的"全电动范围"。

在城市驾驶中，大部分的动力来自于储存的电能。例如，一名轻型的插电式混合动力汽车司机可能会用纯电力模式开车上下班，在夜间充电，准备第二天再进行纯电力通勤。当电池内的电量用尽时，急加速时，或在需要集中供暖或开空调时，内燃机为车辆提供动力。一些重型插电式混合动力汽车的工作方式与此相反，工作行驶使用内燃机驱动，电力用于驱动车辆的辅助设备或控制工作行驶时驾驶室的温度。

加油和驾驶选择

插电式混合动力汽车的电池可由外部电源充电，由内燃发动机充电，或通过再生制动充电。在制动过程中，电动机充当发电机，利用能量来给电池充电。

插电式混合动力汽车燃料消耗取决于两次电池充电间隔期间汽车所行驶的距离。例如，如果汽车不充电，燃油经济性将与同样大小的混合动力电动汽车差不多。如果车辆行驶的距离比它的全电动范围更短，并且在两次行驶之间充电，它可能只使用电力。

节能系统设计

除了蓄电池储能和电动机发电之外，还有多种方式可以将电动机和发动机的动力结合起来。两种主要配置结构是并联式和串联式。一些插电式混合动力汽车使用变速器，允许它们以并联或串联配置运行，根据驾驶状况在两者之间切换，这被称为"混联模式"或"混合模式"。

5.5 燃料电池电动汽车

燃料电池电动汽车（图 5-15）也被称为燃料电池汽车或零排放汽车，是一种采用燃料电池技术来产生运行车辆所需电力的电动汽车。在这些车辆中，燃料的化学能直接转换成电能。"燃料电池"电动汽车的工作原理与"插电式"电动汽车的工作原理不同，即运行该车辆所需的电力是车辆自身产生的。

燃料电池

燃料电池是一种在氢气和氧气之间发生电化学反应的装置。燃料电池的主要组件包括阳极、阴极和电解质。在电解液的作用下，燃料离子，也就是氢离子与氧离子反应产生电、水蒸气和热量。该反应仅在 80 摄氏度的温度下进行，因此也被称为"冷燃烧"。所产生的电能被用来驱动电动机，该电动机又使车辆的车轮旋转。

单个燃料电池的厚度约为 2 毫米，仅可产生 1 伏特的电位差。因此，一组数百个燃料电池被称为"燃料电池堆"，应用于燃料电池电动汽车。

燃料电池电动汽车的主要部件(图 5-16)

1. 储氢罐/燃料箱

燃料电池电动车辆中使用气态氢气作为燃料。这些储罐在 700 巴的非常高的压力下储存氢气。

2. 燃料电池堆

燃料电池堆是燃料电池电动汽车的强大动力,来自储罐的氢气和环境空气中的氧气反应形成电力。

3. 电动机

由燃料电池组产生的电力被供应给电动机,电动机旋转车轮,驱动汽车。

4. 电池组

电池组的功能是存储由燃料电池堆产生的额外电能,并在车辆需要更多能量运行时供应该电能。

5. 控制模块

控制单元监控车辆的整体能量需求,从而调节燃料电池堆、电动机和电池的功能以实现最佳性能。

燃料电池电动汽车的优点

与任何其他传统内燃机相比,燃料电池车辆更有效率。

这些车辆的尾气排放物仅含有水蒸气,因此是无污染的车辆。

燃料电池电动汽车的局限性

在高压下储存氢气是一件危险的事情,在发生碰撞时可能会致命。

燃料电池产生的多余热量很难处理,也妨碍了长期性能。

需要委托具有复杂处理能力的燃料补给站。

5.6 自动驾驶汽车

自动驾驶汽车使用技术来部分或完全取代驾驶员从起点到目的地对于车辆的驾驶,同时避免道路危险并对交通状况做出反应。下图是自动驾驶汽车入门图(图 5-17)。

自动驾驶技术

自动驾驶汽车使用技术和传感器的组合来感知道路、其他车辆和道路上的物体。关键技术(图 5-18)和传感器如下。

激光雷达:一种 360 度的传感器,利用光束来确定障碍物和传感器之间的距离。

相机:常用的廉价技术,但是,需要复杂的算法来解释所收集的图像数据。

雷达:使用无线电波确定障碍物和传感器之间距离的传感器。

红外传感器:允许检测车道标记、行人和自行车,这些在低照明和特定的环境条件下其他传感器很难检测到。

惯性导航系统：通常与全球定位系统相结合以提高精度。惯性导航系统使用陀螺仪和加速计来确定车辆的位置、方向和速度。

专用短程通信：用于车对车（图5-19）和车对基础设施系统，用于发送和接收关键数据，如道路状况、拥堵、事故和改道。专用短程通信可以应用在车队上，一队车可以共同行进。

预建地图：有时用于纠正错误的定位，因为在使用全球定位系统和惯性导航系统时可能出现错误。考虑到绘制每条道路和可行驶路面的限制，依靠预先构建的地图可以限制自动驾驶汽车的路线。

超声波传感器：提供主要用于停车辅助系统和备用报警系统的短距离数据。

全球定位系统：通过使用卫星对车辆位置进行三角测量来定位。

技术推动因素

对于自动驾驶汽车和智能道路系统而言，终端遥测、智能软件和云是必不可少的推动因素。自动驾驶汽车上的车载摄像头和传感器收集大量的数据，这些数据必须实时处理，以保证汽车在正确的车道上行驶，并安全行驶到达目的地。必须实时进行大量本地数据处理，包括将车保持在车道上的必要计算。同时，还有一些可以在云中远程执行的处理任务，例如软件更新和升级学习模型。基于云计算的可扩展高度弹性的基础架构对于处理这种大规模数据处理至关重要，而基于云计算的数据管理系统和智能代理则负责汇总和分析实时遥测数据，例如车辆速度和周围的汽车距离，以启动制动器或切换车道等。请参阅下面的云辅助架构（图5-20）。

基于云计算的网络和连接是另一个重要组成部分。自动驾驶汽车将配备车载系统，支持机器对机器的通信，允许他们在路上学习其他汽车，进行调整，以适应天气变化和道路状况的变化，如绕开路面上的杂物。高级算法、人工智能和深度学习系统是确保自动驾驶汽车能够快速、自动地适应变化的场景的核心。

除了特定的组件之外，云计算基础架构的可扩展性以及智能数据管理和传输能力对于确保正确和安全地处理所有正确的信息是必不可少的。对于目的地和地址数据尤其如此，这可能被视为个人身份信息。例如，如果行驶路径穿越具有次级网络连接的区域，内置智能可以确定数据存储和分析是否发生在云中或车辆上。

References
参考文献

[1] Alexander A. Stotsky. Automotive Engines [M]. New York: Springer-Verlag New York, LLC, 2009.

[2] David Crolla. Automotive Engineering: Powertrain, Chassis System and Vehicle Body [M]. Oxford: Butterworth-Heinemann, 2009.

[3] Nick Prague. Automotive Electrical Systems [M]. iUniverse, 2007.

[4] Mike Westbrook. The Electric And Hybrid Electric Car [M]. SAE International, 2006.

[5] Shawn McEwan. Introduction to Autonomous Cars [M]. Createspace Independent Publishing Platform, 2015.

[6] Anthony E. Schwaller. Total Automotive Technology [M]. Cengage Learning, 2004.

[7] Brad Durant. Electric Cars: The Ultimate Guide for Understanding the Electric Car And What You Need to Know, 2014.

[8] Tim Gilles. Automotive Chassis [M]. Cengage Learning, 2004.

[9] William Manville Hogle. Internal Combustion Engines [M]. Book on Demand Ltd, 2013.

[10] 宋进桂. 汽车专业英语 [M]. 北京: 机械工业出版社, 2013.

[11] 张金柱. 汽车专业英语 [M]. 北京: 化学工业出版社, 2014.

[12] 侯锁军, 王旭东. 汽车专业英语图解教程 [M]. 北京: 北京大学出版社, 2010.

[13] 王锦俞. 汽车专业英语 [M]. 北京: 机械工业出版社, 2017.

[14] https://www.howacarworks.com

[15] https://auto.howstuffworks.com

[16] https://animagraffs.com